WRITERS AND POLITICS

Writers and Politics

CONOR CRUISE O'BRIEN

FABER & FABER

This edition first published in 2015
by Faber & Faber Ltd
Bloomsbury House, 74–77 Great Russell Street
London WC1B 3DA

Printed by Books on Demand GmbH, Norderstedt

All rights reserved
© Conor Cruise O'Brien, 1955, 1959, 1960, 1961, 1963, 1964, 1965
'Conor Cruise O'Brien: An Appreciation' © Oliver Kamm, 2015

The right of Conor Cruise O'Brien to be identified
as author of this work has been asserted in accordance
with Section 77 of the Copyright, Designs and Patents Act 1988

This book is sold subject to the condition that it shall not, by way of
trade or otherwise, be lent, resold, hired out or otherwise circulated
without the publisher's prior consent in any form of binding or cover other than
that in which it is published and without a similar condition including this
condition being imposed on the subsequent purchaser

A CIP record for this book is available from the British Library

ISBN 978–0–571–32425–5

Our authorised representative in the EU for product safety is
Easy Access System Europe, Mustamäe tee 50, 10621 Tallinn, Estonia
gpsr.requests@easproject.com

FOR OWEN SHEEHY-SKEFFINGTON

CONTENTS

Conor Cruise O'Brien: An Appreciaton   *xi*
INTRODUCTION   *xvii*

I

AMERICA

The New Yorker	3
A *New Yorker* Critic	8
Serpents	13
White Gods and Black Americans	17
Free Spenders	23

II

ENGLAND

Orwell Looks at the World	31
Chorus or Cassandra	36

III

FRANCE

Michelet Today	45
The People's Victor	61
Monsieur Camus Changes His Climate	65
Sartre as a Critic	72
A Vocation	76
Communists and *Communisants*	81

IV

IRELAND

1891–1916	87
Irishness	97
Our Wits About Us	101
Somerville and Ross	106
The Fall of Parnell	116
The Great Conger	119
Mother's Tongue	121
Some Letters of James Joyce	123
Queer World	126
Timothy Michael Healy	128

V

FOUR CRITICS

Generation of Saints	139
Bears	144
Re-enter the Hero	149
Poetry, Inspiration and Criticism	154

VI

THE COLD WAR

Critic into Prophet	163
Journal de Combat	169
Varieties of Anti-Communism	174
The Perjured Saint	183

VII

THE UNITED NATIONS AND THE DEVELOPING COUNTRIES

Conflicting Concepts of the United Nations	195
The U.N., the Congo and the Tshombe Government	215
Mercy and Mercenaries	223
Corruption in Developing Countries	230
The Schweitzer Legend	234
Two Addresses	239
ACKNOWLEDGEMENTS	260

CONOR CRUISE O'BRIEN: AN APPRECIATION

by Oliver Kamm

The last time – literally the last time, when he had an advanced stage of cancer – I visited Christopher Hitchens, we talked about the books and writers that had influenced him. He told how, in 1967, he picked up a volume of essays called *Writers and Politics* by Conor Cruise O'Brien in a public library in Tavistock, Devon. Reading it, he formed the ambition to be able to write like that.

I had a similar experience. I never met O'Brien but he was one of the earliest and most important influences on my political thinking and my wish to be a writer. As an undergraduate at Oxford, I picked up one of his books in the Bodleian Social Science Library. It was a collection of essays and reviews called *Herod: Reflections on Political Violence* (1978). His arguments throughout the book were a different face of O'Brien's politics (though he would certainly have claimed they were the same politics in essence) from his volume of the 1960s. In condemning America's war in Vietnam, he was recognisably a writer of the anti-imperialist Left. In his later volume, encapsulating his experience as a cabinet minister in Ireland's coalition government in the mid-1970s, he wrote of the destructiveness of absolutism.

It's a great book. In it, O'Brien not only denounces IRA terrorism, as you would expect from a mainstream politician, but – in a sense quite different from the rationalisations offered by ideological apologists for political violence – seeks to understand it. I mean, *really* understand it – not extenuate it by equivocation and non sequitur. And his thinking leads him to attack the republican mythology at the heart of the Irish state. Few writers have analysed terrorism so acutely or been as effective in undermining its ideological justifications. Here is how O'Brien recounts his thinking:

In the politics of the Republic, I was not quite where I was expected to be. In the Congo time, sections of the British press had assured their readers (quite wrongly) that I was motivated by anti-British fanaticism. My career in America had shown me as opposed to imperialism. So I was expected at least to fall into line with the view that the troubles in Northern Ireland were caused by British imperialism. When instead I said that, in relation to Northern Ireland, it was the IRA who were the imperialists, since they were trying to annex by force a territory a large majority of whose inhabitants were opposed to them, my remarks appeared either incomprehensible or outrageous to a number of people who had liked what they heard *about* me much more than they like what they were hearing *from* me.

As a prophet, O'Brien was fallible. He doubted that the Irish constitution, with its irredentist claims to the whole island of Ireland, could be reformed in order to excise those articles. Yet eventually it was, and politics in Northern Ireland became marginally more normal (or at least less sectarian and violent). What was significant, even brilliant, about O'Brien's analysis was its lucidity in exposing cant. He realised that it was an untenable position for democratic politics both to condemn terrorism and to rely on a romanticised view of how the state had come into being and won its independence. O'Brien was repelled by the 'cult of the blood sacrifice' (expressed most eloquently but chillingly by Yeats in his one-act play *Cathleen ni Houlihan*) which underlay republican thinking. Being O'Brien, he didn't hold back in saying so. It took courage – raw physical courage, and not only political heterodoxy – to say such things in Ireland in the 1970s.

O'Brien had many roles in his long and eminent life. He was diplomat, statesman, politician, historian, literary critic, journalist and polymath. But most of all, he was a public intellectual in the best sense of the term. He applied his knowledge and critical intelligence to matters of great public interest, and he expressed his thinking in elegant, spare prose that argued a case with remorseless logic. He was a great man and a great Irishman, and Faber are to be congratulated in reissuing his work.

O'Brien's written output is best represented by his historical studies. Three of those volumes stand out in my estimation. First, *States of Ireland* (1972) remains the finest historical account of how the Troubles in Ireland erupted. It was a seminal revisionist treatment of the myths of Irish republicanism. If, as many of his admirers (including me) thought, O'Brien eventually went too far in embracing the cause of unionism and underestimated the capacity of a constitutional nationalism to reform itself, he did so with an unflinching humane intelligence.

O'Brien's history of the Zionist movement and Israel, *The Siege* (1986), is also a fine work of scholarship whose analysis stands up well in the light of later events. O'Brien was a friend to and admirer of Israel and often a lonely voice in media circles in explaining the Jewish state's security dilemmas. His downbeat but realistic conclusion was that Israel could not be other than it is, a Jewish state, which merited the sympathy of liberals in maintaining its democratic and secular character in spite of being in a state of permanent siege. Devoutly as he wished for a peaceful solution to the conflict in Palestine, O'Brien believed that a solution was not available. On his analysis, conflicts don't have solutions: they have outcomes. I hope he is eventually proved wrong, and that a two-state solution between a sovereign Palestine and a safe Israel comes into being. But O'Brien's pessimism seems historically well-grounded.

Probably O'Brien's greatest achievement of historical scholarship is his biography of Edmund Burke, *The Great Melody* (1992). Burke is much cited by modern conservatives, and not necessarily accurately. The 'little platoons' that they celebrate aren't what Burke meant by the phrase; he was instead appealing to a notion of a fixed social order, in which each man knew his place. It is far removed from the modern ideals of social (and sexual) equality. Yet O'Brien retrieved the idea of Burke as a Whig of unrivalled historical farsightedness. On O'Brien's telling, Burke foresaw the bloody degeneration of the French Revolution even while celebrating the potential of the American Revolution. Among the gems in the paperback edition of the book is his respectful and affectionate exchange with Isaiah Berlin. O'Brien, as a confirmed Rousseau-basher, will have no quarter with any romantic idealisation of 'the general will.'

O'Brien's was a tough-minded version of liberalism, which stressed the dangers of untrammelled reason. In that respect, he was a worthy inheritor of the tradition of Burke. In his late collection *On the Eve of the Millennium* (1995), he noted that the worst crimes of the twentieth century had been committed by forces that considered themselves thoroughly emancipated from superstition – Nazism and Communism. O'Brien was a man of the Enlightenment, who believed its greatest enemy was absolutism.

His contrarian streak sometimes led him to mistaken and even perverse positions: against European integration; against intervention to stop the aggressive designs of Slobodan Milosevic; opposition in principle, and not merely pragmatic objections, to the Good Friday Agreement in Northern Ireland; and most notably a deep hostility to the American 'civic religion' that celebrates Thomas Jefferson. His book *The Long Affair: Thomas Jefferson and the French Revolution* (1996) depicts America's third president as (and I don't exaggerate) an ideological precursor of Pol Pot.

It's an extraordinary argument and not, I think, O'Brien's finest. His historical revisionism, so valuable a tool, tended to overreach itself. The strict taxonomy that O'Brien set out – the American Revolution extended liberty, the French and Russian revolutions negated it – was, in reality, fuzzier than he allowed. But, again, O'Brien arrived at his conclusions with an intellectual honesty that caused him not to shirk unfashionable sentiments. The reforms enacted by the Constituent Assembly in France from 1789 to 1791 were quite limited, but went in the direction of secularism and the removal of the hereditary principle. Those who believe, crudely, that the American Revolution was good and the French Revolution bad do have the problem of explaining why Jefferson, as ambassador to

Paris, saw these causes as consistent. O'Brien provides his own answer, which may be mistaken (I think it is), but it is an answer: Jefferson's politics were more French than American.

The French revolution of 1789 was admired throughout Europe, including Britain and particularly in Germany, for good reason. It was, like the American Revolution, a historic moment for the cause of reform, secularism and (I use the term without irony) progress. The turning point was war with Austria and Prussia in 1792. This precipitated a second revolution and all that followed: regicide, terror, and the reassertion of autocracy and nationalism. There was no reason that European governments should have sought to undermine the movement of 1789, and in doing so they became steadily more authoritarian at home. The Enlightenment tradition is perhaps more consistent than O'Brien allowed for. But he was brilliant at seeing its darker side. There were idiosyncrasies in his outlook but his was fundamentally an advocacy of a humane and liberal politics. He richly deserves a new generation of readers.

September 2014

Oliver Kamm is a leader writer and columnist for The Times.

INTRODUCTION

"Are you a socialist?" asked the African leader.
I said, yes.
He looked me in the eye. "People have been telling me," he said lightly, "that you are a liberal . . ."
The statement in its context invited a denial. I said nothing.
I knew what the leader meant when he used the word "liberal," and I understood why a charge of "liberalism" was felt to be damaging. In relation to Africa, Asia and Latin America, the European and American liberal has too often been—and is perhaps increasingly—a false friend. Typically, in welcoming the new independence of, say, the African countries, he has warned them lest they fall under the far greater tyranny of communism, and he tends to identify communism with indigenous left-wing movements, thereby consciously or unconsciously identifying liberalism with, for example, the Emirs of Northern Nigeria. He deprecates, or even condemns, the *apartheid* regime in South Africa but advises that any form of sanction against it—for example economic sanctions—is premature, impracticable or otherwise undesirable. His moral worries about forms of government in African countries are unevenly distributed along the political spectrum. His press will have very much more to say about political detentions in "left-wing" Ghana than about the liquidation of entire villages in "democratic" Nigeria or "conservative" Cameroon. The Western liberal, of the kind most often and most widely heard from, uniformly displays acute myopia in face of the various forms of Western puppet government which cover so large a part of Africa, Asia and Latin America; to the sparse news which filters through from these parts he responds with calm agnosticism, in marked contrast to the spasms of moral anguish provoked by the slightest reported misdeed of an African,

Asian or Latin American government which follows an independent line.

To those, outside the rich countries, who are sickened by the word "liberalism," the liberal voice *par excellence* is that of Mr. Adlai Stevenson—the voice that explained to the world that the United States had had nothing to do with the Bay of Pigs invasion; the voice that justified the exclusion of China from the United Nations on moral grounds; the voice that expounded the humanitarian reasons for supporting Belgian policy in the Congo. From this viewpoint Mr. Stevenson's face, with its shiftily earnest advocate's expression, is the ingratiating moral mask which a toughly acquisitive society wears before the world it robs: "liberalism" is the ideology of the rich, the elevation into universal values of the codes which favoured the emergence, and favour the continuance, of capitalist society.

To be taxed with liberalism by one who saw—and had had some cause to see—liberalism in such a light was a serious matter. What was even more serious was not to be able to deny the charge. The country in which I was living at this time was one which was trying to build a socialist society; its spokesmen and its press vehemently rejected Western liberal thought, seen in the light I have described. The country was progressing rapidly, in the development of its economy and in education. Its government showed, as it seemed to me, a greater sense of responsibility to the people—not in a formal sense but in a profound one—than did neighbouring states with more apparently liberal constitutions. I admired the boldness, the seriousness and the single-mindedness with which this government had set about doing what it thought best for its own country, in its state of development, without very much regard for the prejudices or the slogans of its former rulers and their rich and powerful friends. The contrast with the neighbouring countries showed, I believed, that this government had been right to reject a façade of liberalism, masking internal and external exploitation, in favour of a national and popular form of that "plentiful governance" for which mediaeval Europe had longed, from beneath the terrible freedom of the barons.

And yet, as I drove home from my interview with the leader, I had to realize that a liberal, incurably, was what I was. Whatever I might argue, I was more profoundly attached to liberal concepts of freedom—freedom of speech and of the press, academic freedom, independent judgment and independent judges—than I was to the idea of a disciplined party mobilizing all the forces of society for the creation of a social order guaranteeing more real freedom for all instead of just for a few. The revolutionary idea both impressed me and struck me as more *immediately* relevant for most of humanity than were the liberal concepts. But it was the liberal concepts and their long-term importance—though not the name of liberal—that held my allegiance.

When the leader's question forced me to think rather more clearly than I had been doing about my relation to liberalism and to socialism, I did not feel altogether happy about the result. Liberal values, tarnished by the spurious tributes of the rich world's media, today make the rich world yawn and the poor world sick. For my own part I had had so little enthusiasm for them in theory that I was surprised and disconcerted at the depth of commitment to them experienced when, in practice, I met challenges to them.

Not that the experience was altogether new. The Ireland in which I was brought up stood in a peculiar relation to liberal thought and practice: a relation comparable, but by no means identical, to that prevailing among Spanish or Polish intellectuals between the wars. In these Catholic and time-lagging countries the liberal tradition, the tradition of 1848, got less lip-service, and was taken more seriously, than was the case in the industrially advanced countries. This was because the battle of 1848 had not been won. In Ireland the liberal current of the national-revolutionary tradition met the original Rock, the Catholic Church as a social force. Freedom of speech? Politicians, businessmen, trade-union leaders possessed this freedom, in relation to the government, in undiminished measure. In relation to the Church, and areas—such as education—which the Church claimed as its own, they abstained from using this freedom. The thing to be avoided at all costs, one durable politician had pointed out, was "a sthroke of a crozier." Most politicians were nimble in this regard; in a debate a senator from Trinity College drew attention to the fact that, contrary to a Department of Education regulation, children were being beaten in the primary schools for failure at lessons. This was a notorious fact but—since the management of primary schools is in the hands of the clergy—senators chose to deny it and the critic found no support at all. Freedom of the press was subject to similar unacknowledged constraints. The liberal paper was "the Protestant paper," with an entirely urban middle-class circulation; the two national papers competed in displays of orthodoxy, as in other methods of promoting circulation. Both press and radio reported at astonishing length the funerals of bishops: possibly a mechanism for releasing oversuppressed aggression. As for academic freedom, the National University of Ireland, in theory a secular organism, was in practice a clerical domain, and the Archbishop of Dublin proclaimed it a mortal sin for Catholics to attend the only university in the Republic of Ireland which is not under the control of the Catholic clergy. The very word "liberal" was—as in parts of the United States—a suspect one. Here, indeed, two currents joined. Certain elderly Irish ecclesiastics, brought up to think of liberalism as Pio Nono did, were pleased to find, on their American fund-raising tours, that important potential contributors, men of the world and of business, saw liberalism as a pressing *contemporary* danger.

I speak of things as they were; a change for the better may reasonably be expected as a result both of improved living standards and education levels in Ireland itself, and of the liberalizing movement in the Church as a whole since Pope John. But the rate of change is slow: the Irish Church, with that of Spain, remains the heart of darkness of the ecumenical movement.[1]

Outsiders, and some insiders, have discerned in the Irish mind, as in the Polish and the Spanish, a tendency to anarchism, to

---

[1] The criticisms made or implied in this passage refer to the social, cultural and political activities of the Irish Bishops now most prominent and to their spokesmen, not to the whole clergy, in which there is a strong current of sympathy with the ecumenical movement, and not at all to the Irish clergy abroad, many of the best of whom can be regarded, not only as missionaries, but as ecclesiastical *émigrés* from the morose surveillance of their home Hierarchy.

rebellion for rebellion's sake. Where it exists, and it does among intellectuals, this tendency derives, I believe, from the necessities of individual intellectual survival in communities where correct thinking is assumed to be the province of a specialized caste. If we take an intellectual to be a person who prefers to try to do his thinking for himself, even badly, rather than to delegate it to specialists trained to discharge this function with considerable subtlety, then we see that the intellectual, in a priest-led community, must develop strengthened means of defending himself. He acquires in the process special capabilities and special limitations, different from those affecting intellectuals in Protestant/agnostic countries. He is likely to set great store by irony, the versatile, durable and easily camouflaged weapon of every ideological guerrilla; he will take an almost morbid interest in hypocrisy, because of its prevalence among the better-off laity in a priest-led society, because of the natural targets it presents to irony, and perhaps above all because of its peculiar social function in subordinating the meaning of words to the practical needs of the moment. Many Anglo-Saxon intellectuals can, it seems, make reasonable allowances for this last social function, recognizing the utility of a certain amount of hypocrisy as a form of social cement. If deceit is acceptable to win a war, why should it not be equally acceptable, say, to preserve the peace? Or to ensure a greater measure of social justice or social stability? How many lies might not justifiably have been told to avert Hiroshima? Would it not be sensible to accept whole systems of mendacity if thereby the risks of a Third World War could be lessened? It is both the weakness and the strength of the intellectual brought up in a Catholic tradition[2] that he finds it peculiarly hard to accept such pragmatic intimations. On the contrary, he finds it only too easy to say, *ruat caelum* (it is perhaps fortunate, and not accidental, that the Catholic countries today have not the material power to make the sky fall). To intellectuals brought up in Catholic com-

---

[2] This is true of the present writer only in a broad sense. I come of a Catholic family with a number of vigorously agnostic members, including my father; from the age of ten on I attended a non-Catholic school; I then was admitted to "the Protestant University," Trinity College. But everything in Ireland, including Irish agnosticism, is profoundly affected by the Catholic environment and tradition.

munities—whether they accept or not the teaching and standards of these communities—the truth or falsehood of a given proposition is far more important than its social implications. This does not mean that there is not a great deal of dishonesty, both conscious and unconscious, among such intellectuals; there certainly is; but, whatever their personal difficulties, they will think of truth, not utility, as the essential criterion of all propositions.[3]

All this has, of course, its relevance to socialism. In countries which have declared themselves irrevocably committed to socialism, the criterion, in practice, has been utility, not truth; the party press has not hesitated to lie whenever a lie might be useful; intellectuals, especially writers, have been distrusted and dragooned; hypocrisy and sycophancy in their most grovelling forms have been encouraged and rewarded; and all for—it has been hoped—the eventual greater good of the nation as a whole. It is perhaps significant that, so far, the intellectual community subjected to these conditions which has done most to resist and to change them—and to bring on a critique of them throughout much of the socialist world—has been that of Poland. That community, with its distrust of pragmatism, its training in irony, its dash of anarchism, scorn for sycophancy, and skill in undermining the structures of hypocrisy, has accomplished, and is accomplishing—despite all setbacks—an extraordinary work of liberation. By that I do *not* mean "rolling back the curtain," restoring "free enterprise," etc., but simply the setting moving, within the communist world, of currents of intellectual life which had long been blocked. Certainly the Poles alone could not have accomplished this—to the extent that it has been accomplished—but it may be doubted whether, without these indomitable *frondeurs,* the degree of progress in intellectual freedom attained in the past ten years could have come about.

---

[3] This runs counter to a received opinion, especially as concerns the Jesuits and their pupils. The above generalizations refer, however, only to intellectuals and especially to writers. The most famous Irish pupil of the Jesuits, James Joyce, was distinguished, not by any of the devious peculiarities normally attributed to Jesuit education, but by a rigorous intellectual integrity, probably unequalled by any writer of the present century. Of course he rejected much of what the Jesuits told him.

Now, while it would be hard to refute the theoretical proposition that the averting of a Third World War would be worth a good many lies, it is evident in practice that lies, though they may certainly help to win a war, are unlikely means of averting one. The more nearly monolithic the lie-structure of competing power-blocs, the less the possibility of communication between them, and the greater the fear which they inspire in one another. The one great peace which was brought about by the accommodation of monolithic lie-structures—the Hitler-Stalin pact of 1939—lasted less than two years and provided the immediate occasion for the greatest war the world has ever known. Lies, after all, are a means of having one's own way: of winning wars, including revolutionary and counter-revolutionary wars, cold wars and hot wars. Peaceful coexistence, which requires some degree of mutual confidence, demands *ipso facto* a reduction in the lie-content of human exchange. Those who would place commitment to the truth above all expediencies—even the immediate apparent interests of peace or social justice—can claim that only such a commitment can begin to provide that genuinely international, interracial and reliable language without which humanity is likely to destroy itself.

This may be seen as an aspect of a wider phenomenon: respect for facts—and intentness on their relations—as the basis, since the emergence of our species, of our survival and success, at the expense of species dedicated to considerations of more immediate utility. And the importance of the freedoms associated with liberalism lies in the degree of protection they afford to the deployment of the peculiar faculties of *homo sapiens* in relation to the world and to himself. Even after revolutions and counter-revolutions, and their vociferous unanimities, man's need to think for himself, and to hear himself thinking, reasserts itself and redevises codes for its safe, or less precarious, fulfilment.

Unfortunately, as parsons and schoolmasters know, there is something both ludicrous and nightmarish about feeling oneself called on to uphold such a taken-for-granted virtue as commitment to truth. The Good Soldier Schweik put his stubby finger on it:

... Schweik, according to where the lieutenant happened to be, faced eyes right or eyes left with such an emphatic expression of innocence on his face that Lieutenant Lukash looked at the carpet as he remarked:

"Yes, I must have everything clean and tidy. And I can't stand lies. Honesty's the thing for me. I hate a lie and I punish it without mercy. Is that clear?"

"Beg to report, sir, it's quite clear. The worst thing a man can do is to tell lies. As soon as he begins to get in a muddle and contradict himself, he's done for. I think it's always best to be straightforward and own up, and if I've done anything wrong, I just come and say: 'Beg to report, sir, I've done so-and-so.' Oh yes, honesty's a very fine thing, because it pays in the long run. An honest man's respected everywhere; he's satisfied with himself, and he feels like a new-born babe when he goes to bed and can say: 'Well, I've been honest again to-day.'"

During this speech Lieutenant Lukash sat on a chair, looking at Schweik's boots and thinking to himself:

"Ye gods, I suppose I often talk twaddle like that, only perhaps I put it a bit differently."

No one who has read that passage can ever again address, say, an undergraduate audience on the subject of veracity, without looking nervously round in fear of finding a certain potato-face, beaming with insufferable approbation.

If one perseveres in "twaddle"—hoping, like poor Lieutenant Lukash, that one may "put it a bit differently"—it is from a quasi-organic necessity. This is an age of propaganda; all of us who work with words are awash with propaganda, our own and that of others, open and covert. One can hardly fail to have— unless one has ceased to be moved by any human cause—what J. B. Yeats called "a touch of the propaganda fiend" in one's own writing. And yet one also feels the need for an effort of decontamination, the elimination of the lies, not merely of one's political enemies but also of one's political friends and—a more difficult and longer-term task—of one's own. One can come to feel that this effort of personal intellectual survival is a tiny part of the human effort of survival, in which intellectual integrity must remain an essential element.

The essays, articles, reviews and lectures which make up this book contain "touches of the propaganda fiend," efforts at decontamination and occasional attacks of Schweikian "twaddle." They were written at different times, most of them during the past five years, and for different publics: several of them were written—in response to what Dr. Leavis has scornfully called "the exigencies of weekly journalism"—for readers of the two principal English intellectual weeklies; a few were written for a similar public in New York; some for radio listeners in Ireland; and some for university audiences in England and in West and East Africa. Many of them are concerned with writers, and with the visions of society we have through them; some deal with cultural-political phenomena, the activities of periodicals and pamphleteers; some directly with contemporary politics, the United Nations, Africa. Such a collection can have no greater degree of unity than is conferred by the continuity of the writer's preoccupations—or obsessions—some of which I have tried to assemble in this introduction.

All criticism, all political analysis, involves a quest for truth, but few critics, few analysts, could give a philosophically respectable or coherent answer to the question: what is truth? Yet we can identify lies readily enough, and can reasonably hope that, when we have chipped away at these, what remains will be closer to the indefinable truth. A certain amount of chipping away goes on in the pages that follow. It will be seen that the chipping is mainly, though not exclusively, at the expense—or for the benefit —of Western cultural and political edifices. There are, I think, adequate reasons for this. The English-speaking critic and analyst is—or should be—led to criticize and analyze the phenomena of his own contemporary culture, which is increasingly dominated by values prevalent in the United States of America. The distortions and misleading façades which he will most often encounter —I use this verb advisedly—are pro-American and anti-communist distortions and façades. He will of course be aware that in the communist world, and in the poor world of Asia and Africa, there are also distortions and façades, usually much more blatant, and therefore less insidious, than those prevalent in the West. As far as outside criticism can do something to demolish the mendacities of the communist world and the poor world, that effort is being vigorously made by many writers, and I have not felt any great need to add my amateur efforts to those of the numerous professional critics of communist practice. My own guess is that the liberation of the communist world, and of the poor world, from their crude forms of mendacity, will have to proceed from within and that the liberation of the Western world from its subtler and perhaps deadlier forms of mendacity will also have to proceed from within. Whether these liberations make much progress or not will obviously depend mainly on mighty economic and social forces, but also a little on the efforts of individuals. From the other side we can hear a few writers, Poles, Russians, Hungarians and others, busily chipping away. Our applause can neither encourage nor help them. What might help would be that, from our own side also, should be heard the sound of chipping.

Legon, January 16, 1965   CONOR CRUISE O'BRIEN

I

AMERICA

THE NEW YORKER

A recent issue of *The New Yorker* carried a full-page colour advertisement showing the back of a man looking out to sea, where a sailing ship is foundering in a purple storm. The man is wearing a bowler hat and a black suit; the set of his shoulders is military or paranoid, his arms hang stiffly at his side; what can be seen of his head is spongy and striated like a tree fungus; and across his back, about the level of the base of the lungs, are a Vienna roll and a sherry glass containing a colourless liquid. Below this picture, attributed to René Magritte, is the legend:

John Milton on the victory of truth.
Though all the winds of doctrine were let loose to play upon the earth, so Truth be in the field, we do injuriously . . . to misdoubt her strength. Let her and Falsehood grapple; who ever knew Truth put to the worse in a free and open encounter. (*Areopagitica*, 1644) Great Ideas of Western Man . . . one of a series. (*Container Corporation of America*)

At the side of the picture is a longer text which reads in part:

This is Truth, mysterious . . . He is in truth somebody; there are in him two elements simple and pure . . . to wit, a loaf of bread and a glass of water. The person who is vested with Truth is impassive. He gives the feeling that the spectacle of the unleashed forces of evil has no power to infringe upon his integrity. The contrast between the firmness of this personage and the disorder, the fury, of the elements, is the same as the contrast between the doctrinary tempests unleashed against the Truth of which Milton was thinking.

Neither Milton nor the Container Corporation would "make" *The New Yorker* on the merits of their prose alone, yet their conjunction is in some ways characteristic of the culture which has produced *The New Yorker*. The canners' commentary on Milton sets out rather plainly two of that magazine's basic assumptions. The first is that the standpoint of the detached observer is particularly meritorious, and close to the truth. "So

Truth be in the field," said Milton; but the admen's fungoid effigy of Milton's Truth is not in the field—he is behind a parapet firmly watching other people drown. The second assumption is that the standpoint of the detached observer is associated with successful commercial activity. As the canners' publicity encapsulates the *Areopagitica* and other Great Ideas of Western Man, so *The New Yorker*'s own prose runs in a thin channel between thick rich banks of advertising.

When "the doctrinary tempests" of McCarthyism were unleashed, the editorial policy of *The New Yorker*—though not the tendency of *New Yorker* writers—was to say as little as possible about it and let truth and falsehood do their grappling somewhere else, out of earshot of the advertisers. This policy was laid down by Harold Ross, builder and editor of the magazine, whose biography has now been written by Mr. James Thurber.* "Harold Ross," Mr. Thurber tells us, "inherently cautious, fundamentally conservative, stuck resolutely to his original belief that the *New Yorker* was not a magazine designed to stem tides, join crusades, or take political stands. He was not going to print a lot of 'social-conscious stuff,' because his intuition told him that, if he did, he would be overwhelmed by it. . . . He didn't encourage, he even discouraged, pieces on McCarthyism . . ."

Since Ross's death in 1951, the magazine under William Shawn's editorship has changed in minor ways: certain verbal quirks, mainly "plain man" gestures, are no longer inflicted on contributors' prose; there are fewer commas and less prudishness; writing is less nervous and more relaxed (not altogether a gain). But basically *The New Yorker* remains what Ross made it. It still wants, as it did in his day, "superior prose, funny drawings and sound journalism, without propaganda." Its many admirers still think of it as being, in the words of a provincial tribute which Ross valued enough to frame, "a supposedly 'funny' magazine doing one of the most intelligent, honest, public-spirited jobs, a service to civilization, that has ever been rendered by any one publication." Any reader of *The New Yorker* will give at least two cheers for that sentiment; but those who give two and those who give three are apt to regard each other with suspicion if not with aversion. "Are we important?" Ross once asked Thurber. And to this, even a two-cheer man would have to an-

* *The Years with Ross.*

swer, with some reluctance, "Yes." The magazine has published, over more than thirty years, too much good writing, too many brilliant drawings, for any other answer to be possible. *The New Yorker* is an important part, not only of American culture, but of Western culture generally.

Mr. Thurber's portrait of the man who made *The New Yorker* is therefore worth serious attention. It is an admiring and friendly portrait—a "long fond view," he calls it—but being by Thurber it does not leave out the warts. There are so many of these, that the portrait finishes by looking like one of those distressing medical phenomena, where the patient is entirely encased in a hard scaly hide. There is a story of Dorothy Parker's called "The Old Gentleman" in which a sorrowing daughter tells a series of anecdotes about her late father, all intended to illustrate his lovable eccentricity and all in fact building up a picture of a selfish monster who had systematically exploited her. *The Years with Ross* is rather like "The Old Gentleman." The editor of *The New Yorker* was splendidly uneducated ("Who's William Blake?") and impatient with foreigners for not understanding English ("Goddam it, I'm speaking slowly and clearly enough," he yelled). He took an interest in the home lives of *New Yorker* writers; for example, he tried to stop Thurber marrying again, for fear "that if I became happily married something bad would happen to my drawings and stories." He watched anxiously over the creative impulse ("if you pay a writer too well he loses the incentive to work") and over morals (". . . Ross, discussing some guilty pair, said, 'I'm sure he's s-l-e-e-p-i-n-g with her.' He was the only man I've ever known who spelled out euphemisms in front of adults"). He had a limited gift for repartee: "Ross was better at parry than at thrust, and that is why he learned to use so often his familiar 'You have me there' and 'A likely story' and 'That I'd have to see.'" Lovable though his character was generally, stress would occasionally bring out a darker side. A junior employee got married, had children, needed a raise, which Ross refused to okay. When Thurber remonstrated with him, " 'I haven't got time for little people,' Ross snarled"; later apologized and murmured something about his physical troubles. The same physical troubles were responsible for an impulsive rebuke to the near-blind Thurber: "Ross snapped, not out of his heart but out of his ulcers, 'If you could see, you would know what we mean.' "

David Cort began his review of this book in *The Nation* with the words: "It is incredible and outrageous, but nevertheless a fact, that the generation of American culture between the world wars was strongly affected by the character, manners and will of one Harold Ross, late editor of *The New Yorker* magazine, the nominal wheelhorse of American sophistication." Whatever they may think about sophisticated wheelhorses, many readers of *The Years with Ross* will be likely, even if they do not share Mr. Cort's indignation, to feel the force of the contrast which he points out. How could somebody like Ross invent something like *The New Yorker?* And how, having invented it, could he successfully edit it, and give it the stamp which it still bears? The answer, no doubt, is that nobody else could have done these things. The point about Ross is that he was an energetic lowbrow who knew how to hire the right highbrows and, having hired them, to see that they would write in a manner that would seem highbrow, but not offensively so, to lowbrows with highbrow leanings. He was a great editor because he effectively and shrewdly represented a great number of potential readers—whom the *New Yorker* writers, left to themselves, would have alienated. An important source of *The New Yorker*'s financial strength today is that great class which thinks itself entitled not merely to appear but actually to *feel* cultured, without undergoing any dull and painful preparation, such as being educated. The conquest of this class was Ross's achievement. The achievement of certain *New Yorker* writers and artists—notably Thurber himself—was that, within the limits imposed by Rossism, they managed to produce so many extraordinarily good things. But some went under, and some of the best; Mr. Thurber has curiously little to say about Dorothy Parker. And the magazine as it is today, luxurious and air-conditioned, seems sterilized by money; not that it does not still carry good writing, but that its exclusion of controversy—not quite total, it dislikes bombs—gives a general impression of unnatural constraint, of something less adult, less honest and less free than, say, *L'Express* of Paris. It is true that it is not brainwashed like *Krokodil*—because *Krokodil* has its tiny cerebellum scrubbed with red carbolic—but it smells suspiciously clean. The worst result of the cleaning is the acceptance and even admiration of Rossism by good and intelligent men. "We were all asked, a hundred times," Thurber tells us, " 'What will happen to the *New Yorker* now that Ross is dead?' We had our separate answers to that, but Joe Liebling's is perhaps the one that will last: 'The same thing that happened to analysis after Freud died.'" It seems from the context that neither Liebling nor even Thurber saw anything ludicrous in that comparison.

A *NEW YORKER* CRITIC

———•◦•———

Mr. Dwight Macdonald was once one of the boldest of American political commentators, and is today one of the wittiest and—in detail—most lucid of American literary critics. The present volume is a collection of his critical essays—about half of them being reprinted from *The New Yorker,* on which the author has been a staff writer since 1951. It follows that *Against the American Grain* is not as much against the American grain as all that.

The New Yorker is an established and highly esteemed part of American middle-class culture, and its 400,000 regular buyers—most of whom probably read some part of it—are assumed to include many of the leaders of American economic, political, social and cultural life. Now on many matters, such as art, music or literary criticism, these are, on the whole, very tolerant people. You could say *almost* anything about Mark Twain, James Joyce, James Agee, Ernest Hemingway, James Cozzens, Colin Wilson, the English of revised Bibles, or Webster's *New International Dictionary*—to list most of Mr. Macdonald's subjects—without causing a *New Yorker* reader or advertiser to wince. If, however, your favourite authors happened to be Mao Tse-tung and Fidel Castro and you tried to say so in *The New Yorker,* then you *would* be going "against the American grain" and you would not be likely to go very far. Even on Mark Twain etc. certain writers could, by making or implying certain kinds of radical criticism of American capitalist society, contrive to set some important American teeth on edge. Jean-Paul Sartre, writing on any one of Mr. Macdonald's subjects, would be likely, from his first paragraph to his last, to rasp the nerves of most *New Yorker* readers and all *New Yorker* advertisers. In Mr. Macdonald's case, however, the continuity of his association with *The New Yorker* suggests that his grating does not go beyond that threshold where "literary criticism" shades into "politics" and Mr. William Shawn becomes conscious of pain.

This raises questions of varying degrees of interest. Why does so agreeable a critic want to go against the grain at all? Why, if he wants to go against the grain, does he not succeed in this comparatively simple enterprise? And why does he think he has succeeded where he has in fact so pleasantly failed?

The answer to the first question is simple. Mr. Macdonald is concerned about the impact of "a novel kind [of culture] that is manufactured for the market"—which he calls Masscult—on higher forms of culture. This is the pressure against which he would rebel, the grain against which he would work. His remarks about the nature of Masscult do not now sound novel, as he is aware:

As an earlier settler in the wilderness of Masscult who cleared his first tract thirty years ago . . . I have come to feel like the aging Daniel Boone when the plowed fields began to surround him in Kentucky.

But what is interesting in this collection of essays is not his rather confused analysis of Masscult—confused by a tendency to run together "the masses" and those who manipulate them—but his detailed investigations in a middle area: "not," as he says, "the dead sea of masscult but rather the life of the tideline where higher and lower organisms compete for survival." Part of this tideline is taken up by Midcult, of which Mr. Macdonald analyses and exposes four "typical products . . . Ernest Hemingway's *The Old Man and the Sea*, Thornton Wilder's *Our Town*, Archibald MacLeish's *J.B.*, and Stephen Vincent Benét's *John Brown's Body*." Mr. Macdonald disposes of these hollow masterpieces—all "hailed" by most American critics in their day—mainly by quotation and comment. Thus he quotes a Wilder sage: "There's something way down deep that's eternal about every human being." And he comments: "The last sentence is an eleven-word summary, in form and content, of Midcult. I agree with everything Mr. Wilder says but I will fight to the death against his right to say it in this way."

On this tideline "lower organisms" have the best of it. Here even good writers, like Twain and Hemingway, become corrupted; the English language is debased by the indiscriminate lexicography of the third Webster's: even the classics are defiled by cultural wholesalers: "a hundred pounds of Great Books: four hundred and forty-three works by seventy-six authors, ranging chronologically and in other ways from Homer to Mortimer J.

Adler." Mr. Macdonald sees all around him "a tepid ooze of midcult" and feels that "there is something damnably American about it all." If this indeed is "the American grain," then the question of why a critic like Mr. Macdonald feels the need to go against it is easily answered.

The second question is harder: why the American public so cheerfully supports Mr. Macdonald's form of un-Americanism. The most obvious, but not necessarily the most accurate, answer is that the public for which Mr. Macdonald is writing, the *New Yorker* public, is "different," Stendhal's "happy few," above both Midcult and Masscult. That, clearly, is how Mr. Macdonald would like it to be. He now—breaking with his socialist past—favours an "attempt to define two cultures, one for the masses and the other for the classes." He adds in a footnote that by "classes" he doesn't mean "a social or economic upper-class but rather an intellectual elite."

Now readers of *The New Yorker* undoubtedly belong to "a social or economic upper-class" (both, indeed). Do they also constitute an intellectual elite? Mr. Macdonald would not maintain that they do, but he is uneasily defensive about *The New Yorker*. At one point he maintains that it is "a Midcult magazine, but one with a difference. It, too, has its formula, monotonous and restrictive, but the formula reflects the tastes of the editors and not their fear of the readers." Later, he speaks of *The New Yorker* as "a plot of artificial grass, fenced off from American mass culture" in which "some freedom of expression is possible."

The theory that the people who run *The New Yorker* are working in some kind of privileged sanctuary, where they can afford to be indifferent to the reactions of readers and advertisers, hardly belongs on the same intellectual level with most of the rest of Mr. Macdonald's writing. *The New Yorker* is, in fact, an immensely successful commercial enterprise, and such successes are not obtained in the amateurish and absent-minded manner which Mr. Macdonald suggests. The key word in his remarks about *The New Yorker* is "restrictive" and this, significantly, he does not amplify. In practice, we know that "restrictive" means that politics are out, and that "politics" means the kind of politics that annoys advertisers and rich readers—the kind of politics in which Mr. Macdonald himself was once so passionately engaged. Within this enclosure, once this taboo is respected, the writer enjoys a certain kind of freedom. He is free, as Mr. Macdonald quite rightly says,

to express himself without regard for the conventions of American journalism, taking the space he needs, using long sentences, interesting syntax, and difficult words, and going into all kinds of recondite by-ways simply because the subject seems to lead there.

Indeed, he seems to be encouraged to do all these things—*The New Yorker,* above all, is a magazine of conspicuous leisure. More than this, the writer can even assail, as Mr. Macdonald repeatedly does, the general level of American culture. The *New Yorker* reader, knowing he is not as other men are, lends a complacent ear to this kind of thing, within limits.

The limits are that no political remedy is sought or implied—Mr. Macdonald is sound on this—and that there is no implication that this form of decadence is peculiar to the capitalist world. Mr. Macdonald constantly reminds us that things are worse in Russia; this not merely keeps him right with the Congress for Cultural Freedom, but also reassures his readers. His prose remains free to flow in just as leisurely a current as he wishes, channelled between those fat walls of advertising which symbolize the limitations of his freedom. I do not claim that Mr. Macdonald is in any way insincere in this—his anti-communism is just as sincere as his other attitudes—but I don't think he fully realizes the coercive force of the restrictions which he has accepted and to which he has adapted himself. *The New Yorker,* which he tries to use as a vantage point, belongs precisely to that region which he is trying to study: "the tideline where higher and lower organisms compete for survival." Mr. Macdonald, a higher organism if ever there was one, should watch out for faceless creatures in that tepid pool of his. He tells us in one of the most moving of his essays what Midcult did, through *Time* magazine, to so gifted a writer as James Agee. Mr. Macdonald stands in similar, but more insidious, danger from the particular organ of Midcult which has got hold of him.

In Mr. Macdonald's inability to dissociate himself from the *New Yorker* perspective is to be found the answer to our third question: why he feels he has succeeded in rebelling. By setting up the self-flattering idol of "an intellectual elite," he feels that he has extricated himself, whereas what he has really done is conform to the totality of the culture against which he thinks he is in revolt. Although he cannot believe that his readers are such an elite, they believe it, and take comfort from him. They are not irritated by his words, which seem to them points well taken, at the expense of their social, and therefore their intellectual, inferiors. They are like prosperous parishioners listening to a sermon on the evils of drinking red biddy. He in turn, in the political apathy, or aphasia, which seems to have overcome him on losing his Trotskyite faith, has been visited by an illusion of social and economic weightlessness, believing himself to be outside the system which he is describing, and of which he is, apparently without knowing it, a functioning part.

There was a time when Dwight Macdonald, in his prickly and indignant independence, might have been thought of as an American Orwell. Through accepting "restrictions" such as Orwell never accepted, he is in danger of turning into a critical dandy, the literary image of that "Eustace Tilley" who lifts his ridiculous monocle every year on the cover of the magazine for which Mr. Macdonald writes. Mr. Macdonald has not quite fallen for the kind of nonsense symbolized by "Eustace Tilley," but his choice of "classes" against "masses" makes the monocle—emblem of pretentious myopia—a disturbingly appropriate symbol to appear above his recent writing. Like Burke according to Paine, this gifted liberal "kisses the aristocratical hand that hath purloined him from himself."

SERPENTS

―――――•◆•―――――

When Deganawida was leaving the Indians in the Bay of Quinté in Ontario, he told the Indian people that they would face a time of great suffering. They would distrust their leaders and the principles of peace of the League, and a great white serpent was to come upon the Iroquois, and that for a time it would intermingle with the Indian people and would be accepted by the Indians, who would treat the serpent as a friend. This serpent would in time become so powerful that it would attempt to destroy the Indian, and the serpent is described as choking the life's blood out of the Indian people. . . . and he told them that when things looked their darkest a red serpent would come from the north and approach the white serpent, which would be terrified, and upon seeing the red serpent he would release the Indian, who would fall to the ground almost like a helpless child, and the white serpent would turn all its attention to the red serpent. . . . And Deganawida said they [the Indians] would remain neutral in this fight between the white serpent and the red serpent.

Mad Bear, the Tuscarora Indian who related to Edmund Wilson the long allegory which includes the story of the serpents, is one of the leaders of a messianic and nationalist movement which has developed in recent years among the Iroquois "Six Nations" in New York State and Canada, and apparently affects in some degree other Indians in regions as far afield as Florida, Wisconsin and even Arizona. Socially, this movement draws strength from the resentment created by the impact of industrial society—particularly the physical and legal impacts of great engineering projects, "thruways" and seaways—on the Indian reservations with their ancient treaty rights, never fully observed and never completely rescinded by the white man. Politically, the movement is strongly affected by the activities of the "newly emerging nations" not only in Asia and Africa but also in Latin America. *Apologies to the Iroquois* contains a photograph of Fidel Castro receiving Mad Bear in Cuba in 1959, and according to Mr. Wilson, Iroquois nationalists hope that Cuba will sponsor the admission of the Iroquois League to the United Nations. Culturally, the movement is traditionalist and pagan in tendency. The dances and ceremonies of the Longhouse are revived and there are even those—as yet a minority, it seems—who want to return to the Sacrifice of the White Dog. Other sacrifices are not altogether to be excluded. Brigadier Holdridge, a paleface sympathizer with the Indian nationalists, once campaigned in favour of hanging Harry Truman, General Bradley, Cardinal Spellman and John Foster Dulles. We have no means of knowing whether this program appealed to Indians more than to other sections of the population, but the Brigadier recently counselled violence to the Indians specifically: "to resist with all their power, even to gunfire, if necessary, in defense of their territory."

Apologies to the Iroquois is an extremely interesting, attractive and yet finally unsatisfactory discussion of these questions. The interest and attraction derive from Mr. Wilson's well-known and unflagging powers of observation and description, and especially his watchful respect for individual members of an alien culture: the unsatisfactory character is probably the result of the peculiar requirements of *The New Yorker,* in which most of the material originally appeared. The more obviously irritating characteristics of *New Yorker* reporting—artfully-artless meandering, and an affection for detail above and beyond the call of duty—are certainly not dominant here, but the reader is conscious that something of the kind has been expected, and that something better has been lost by reason of this expectation. "The nationalist movement of the Iroquois," writes Mr. Wilson, "is only one of many recent evidences of a new self-assertion on the part of the Indians. The subject is much too large and complicated even to be outlined here, but . . ." No doubt it is large and complicated, and no doubt there is much to be said for Mr. Wilson's method of confining himself to a few tribes and a few concrete problems, rather than indulging in generalizations about Indian movements. Yet as a long description of a dance follows a long account of a lawsuit and these are followed by another lawsuit and another dance, it is possible to feel that room could, after all, have been found, if not for an outline of American Indian nationalism today, at least for something more than the shrewd, tantalizing hints scattered through the three hundred pages of this volume. Not that there is anything frivolous about either the lawsuits or the dances: it is the slow, restless oscillation from subject to subject, *The New Yorker's ton de bonne compagnie,* that is frivolous. But the white serpent has come to crave this cunning mixture of information and distraction, and even Mr. Wilson must sacrifice to him.

In Mad Bear's allegory there is also a black serpent, who eventually defeats the red and white serpents, and whose victory is the prelude to the return of the Indian messiah, Deganawida, and the restoration of the Indian nation. The culminating moment is already at hand. The big war between the red and white serpents is due to begin in 1960, and as a result of it the United States is to come to an end and a great light will come to the Indian people.

No doubt such fantasies are common to all oppressed peoples—and a people can still feel itself oppressed even if no one is any longer conscious of oppressing it. Nor is there anything new in what is represented by the red serpent—a sporting flutter on the enemy of one's enemy. "England's difficulty is Ireland's opportunity" was for long the watchword of the most irreconcilable "minority people" in Western Europe. What is probably new, however, is the role of the black serpent—the feeling that a general victory of oppressed non-white peoples is at hand. Mr. Wilson writes:

They know that they came from the Orient . . . and they know what has been happening in China. They also know that India has freed herself, that Ghana is now a free state, and that the Algerians are struggling to become one. They have sensed that the white man has been losing his hold, and, like the rest of the non-white races, they are sick of his complacency and arrogance. They find this a favorable moment for declaring their national identity because, in view of our righteous professions in relation to the Germans and Russians, they know that, for the first time in history, they are in a position to blackmail us into keeping our agreements and honoring their claims.

Cold war, unlike hot war, has probably more beneficiaries than victims, but it resembles hot war in that those who are most apt to benefit are those who manage to avoid taking part in it. The American Indians, like so many African and Asian peoples—but unlike the people of Tibet—may greatly gain, materially and politically, from the cold war. Agreeable as this is, it is not without its dangers, even for the beneficiaries. All weak peoples are apt to cherish a sense of superior virtue, corresponding to the magnitude of the crimes they have been powerless to commit. This sense, in times of oppression, is a relatively harmless consolation. On the emergence of freedom it becomes a costly delusion. Atavistic practices, being felt to guarantee the tribal distinctness—and therefore superiority—become more cherished than intelligence or even common sense. The reverses brought about by this scale of preferences will in the long run, if there is one, overthrow it; in the short run they are more likely to intensify atavism: "The Sacrifice of the White Dog was not, it seems, enough. . . ."

Logically, the discredit of racism should have done nothing to make primitive animism respectable. In practice the white man's shame does tend to have that effect. The eighteenth century pronounced the Savage noble, in cheerful ignorance of how the Savage behaved; the twentieth century, having had the opportunity to study all varieties of savagery, refuses to pronounce a value judgment at all. The resources of civilization have, apparently, become exhausted quicker than Mr. Gladstone would have thought possible. It is only "apparently," of course; the anthropologist who writes as if he thought that the practices of headhunters were no less valuable and no less commendable than the proceedings of the Royal Society is playing a scientific game, which most of his readers understand. But members of the communities studied might be forgiven for taking the game seriously, for reaching the conclusion that Western civilization, having studied what it wrongly took to be a primitive form of society, had been forced to see that this society was in fact an alternative civilization, of no less value than that of the declining West. The relativist anthropologists of the twentieth century may be seen in retrospect to have been no less disastrous than the absolutist ethnologists of the last century. For something like the dream which haunts Mad Bear—and no doubt many other Mad Bears in other parts of the world—may very easily come true. The red and white serpents may indeed destroy each other, and the black serpent may inherit the earth. In the perspective of human history this need not be an unmitigated disaster—except for amateurs of a particular pigmentation—provided that the transit of civilization has already been successfully accomplished. But it will be a pity if the survivors of the human race are in such a mental state—as a result, among other things, of anthropological "respect"—that they fancy their survival to be a result of their persistence in sacrificing dogs.

WHITE GODS
AND BLACK AMERICANS

In Accra recently a Nigerian company, under the direction of the brilliant young artist Demas Nwoko, presented a dramatized version, in Yoruba, of Amos Tutuola's *The Palm-Wine Drinkard*. The highlight of the evening was "The White Gods," a European couple, as they appear to a simple West African, interpreted by a very sophisticated West African. Lank straw-coloured hair hung round their pallid masks; they seemed all knees and noses, their movements angular, their courtship birdlike, their voices shrill and sad. They were felt to be benevolent, in a sense, and powerful, in a sense, but the benevolence and the power had strayed in different directions, and all this was somehow conveyed by the movements of these dislocated dolls. The audience before which these figures mopped and mowed was black and white. The black part laughed heartily, in frank, spontaneous recognition. As for the white part, we laughed too, but later and less. It was disconcerting to feel oneself seen in this way: one felt naked, awkward, ruffled. *Les Blancs riaient, mais jaune.*

And here is James Baldwin describing, in *Another Country*, a white man dancing with a black girl:

Ida and Ellis had begun a new dance; or, rather, Ida had begun a new cruelty. Ida was suddenly dancing as she had probably not danced since her adolescence, and Ellis was attempting to match her—he could certainly not be said to be leading her now, either. He tried, of course, his square figure swooping and breaking, and his little boy's face trying hard to seem abandoned. And the harder he tried—*the fool!* Cass thought—the more she eluded him, the more savagely she shamed him. He was not on those terms with his body, or with hers, or anyone's body. He moved his buttocks by will, with no faintest memory of love, no hint of grace; his thighs were merely those of a climber, his feet might have been treading grapes. He did not know what to do with his arms, which stuck out at angles to his body as though they were sectioned and controlled by strings, and also as though they had no communion with his hands—hands which had grasped and taken but never caressed.

Reading this I was instantly both reminded of the White Gods and struck by a contrast. Those arms "sectioned and controlled by strings" are exactly those of the White Gods, but the spirit of the scene is very different. The laughter of the black audience at the White Gods had no more hatred or bitterness than the laughter of an English Edwardian audience at the Dixie Minstrels: some contempt, yes, some affection too, in both cases. In Baldwin's tone there is neither amusement nor affection; there is cold contempt with a touch of something else, either pity or cruelty. True, this white character is a particularly unsympathetic one and he is supposed, at this moment, to be seen through the eyes of a white woman. But she is a white woman invented by James Baldwin and her vision and her tone are characteristically and unmistakably Baldwin's.

It is not surprising that a West African and an American Negro should contemplate the jerky progress of the Caucasian with quite different emotions. The historical experience of the American Negro has been far more bitter; his present, though in absolute economic terms more prosperous, is socially and psychologically much harder to bear. The West African's house is a modest one, but he is master in it; the American Negro lives in the basement of a rich man's house, as a poor relation.

The relationship makes the poverty much more bitter. "That's part of the dilemma of being an American Negro," said James Baldwin in a radio interview;

that one is a little bit colored and a little bit white, and not only in physical terms but in the head and in the heart, and there are days when you wonder what your role is in this country and what your future is in it. How precisely are you going to reconcile yourself to your situation here and how are you going to communicate to the vast headless, unthinking cruel white majority: that you are here, and to be here means that you can't be anywhere else. I could, my own person, leave this country and go to Africa, I could go to China, I could go to Russia, I could go to Cuba, but I'm an American and that's a fact.

It is Baldwin's achievement that he has convinced an important section of his white fellow-countrymen that he "is there." He has not only made them see him, but made them see how *he* sees *them*—a feat which no American Negro writer, not even Richard Wright, had ever before succeeded in performing. His fellow-countrymen had seen him as a specialized abstraction: not seeing "a man" or "another American," but only "a Negro," that is to say, a phenomenon about which the most important facts were certain physical characteristics. The presence of these characteristics reduced "him" almost to "it": an object about which one held certain views, possibly even liberal views, and whose movements were restricted to certain grooves, both in the mind and in the city. When this object flew from its groove, when America discovered Baldwin discovering America, the effect was something between that of a clear message from a mind in Outer Space and that of a stinging rebuke from a deaf-mute.

It was not that other American Negroes, from the late and great W. E. B. Du Bois to Richard Wright, had not written, and written well, about the Negro situation. What Baldwin did was to shift the ground, to talk about *American* situations, human situations in America. He threw away the placards of the "literature of protest"; he tells us in *Nobody Knows My Name* how he did that and how he had to quarrel with Richard Wright about it. He wrote without flattery, either of the white people or—what was harder—of his own people. The hatred and fear of whites which had inevitably marked his youth dissolved into his imagination, leaving his consciousness unusually clear, his tone calm and casual. "What white people have to do," he said, "is to try to find out in their own hearts why it was necessary to have a nigger in the first place, because I'm not a nigger, I'm a man, but if you think I'm a nigger it means you need it. Why?"

If white Americans—and other whites—are having to give increasing attention to this question, this is obviously not just because of Baldwin, or any other writer. But it is Baldwin who made this question explicit in this particular way, not thundering at injustice but probing for the roots of a sickness. He has made white men listen to him, and simply because of this—so deep is the alienation of "black" from "white" America—he has made some Negroes suspicious of him. Their suspicions have been summarized for them by another important American Negro writer, Julian Mayfield—who himself admires Baldwin—in these words:

There must be something wrong with Baldwin because his books are on the best-seller list and his articles appear in prestige, mass-circulation magazines. Worst yet, he's always on television giving his opinion about this or that; and although I usually say "hear, hear" to his ideas, tell me—since when did Mr. Charlie White Man Boss become so interested in the opinion of any black man but an Uncle Tom? And why should Baldwin be writing about "queers" all the time when there are so many more important things to concern Negro writers?

If Baldwin is a "queer" Uncle Tom, he must be a very queer Uncle Tom indeed. He told his New York television audience, for example, in May 1963, that he would have trouble convincing his nephew to go to Cuba "to liberate the Cubans in the name of a government which now says it is doing everything which it can do but cannot liberate me." Mr. Mayfield rightly stresses—in relation to the role of spokesman for his people which has been almost forced on Baldwin—the importance of an article which Baldwin contributed to *The New York Times Magazine* in March 1961 and which is now reprinted in *Nobody Knows My Name* under a new title, "East River Downtown." This article was about the violent demonstration which a group of American Negroes staged in the gallery of the United Nations Security Council, after the news of the murder of Lumumba. Some prominent American Negroes were shocked at this behaviour, and Dr. Ralph Bunche made himself their spokesman; James Baldwin spoke up for other and much more numerous Negroes. At a time when the newspapers made "Communist-inspired" the prescribed epithet for the demonstration, Baldwin condemned "the American assumption that the Negro is so contented with his lot here that only the cynical agents of a foreign power can rouse him to protest." And he told the readers of *The New York Times*—not at all accustomed to such thoughts—that a young American Negro today will not "settle for Jim Crow in Miami" when he can "feast at the welcome-table in Havana."

It is true, and it is significant, both for Baldwin's hostile critics and for his friends, that when he has made his point about Miami and Havana he adds the words: "These are extremely unattractive facts . . ." Thus discreetly, and without loss of dignity, he intimates to his reader that he is not a Communist, and that—at the least—he would wish to be a loyal American. (In his earlier writings he uses "we" in speaking of Americans generally, both black and white. I have not noticed this pronoun, thus used, in his later work.) Such words are passwords, the minimum guarantee without which his voice could not be so widely heard; the fact that he can give, and has given, this password is what makes him distrusted by some, like Mr. Mayfield's querist, among the Negro left. In a community whose "leaders" have so often turned into the tools of its oppressors, it is natural enough that people should worry about Mr. Baldwin, lest he too be "got at"; that there should be a sharp intake of breath every time he is heard from, or heard about, at a meeting organized by the Congress for Cultural Freedom. Yet because Uncle Tom is an anticommunist, it does not follow that Mr. Baldwin, to be justified, must be a Communist, or pretend to be a Communist, or even sedulously refrain from letting it be known that he is not a Communist. He could not follow such lines without ceasing to be himself, without losing what one of his angrier critics, with perhaps unconscious felicity, called his "excruciating detachment."

Why should he write so much about homosexuals instead of the "so many other important things to concern Negro writers"? He writes, of course, about what is important *to him*, not about what should interest "Negro writers" as a class, and he has denied that he belongs to such a class: "I am a writer. I am not a Negro writer." In the same sense Mauriac denied being "a Catholic novelist," gave scandal to Catholics by writing about sex and money; Yeats, although a good Irish nationalist, could not pretend that he found gerrymandering in County Fermanagh more interesting than sex and magic. Yet Mauriac remained a Catholic, Yeats an Irishman and Baldwin a Negro. When Baldwin writes about homosexuals he writes with a Negro's sense of another "outlawry," and also, it seems, with some sense of release at a transposition of values: escape into a world where the colour of a man's skin is less important—in reality, not just in theory—than another attribute, in this case a particular sexual bent. It is not as simple as that—exploitation of black boys by white homosexuals is one of Baldwin's themes—but in general, homosexuality, in

Baldwin's work as in Proust's, is felt to provide an alternative set of hierarchies and values to those of the larger society. Proust felt torn by this; Baldwin is less torn because, by the nature of his situation, he cannot feel himself to be a part of the white, heterosexual Anglo-Saxon Protestant culture under which—not in which—he grew up.

Even Baldwin's harsher critics among American Negroes show some affection and admiration for him. The respected left-wing intellectual Negro quarterly, *Freedomways,* devotes some space to him regularly—many of my quotations are taken from its pages—and its contributors oscillate between rebuke and applause. If a reviewer finds Baldwin's style "self-conscious and affected" and himself "disturbingly responsive to the Seducers," Mr. Mayfield, in the same issue, more pertinently observes Baldwin's "ability to capture in beautiful, passionate and perceptive prose the essence of Negro determination to live in the American house as a free man or, failing that, to burn the American house down." But the most moving and I believe the most representative comment is the reply of a very militant American Negro, Mr. Sylvester Leaks, to Baldwin's claim to be just "a writer":

The Negro people love Mr. Baldwin. And rightly so! He is of us. And no matter what you say, Jimmy—Oh! yes you are—Oh! yes you are a Negro writer!

FREE SPENDERS

———◆———

It is not possible to be thrifty and yet hold a high position in the corner gang.
—WILLIAM FOOTE WHYTE

Mr. Whyte, one of the numerous American sociologists whose case histories and findings are used by Mr. Vance Packard in *The Status Seekers,* tells the story of two boys in the Italian slum "Cornerville": "Chick went on to 'Ivy University' and law school to become a successful lawyer. Doc, in contrast, made little progress, continued to hang out nightly with the street-corner gang." Mr. Whyte found that the difference in intelligence and ability did not explain their different careers. The explanation lay in different attitudes to money. Chick was thrifty and ignored gang opinion. "In contrast, Doc, to maintain his prestige as leader of his street-corner gang, had to be a free spender."

According to the classic American tradition, it is Chick who has adapted himself to American (Protestant) values, Doc who clings to a feckless European (Catholic) way of life. Almost any nineteenth-century version of the story would carry some such implication and many Americans today—probably a majority—would take that nineteenth-century implication for granted. But that is not the way in which the story can be fitted into the world of *The Status Seekers* and Mr. Griffith's *Waist-High Culture.* That world is dominated, not by Chick's values, but by Doc's. Chick can move from the corner to a country club—one that takes Italians—but at the club level he will find that he now cannot avoid being "a free spender" and looking after his "prestige." Mr. Philip Starr, of Yankee City, who, like Chick, pushed his way up from the lower class to the top, was so determined to win prestige at his new level that he "sought to make his parents seem upper class, too, by disinterring their remains in the city's lower-class cemetery and reburying them in the city's upper-class cemetery." Nearer, my God, to thee.

The point of *The Status Seekers* is not so much that snobbery is a powerful force in American life—it is in every society including the Soviet Union—as that uncontrolled snobbery, in American conditions, involves such human and material waste as to threaten the coherence, and eventually the survival, of American society. In conditions of plenty, of corporate might and community weakness, brains are diverted from education into advertising—the comparative salary figures quoted by Mr. Packard are convincing on this point—and there used to promote the diversion of material resources into a profusion of status symbols. The cultural impoverishment that results from the eclipse of education by salesmanship is Mr. Griffith's main concern in his misleadingly named *The Waist-High Culture*. ("Have we sold our birthright for a mess of pottage that goes pop, crackle, snap?") And Mr. Emmet Hughes in *America the Vincible* is preoccupied by the collective weakness and drift of this enormously and often absurdly productive society, confronted, as it is, by an ambitious and disciplined rival. In the picture that emerges from the three books, America today looks rather like a "corner gang" of free-spending, prestige-minded Docs, resenting—in the rising, confident, thrifty Soviet Union—a collective Chick.

Many will say—many are saying—that this is a grossly distorted picture. They point out, with justice, that America can give her workers and farmers a far higher standard of living than these classes have in the Soviet Union, and that this standard of living is based on higher efficiency all round. They point out also that hardly anyone in America wants or would accept the harsh regimentation by which the Soviet Union maintains a high rate of saving. None of these three writers—who are representative of a growing volume of radically critical comment—would dispute any of this. None of them wants to see this country turn into anything like the Soviet Union.

They are all successful journalists—Mr. Griffith and Mr. Hughes are both senior *Time* men—and, despite the example of Mr. Whittaker Chambers and one or two others, good journalists are probably more resistant to the attractions of communism than are members of most other professions. Scientists, engineers, most teachers, actors, managers, doctors, soldiers can all carry out their functions in a communist society, often with an agreeable improvement in status or pay. But the journalist's function is largely suppressed: he is told by his political superiors what sort of facts to find and what comments to make on them. At a recent international gathering it was proposed to endorse the right of journalists to "seek" information. The communist countries wanted an amendment: delete "seek" and substitute "gather." Good journalists, like these three, are, by fundamental preference, "seekers" rather than "gatherers." They know by professional experience that even in Western societies, the theory of "seek" often covers the practice of "gather," but they know also, and show by their practice, that the amount of "seeking" possible is vastly greater than anything permitted in communist societies. They are therefore anti-communists by profession—as distinct from the professional anti-communists who often, like the late Senator McCarthy, are not seriously worried about communism at all. When journalists of this type radically criticize American society they do so, not in order to exalt its principal rival, but in fear lest that rival and his techniques of regimentation may be about to prevail. They all—although with various reservations—seem to think that is what is now happening.

"In this time of transcendent challenge and danger to our way of life," writes Mr. Vance Packard, "it seems clear that we can endure and prevail only if the vast majority of our people really believe in our system." By the American "system" he means the ideals of independence of mind, equality of opportunity, democracy in social life, etc. As the whole tenor of his book is that his fellow-countrymen profess to believe in these things, but mostly act as if they did not believe in them, the corollary seems clear. "We must, then, seriously ask ourselves," writes Mr. Thomas Griffith, "whether our society, despite its deceptive vitality, has not entered a parabola of decline, less and less able to cope with what it must face." And Mr. Emmet Hughes—formerly a speechwriter for President Eisenhower—ends his long survey of what he considers to be the bankruptcy of American policy with two alternative drafts of a letter to his children, to be dispatched in 1976. One of these is written on the hypothesis that there is no radical change in present practices, and it describes the grim process and results of America's decline. The other and happier draft is based on the premise that a sudden change of heart and practice arrests the decline. There is little in *America the Vincible* to suggest that it is the second draft which will be dispatched.

What is a non-American to make of these American prognostications? For anti-Americans of right and left there is no problem; shop stewards in Glasgow and colonels in Algiers can mark the same passages with the same glee, and range *America the Vincible* beside their well-worn Mao. Uncritical apologists, including the various dollar-parasites, will also find it easy to take up a position: "healthy American self-criticism . . . American tendency to hyperbole . . . no reason to question fundamental soundness."

But what are the rest of us to think? Can we, as some suggest, write all this off as merely modish debunking? Is it merely stunt-writing aimed at a public frightened by the footprint of a sinister Man Friday in the technological sands? The honest answer of anyone who reads these three books must, I think, be: "on the whole, no." It is true that Sputnik and its successors prepared a public for inquiries of this kind; and true also that, most especially in the kind of society these writers describe, the existence of the public is apt to produce the inquiry. But that is quite a different matter from saying that the results of the inquiry are distorted.

Mr. Packard's manner may be more cheerful than his facts warrant—although the facts have their circus side: it is hard to be solemn about the posthumous migrations of the Starrs. But his findings seem quite genuinely related to a mass of American sociological work over the past ten years or so—the sort of work that has been criticized by Mr. C. Wright Mills in *The Sociological Imagination,* not for being sensational, but for being too timid, limited and academic. Mr. Griffith's book, on the other hand, consists mainly of personal impressions about American life, the personal impressions of the foreign editor of *Time. The Waist-High Culture* is a much sadder book than *The Status Seekers,* as if Mr. Griffith felt the quality of what Mr. Packard was describing in terms of quantities. And just as it would be hard to challenge the general factual basis of *The Status Seekers,* it would be hard to impugn the sincerity in Mr. Griffith's dry, sad tone—the tone that is there when the reassuring amplifiers of that style which he calls "Third Person Authoritative" are switched off. It is the tone of a well-informed passenger who believes the ship is sinking but doesn't want to start a panic. Mr. Hughes in *America the Vincible* talks louder and with more than a touch of rodomontade in the opening generalities—but his anger rings true and his argument is close when he gets down to the known facts of the Dulles years. These three witnesses cannot be dismissed as hostile, as alarmist or as pandering to a national craze for self-denunciation.

"Our society," writes Mr. Griffith, "must find a way first to conceive the common good, and then to honor and reward in proper proportions those activities which best serve, not individual employers, but the community's aims." The stranger can but agree, thinking perhaps of New York, probably the richest city in the world, with its myriad individual success-stories and its municipal failure, its shining towers and dirty ill-lit streets, its treasure-houses of art and its crowded, frightening schools, its brains on Madison Avenue and its despairing bedlam on the Bowery. New York is not America, granted, and Mr. Griffith and his like want to stop America from multiplying the image of New York's anarchy. We outsiders can only wish them luck, knowing that so much of our own luck is bound up with their success. We have the same kind of interest in their attempt to bring on a "tightening" of American society, as we have in the attempts of those who are trying to "loosen" Soviet society—and the same almost complete lack of influence over both. Unless Doc can be made to sober up, and Chick to relax a little, the end of the story—the end for us too—is not hard to guess. Not that we should exaggerate Chick's malevolence. "Doc," we can imagine him saying, "was his own worst enemy."

II

ENGLAND

ORWELL LOOKS AT THE WORLD

"I knew that I had a facility with words and a power of facing unpleasant facts, and I felt that this created a sort of private world in which I could get my own back for my failure in everyday life." These words, about himself as a boy, Orwell wrote when he was already near his death; and they are both true and an example of their own truth. Not that objectively Orwell was a failure, at school or in life. But he did feel himself to be a failure; he did want to get his own back; he had the ability to face unpleasant facts and knew that ability to be, in his own carefully chosen word, "a power." In the same sentence he demonstrates his possession of that power by facing two facts about himself: his sense of failure and desire to get his own back. "I am going to tell you some facts about yourself," he says in effect to the left-wing intellectuals who were for long almost his only readers, "but first you must recognize that I face unpleasant facts about myself, and face such facts in person—facts like bullets. These are things that most of you are very little inclined to do. Through my skill with words, and the power which such skill exerts over people like you, I am now going to compel you to face at least some of the facts which you are trying to hide from yourselves and others."

Most of those addressed—perhaps on this page I can say "most of us"—responded to this challenge, I suppose, in one or both of two opposite ways. The first way was to admit that Orwell's criticisms were largely true: that left-wing intellectuals were, too often, intellectually dishonest, selective in their moral indignation, furtive worshippers of power, and startlingly ignorant both of political realities and of the working class. The quantity and quality of this acceptance no doubt varied. You could, for example, accept Orwell's indictment as being true about your friends but not about yourself. Or you could, if you wanted to, drop being a leftist—for motives probably even less admirable than those which had taken you to the left—have your eyes conveniently "opened" by Orwell's fearless honesty. Some of Orwell's American admirers in the fifties may have been, in reality, more impressed by the arguments of Senator McCarthy than by those of *Animal Farm,* but an Orwellian conversion lent dignity to retreat. There were certainly also, among those clever and anxious people whom Orwell addressed, those who actually enjoyed submitting to the punishment which he inflicted:

> *Come fix upon me that accusing eye*
> *I thirst for accusation.*

But the main reason why many intellectuals accepted the truth of Orwell's accusations is that so many of these accusations were true, and the lucidity of Orwell's prose made their truth inescapable. Intellectuals are probably not more dishonest than other people; their resources for self-deception are of course much greater, but then so is their compulsion to self-criticism: greater forces committed on both sides, and the result equally uncertain. But one characteristic which the intellectual must have, or he ceases to be an intellectual at all, is the ability to see when a real point has been made in debate. It was impossible for anyone with that ability not to notice that Orwell kept scoring direct hits. You knew that certain things he said were true, because you winced when you heard them.

There can be little doubt that Orwell did change the minds of quite a few people through whom he changed the minds of many others. He cleared out a great deal of cant, self-deception, and self-righteousness, and in doing so shook the confidence of the English left, perhaps permanently. The right, as everyone knows, paid no attention to him except for the valuable ammunition he was to supply against communism, and retained its own variety of cant, almost undamaged. But the cant of the left, that cant which has so far proved indispensable to the victory of any mass movement, was almost destroyed by Orwell's attacks, which put out of action so much cant-producing machinery in its factories: the minds of left-wing intellectuals. His effect on the English left might be compared to that of Voltaire on the French nobility: he weakened their belief in their own ideology, made them ashamed of their clichés, left them intellectually more scrupulous and more defenceless.

There was, of course, and is, a second way of responding to Orwell's challenge: you could question his impartiality and therefore his right to judge. But Orwell has been accused of being essentially a reactionary writer whose work both "objectively" strengthened, and was intended to strengthen, the existing order. On this view the critique of that order which his works contain is held to be perfunctory, a sort of diversion to draw attention from the real attack, which was directed against the left. In its extreme forms, this accusation is very easy to refute. Anyone who calls Orwell a fascist—and I believe the thing has been done—knows nothing at all about either him or his life. Orwell's life, and the Spanish wound which shortened that life, refuted such absurdities. But if no human type, except perhaps the Communist party member, could be more remote from Orwell than is the fascist, it is also true that he is very far indeed from being "progressive."

Sir Richard Rees, in his sympathetic and enlightening book,* brings out well the "old-fashioned" side of Orwell—the deep English patriotism, the distaste for machinery and modern psychology, the love of the country, of animals, even the lingering nostalgia for the Edwardian age. These qualities, in Orwell's work, growl in many asides, and growl increasingly often. It is a Tory growl: each quality in itself, obviously, is not necessarily Tory, but grouped together they do form a Tory pattern. It is not surprising that Orwell should have taken pleasure in defending Kipling against leftist criticism (his important essay on Kipling is unaccountably omitted from the present volume† of collected essays, the title of which is misleading). If we add to the list a chivalrous but rather insensitive attitude towards the underdog and a tendency towards self-immolation, what seems to emerge is the character of an English conservative eccentric.

The character is on the whole an attractive one, and has done much to make English life more decent—a favourite word of Orwell's. The limitations of the viewpoint it implies are probably more obvious to foreigners than they are to the English. Orwell seldom wrote about foreigners, except sociologically, and then in

---

* *George Orwell.*
† *Collected Essays.*

a hit-or-miss fashion otherwise unusual with him; he very rarely mentions a foreign writer and has an excessive dislike of foreign words; although he condemns imperialism he dislikes its victims even more. Indeed he sometimes goes beyond dislike; he rises to something like hysteria. In *Shooting an Elephant,* he records fantasies about sticking a bayonet into the belly of a sniggering Buddhist priest. This is the kind of fantasy that Orwell himself found sinister in *No Orchids for Miss Blandish*. It is really more disquieting in *Shooting an Elephant:* not that sadistic fantasies are unusual, even in good and gentle men, but that quite unmistakably Orwell was much more likely to have this kind of fantasy about a Burmese than about an Englishman.

I do not suggest that it is morally better to have such fantasies about an Englishman. The point is that if sadistic fantasies are unevenly distributed by race or nationality, the consequences are more likely to be political—and therefore contagious and dangerous—than if they remain purely personal.

Orwell of course was too decent and clear-headed to support any racialist or imperialist program. The presence in his make-up of the kind of feeling that inspires such programs led to no more than a certain deadening of his feeling and understanding where most of the population of the world was concerned. He turned towards foreigners, especially Asians, that part of his mind which brooded darkly about sandals, beards and vegetarians. He could not "think himself into the mind" of any kind of foreigner and he seldom tried to do so. He never thought it worth while to imagine seriously what it would be like to belong to a people with a quite different historical experience from that of the English. As far as he considered such matters at all, I think he felt that not to be a product of English history was a sort of moral lapse.

Many people, quite obviously, are not less insular today than Orwell, but no one of comparable intelligence can now attain that degree of insularity—short of being whimsical like Mr. Evelyn Waugh or Mr. Kingsley Amis. During almost all of Orwell's writing career, England was sufficiently central to the world's political and economic life for an Anglocentric view of the world not to be seen as an eccentric one. Since then, the McCarthy years, the "thaw" in Russia, the rise of African nationalism, the Common Market in Europe, the ferment in Latin

America, the Russian-American space race, emanations of Communist China and, in a different category, the Suez experiment and its failure have made a world in which much, though not all, of Orwell's writing must seem, to readers outside these islands, somewhat provincial.

We are near enough now to 1984 to see that the world then, whatever it may be like, will not be very like Orwell's imagining of it. Is it fantastic to see in Orwell's *1984* the reflection of a feeling that a world in which the pre-1914 British way of life had totally passed away must necessarily be a dehumanized world? And is it altogether wrong to see the inhabitants of *Animal Farm* as having points in common, not merely with Soviet Russians, but also with Kipling's lesser breeds generally, as well as with Flory's Burmese who, once the relative decencies of the Raj are gone, must inevitably fall under the obscene domination of their own kind?

To insist on the limitations of Orwell's thought is only to establish the limits within which we admire him. How much there is to admire, how much we owe to him, every page in these collected essays reminds us. That spare, tough prose has not aged; that clear eye sees more than ours do even if there are things which it cannot see through, and which we now can see from the other side in time. What political writer now cares as much as he did, both about what he is writing and about how he is writing it? Subsequent writers who exploited anger seem far off and apathetic compared with this careful writer who tried so hard to keep his judgment and his language from being clouded by an anger as real as Swift's.

CHORUS OR CASSANDRA

Stalin and the Kulaks:
... we believe that from its own point of view the Russian Government has often been quite unnecessarily repressive. That, one may notice, is the view of Stalin who put an end to the very misguided efforts to expropriate the whole kulak class by terrorism. (*NS & N*, July 4, 1931)

Hitler enters Rhineland:
... it would be folly to reply by a mere *non possumus* ... the sane policy would be to invite her [Germany] back into the League on terms which will do justice to her and ensure that she is a better neighbour. (*NS & N*, March 14, 1934)

Mussolini and Abyssinia:
Last month the Duce was convinced that he had nothing to fear from the League whatever he did. Today he must be disillusioned. Italy's arrogance has completely isolated her. When it comes down to brass tacks the League Powers will cooperate in economic sanctions. (*NS & N*, late 1935)

Spanish War:
It is fairly evident that the Spanish fascists are in full retreat. Their desperate acts defeat their own ends by irritating public opinion against them. (*NS & N*, May 1936)

Munich:
If Mr. Chamberlain is prepared for the results of isolation let him say so. We for our part regarding war as the greatest of all catastrophes and recalling the results of one war to prevent Germany from holding the hegemony of Europe, would applaud and support such a decision. (*NS & N*, March 1938) The question of frontier revision should at once be tackled. (*NS & N*, August 1938) Nothing we or anyone else could do would save Czechoslovakia from destruction. (*NS & N*, August 27, 1938) In the last resort there is no doubt that Britain as well as France and the whole democratic world would stand by the Czechs. (*NS & N*, early September 1938) The Murder of a Nation. (*NS & N*, September 21, 1938)

Chorus or Cassandra   [37]

It is characteristic of the honesty which, at more than one level, has come to be expected from the *New Statesman*—and which makes people like writing for it—that the above material, so rich in ammunition for the paper's enemies, can be taken from two books commissioned by the paper itself for its jubilee.* Mr. Hyams, a contributor to the *New Statesman* but not a member of the staff, chronicles, and often perceptively criticizes, the strange, and strangely successful, sequence of contradictions, made acceptable by a consistent and agreeable tone and style, which the *New Statesman* offered to its puzzled and increasingly anxious readers in the thirties.

Mr. Hyams concedes the contradictions, the illusions and what amounts to the moral and political Micawberism of the paper in the early years of Mr. Kingsley Martin's editorship—up to, in his view, the mid-thirties. He writes sympathetically and well of the conflict between pacifism and anti-fascist socialism in the mind of the nonconformist radical in the context of the early thirties. He reveals, in effect, the split in the British left-wing mind between the harsh Marxist assumptions about the nature of society and the English will to believe that most people are pretty decent chaps really. Mr. Hyams makes a very good point indeed when he speaks of a capacity which Mr. Kingsley Martin shares with many of the rest of us inside and outside the British left: the "capacity to be surprised and angry when the man whom he expected to punch him on the nose, punched him on the nose."

All this part of Mr. Hyams's study seems to me clear and fair. It is with his "Came the Dawn" that I regretfully part from him. He tells us that "halfway through the decade" the *New Statesman* "gave us a clear lead by making a choice between two conflicting sets of principles." He does not, however, establish that on any really important and critical issue of foreign policy in the thirties (except perhaps that of co-operation with the Churchill wing of the Tories) the *New Statesman* did give a clear lead at any moment when a clear lead would have been of much use. The original clear lead of which he speaks was an editorial of September 1935, in which the *New Statesman* endorsed the principle of League sanctions, even at the cost of war, against Italy. Mr. Kingsley Martin, according to Mr. Hyams, "had become

* Edward Hyams, *The New Statesman: The History of the First Fifty Years; New Statesmanship,* chosen by Edward Hyams.

willing to give the policeman a truncheon; and by that change had given the *New Statesman* a 'hard' policy in what was to come." Now first of all, Mr. Kingsley Martin did not have a truncheon to give to the alleged policeman; second, he must have known that the League was not a policeman at all but, generally speaking, the expression of whatever policies could be agreed on by Britain and France (just as for most practical purposes today the United Nations is the expression of whatever policies can be agreed upon between the United States and a sizeable segment of Afro-Asia).

The League could perhaps have been, and the United Nations is, a useful mechanism of international adaptation, but to regard either of them as an impartial executive "policeman" carrying out the will of the international community as a whole is to take the wish for the reality. (The *New Statesman* sought to do this after the war when it took up the so-called Baruch plan for preserving the American monopoly over atomic weapons under the cover of an international organization in whose main organs the influence of the United States would have been securely predominant.) Unconditional pacifism had passed; unconditional euphoria was more tenacious.

On the Spanish War, the *New Statesman* had a clearer line than it did on anything else in these crucial years, perhaps partly because the anti-Catholic element in British nonconformity outweighed the tendency to pacifism. But even here, at its hardest, the hard policy is not very formidable. "In the long run," writes Mr. Hyams, *"New Statesman* writers were forced to see that the whole policy of non-intervention had become a plain fraud and to attack it as such." Why run so long? And why have to be forced in order to see? The "toughest" episode of this period was the refusal to print Orwell's articles describing what he had seen in Spain: "Kingsley Martin did not disbelieve what Orwell had written, but he decided against publishing it." Superficially, his reasons for doing so—"damaging the cause"—seemed like those usually attributed to the Jesuits, whom he disliked. In reality, however, I believe that the refusal may well have been motivated not by counter-Jesuitry, but by a temperamental unwillingness to see unpleasant facts.

Then came Munich, the issue on which the *New Statesman* took a resolute and uncompromising stand, in retrospect. Mr.

Hyams's account of the paper's role in the Czechoslovakian crisis should be read in full, but the quotations at the head of this article plot the leading points on the graph: the idea of Britain's dropping all European commitments and accepting German continental hegemony, the acceptance of the need to revise Czechoslovakia's frontiers, the assertion that Czechoslovakia cannot be helped in any way, the optimistic assumption about what Britain and France will nonetheless do, and finally the thunder of moral indignation when Britain does avoid commitments, the frontier is revised, nothing does save Czechoslovakia, and the British and French governments do what, on the basis of their previous record, they were most likely to do.

Mr. Hyams shows this record side by side with Critic's London Diary for the same period, in which Mr. Kingsley Martin

> talks intimately, an anxious friend, to readers with whom he shares his perplexity and who cannot fail to see that he is in the same state of mind as themselves, that he no longer has any certainties left. It is journalism at its most honest and its most moving.

Moving certainly, and even a part of the memorable literature of the time. But one may well ask: "Moving what, where?"

It is understandable enough that Mr. Hyams, in describing the *New Statesman*'s dilemma—which was also the dilemma of not a few others—in the autumn of 1938, should tend to forget about the famous "hard" policy which we were promised from "the middle of the decade." The *New Statesman* was obviously by no means alone in going through its agonizing reappraisals at the time, and hard policies, like others, are open to be reconsidered. What is a little surprising in the light of the *New Statesman*'s own record is Mr. Hyams's definition of what the *New Statesman*'s hard policy, as distinct from the policies of the other papers, actually meant:

> It is my belief that the almost startling success of the *New Statesman*, from the thirties onward, can only be explained by reference to the fact that its Editor, having thought instead of felt, took a clear decision, as I shall show, between two opposing principles, and out of that decision gave his paper a "hard" policy. The rest of the Press, as far as I know without exception, simply went on behaving like its own readers, went on waffling, went on advocating mutually incompatible policies, or else advocating the basest solution to every political problem.

With the honourable and important exception of the bit about "the basest solution" every word of this description applies, on Mr. Hyams's own showing, to the *New Statesman and Nation* over the period in question.

On concluding his description of the evolution of the *New Statesman*'s attitude to Czechoslovakian frontier revision and allied matters, he makes the following comment:

However, as soon as the Chamberlain-Daladier capitulation to Hitler, entailing a brutal sell-out of the Czechs, was an accomplished fact, the *New Statesman* supported the National Council for Labour in its declaration that this deal was a "shameful betrayal" and rounded on Chamberlain for doing what did, indeed, run counter to the policy the paper had been advocating for years, yet what it might seem to have justified by its single lapse into pessimism, into a devastating honesty.

If I understand this oddly constructed sentence—and I am not sure that I do—Mr. Hyams is here treating what he regards as an encounter with honesty—of the devastating sort as is so often unfortunately the case with honesty—as a "lapse." We must also note that, on Mr. Hyams's own showing, it is not a question of a single lapse into "pessimism." Of the quotations I have collected, three point to what the *New Statesman* later called a "sell-out," although, of course, a "brutal" sell-out was at no time envisaged.

In fact there is a fairly close parallel between the attitude of the *New Statesman* on Munich and the attitude of the Eisenhower/Dulles government to the Hungarian crisis, eighteen years later. Both, on their declared principles, were committed to a stand. Both, for a variety of quite sound and creditable reasons, feared the risk which such a stand entailed. Both, while the issue of possible involvement remained undecided, took a cautious position. On Czechoslovakia, the *New Statesman* wrote what we have seen; on Hungary, as long as Mr. Nagy's government remained in power in Budapest, Mr. Dulles's officials in the corridors of the United Nations used all their great influence against any possible effort to help him. Once the Germans had been given the Sudetenland, once the Russians had occupied Budapest, the *New Statesman* and the State Department waxed, in their respective situations, morally indignant.

The point is not that the *New Statesman* was "soft on communism" as its usual critics allege; the point was that with a sort of instinctive cosiness it usually preferred settling down among the hopeful illusions of its readers—including you and me—to losing popularity and "influence" by rasping those illusions. "It was better," says Mr. Hyams, "to eschew judgements so sharp and clear that they would bounce off wooden heads, to be less uncompromisingly scientific and more rhetorically woolly." The paper did not—it does not—care for the commercial rewards of circulation; it did care for popularity and, above all, for "influence"—too often influence in the Lafayettian sense of leading the people where they thought they were going—reflecting, as Mr. Hyams says, their "preoccupations." This, surely, is the real treason of the clerks: that leaders of opinion, instead of showing to the very best of their ability and knowledge how things actually are, should, in the interests of something or other which usually looks pretty shabby in retrospect, present them with a version which is thought to be better for them or more suited to their limited capacity of understanding, their "wooden heads." Plato's Noble Lie is really just another lie, the nobility being in the vocabulary of the liar.

To many, perhaps to most, readers much of this may appear unfair; and indeed, though true, it would be unfair if left without qualification. There was, and is, much more to the *New Statesman* than a line of editorial policy; and more to editorial policy than the single theme I have discussed. There is a consistently high standard of writing in every department; there has been, ever since Mr. Kingsley Martin became editor, a firm and decent attitude on racial and colonial questions; there was, in Critic's page, perhaps the most successful, and certainly the most urbane, feat of personality-projection in the history of journalism; the book reviews carry weight even with those who dislike all the rest of the paper; finally, even those who dislike the paper's editorial policies like reading it because of its good humour, its good manners and its intelligence (even when, as often, deluded, it is deluded in an intelligent way). It has earned the right, in its fifty years of vigorous life, to be regarded as a great paper—I, perhaps, have earned the right by what I have also said above, to call it so to its face. And it was Mr. Kingsley Martin—inconsistencies, illusions and all—who made the *New Statesman* a great paper.

Why concentrate, then, in the bulk of the article, on a few errors of judgment in editorial policy? Because the paper claims to lead, and to have led, opinion, and because, above all, it is only too apt to claim—and Mr. Hyams has claimed for it—that in this period, when all other leaders of opinion were giving false leads, it alone maintained a sound, bold and consistent policy. This claim is untrue, although of course the *New Statesman* has a better record than, say, *The Times*. Mr. Freeman, like the editors of most other successful papers, could cover the walls of his editorial room with extracts from old issues which involve illusions and inconsistencies. It might be a good idea if he did. The notion that the *New Statesman* played Cassandra in the thirties ought to be firmly discarded; it was no more than chorus in the tragedy. One would have to imagine, though, a cheerful chorus, in good health and spirits, and generally sanguine about the outcome: "The King must persist in his investigation. The clerical interests, headed by the sinister and shortsighted Archbishop Tiresias, must be obliged to divulge the information they are improperly holding back. There is every reason for confidence that by holding firmly to his present course—despite the inevitable prophets of doom—Oedipus will stabilize the situation and ensure a peaceful and productive future for his family and for Thebes."

III

FRANCE

MICHELET TODAY

Aspects of The French Revolution

> *Luckily, time is marching on. We are a little less stupid. Messianism, the mania of incarnations so carefully inculcated by Christian education, is passing away. We are beginning to understand the advice which Anacharsis Clootz, about to die, gave us: France, cure yourself of individuals.*

These words, dated November 1869, are the conclusion of Michelet's introduction to the fifth volume of his *History of the French Revolution*. He was speaking of Robespierre, with Napoleon III in mind, and as far as Napoleon III was concerned he was a shrewd enough tipster. In the wider sense in which he wrote, his words reach us, ninety years later, with an effect of more than Sophoclean irony. This Tiresias, prophesying the downfall of the King, cannot know how his words sound to us. From the vantage point which the passage of time—invoked by him—has conferred on us, his prophetic rage resembles the rage of the Greek king against the reluctant witnesses. For by the standard which he himself invokes, that of temporal progress, it must now seem to us that Napoleon III was right. The advice of Anacharsis Clootz has once again been enthusiastically rejected. The present regime does not repudiate its obvious likeness to the Second Empire. An official exhibition, "Napoleon III and the Imperial Family," held this summer in the Invalides shows every phase in the life of Napoleon III except the final one—no Ems telegram, no Franco-Prussian war, no Sedan. Officially the Débâcle did not take place; certain visitors to the exhibition probably came to the conclusion that Napoleon III is still reigning, and in a way they are right. As for Robespierre, that "Hymn to the Supreme Being" which symbolized his brief Revolutionary monarchy was restored this year to a place of honour in the Fourteenth of July celebrations in Paris. If Michelet was as wrong about eternity as he was about time, he must be suffering intensely.

In fact, of course, our advantage is illusory, our point of time no more privileged than his, and there will no doubt be future dates from which he will seem to be "right" and we "wrong." Where he *was* wrong was not in what he prophesied but in prophesying at all, in believing that the historian knows enough to prophesy. And even that he did not wholly believe; his prophetic activities were in part polemical, like those of so many other prophets, curses rather than predictions.

Michelet's polemics—which pervade his historical writings—seem to many modern historians an even greater crime than his prophesies. "Absolutist thinker," says Professor Pieter Geyl,* "illusionist and self-deceiver," "repulsive sentimentality," "impotence of the judgment in the face of emotion and sentiment." Most historians, outside France, would probably concur in those opinions; some would deny Michelet the title of historian altogether, call *The French Revolution* an epic pamphlet, a work of art inspired by historical events, anything but history, for accuracy is the essence of history, and accuracy is said to require scientific detachment, not passionate involvement.

It is going to be my contention in this essay that, while every one of Professor Geyl's harsh judgments can be sustained on aspects of Michelet's work, Michelet remains not merely a very great historian but, within certain limits, an exceptionally honest one. His kind of honesty sustains a greatness which his very intelligent and competent modern critics cannot reach because—assuming an equality of talent—their principles would inhibit them. It is fair to add that they do not choose to aim at greatness. They would adapt to their own use the tribute which Vigny paid himself in comparison with Hugo: "What is important is not to be a *great* poet, but to be a pure poet." And certainly Michelet is in history what Hugo was in poetry. Each, as well as being poet or historian, was also politician, prophet, philosopher, showman, pamphleteer and even at times something of a buffoon. Modern poets and historians are apt to be purer, and duller.

The case that needs to be established is not that Michelet is vastly more entertaining than most modern scientific historians—no one who has read Michelet's *French Revolution* and, say, Professor Thompson's account of the same events, would care to

---

* In *Debates with Historians*. Professor Geyl's essay on Michelet is, like his other essays, extremely shrewd, although I think it suffers from a lack of sympathy with the subject.

dispute that. What will be disputed is the claim hereby made that Michelet is in some ways more honest and therefore more scientific than most modern scientific historians.

The root of Michelet's greatness was that he felt passionately about history—specifically about the French Revolution—and the kind of honesty which distinguishes him from many modern historians is that he said clearly and openly what he felt. The tendency of the scientific historian—perhaps less a tendency than a convention imposed by academic public opinion—is towards impassivity. Some Buster Keatons of historiography can attain genuine and total impassivity: they record the facts, and nothing more. Yet what facts, and why record them? How select the facts if you care nothing about them, one way or another? You can, of course, rely on "what seemed important to contemporaries," but all you know about is what a tiny minority of contemporaries said they thought important. For this reason an intelligent section now tends to fall back on "the history of public opinion." What was done is doubtful, what was thought unknowable, what was published remains and can be classified, with the minimum intrusion of modern preoccupations. This is a respectable and useful, but limited, activity. There are others who are known to have strong opinions on historical subjects but who separate their opinions—or perhaps rather the expression of their opinions—from their scholarly activity as much as possible. The opinions, hot and strong, go into newspaper articles, radio, television; the serious historical writing is tightly buttoned, ostentatiously unemotional. This convention no doubt has considerable merits. The plain dry style implies the acceptance of rigorous standards, submission to ascertainable facts, the aspiration of historiography towards the status of an exact science. Yet, as in all systems of strict convention, hypocrisy, the nemesis of puritanism, is never far behind. Under this Recording Angel mask, "X" the historian is still "X" the man, often "X" the journalist. His emotions, interests, prejudices are with him as he selects and relates facts, sifts conflicting accounts, attributes degrees of credibility to sources. And he is working in a field, the human past, in which human emotions, interests, prejudices are pervasively relevant; a field moreover in which the arbitration of experiment is impossible—except perhaps in a few peripheral areas, like pachydermatous Alpinism. Class war, religious war, national war all rage in historiography as they have raged in history. With Michelet and

Carlyle the war was in the open country. Among modern scientific historians it is siege warfare, unrelenting hostilities masked by long periods of apparent quiet. Then through the ideological slit-window in the massive fortifications of fact comes the crossbow bolt to transfix German, or Jew, or Jesuit. That, or the collapse of a long section of the curtain-wall shows that Tory sappers have succeeded in undermining a Whig position long considered impregnable.

When, therefore, a modern scientific historian rebukes Michelet for prejudice and emotionalism, what he really objects to is Michelet's *unguarded expression* of prejudice and emotion. But the reader should surely be grateful for these unguarded expressions, for they put *him* on his guard. With Michelet he knows exactly where he stands, as he often does not know with the modern historian. He knows that Michelet has a passionate love of France and a passionate hatred of kings, and that the intense emotional significance which the Revolution had for him was that it meant the liberation of that which he most loved from that which he most hated. A modern reader will see an obvious psychoanalytical explanation for that, which will further increase his understanding of what the French Revolution meant to Michelet, what must be allowed for in reading Michelet's *French Revolution*. Of course, if those who wish to purify historiography from the taint of emotionalism were strictly consistent, they would require all honours students in history to undergo psychoanalysis, as a condition of being allowed to proceed to a degree. But then if this were done the results might go far beyond the elimination of the last traces of Micheletism: no history might any longer get written at all.

Michelet does not limit himself to telling us in general terms what he felt about the Revolution. He answers at almost every turn the vulgar query which historians usually ignore: "What would *you* have done, chum?" He tells us exactly where he would have sat in the Convention: between Cambon and Carnot. He would have been, that is to say, a man of the Mountain, but neither a Girondin nor a Jacobin. He would have voted in favour of war, of the assimilation of Belgium, of the death of the King. ("He was still sure he *was* King, in spite of all that had happened . . . *That* is what they had to kill.") He would have been *for* the tenth August, but *against* the second June: that is to say, in favour of the insurrection of the Paris streets to bring down the monarchy, but against the same kind of insurrection to purge republican institutions. He excuses the institutions of the Terror as forced on France by fatality, but does not condone the September massacres, or the mass executions of Prairial and Messidor. Against the triumvirate, but also against the Thermidorian reaction, he leaves his reader in some doubt about where exactly he stands only in one important situation: on Thermidor itself. From his position in the Convention he would have had to vote for the death of Robespierre, Couthon and Saint-Just: *la mort sans phrases,* in the sagacious proposition of Sieyès. *La mort sans phrases* but also, for Michelet, *la mort dans l'âme,* for Thermidor is the end of the Revolution and the end of his book. The last paragraph of his great work runs as follows:

Not long after Thermidor, a man who is still living and who was then ten years old was brought to the theatre by his parents. As they left the theatre he admired a long line of sumptuous carriages such as he had never seen before. Attendants in short jackets, hat in hand, said to the spectators as they came out: "Need a carriage, *master?*" The child did not quite understand this new expression and asked what it meant. All they told him was, that there had been a great change because of the death of Robespierre.

Michelet is certainly honest, in the sense that he declares his interest openly, puts his ideological cards on the table. But to call him "an honest historian" would be only a play on words unless he is also found honest in relation to the facts, unless he consistently relates events which do not suit his thesis. How far is Michelet in that sense an honest historian? Here it is necessary to make a distinction. As historian of the Revolution, of what happened inside the Revolution, he is remarkably honest, because he is anxious to be just to all parties, is acutely concerned and even torn by their disputes, has a keen sense of political tactics and of the working of assemblies, an uncanny intuition into the psychology of power, and the literary ability to say precisely what he means. Few historians have had such equipment and very few have had, in addition, what Michelet pre-eminently had, the stamina to grapple with the enormous basic literature of a long and extremely articulate revolution. He worked harder to find the truth than anyone had done before in this field, and indeed he pays himself an eloquent and deserved tribute. He writes in a footnote to his opening chapter on the September massacres:

> If I may be permitted to say so, I am walking alone in these gloomy regions of September. Alone—no one before me ever set a foot there. Like Aeneas in Hades I walk with my sword unsheathed, driving off vain shadows, defending myself against the lying legions which surround me. I have brought to bear [on these lies] an inflexible critical method, checking them by various tests, by which they fall, especially by a rigorous chronology of days and hours.

This language, un-British though it may be, is on the whole justified in relation, not only to September, but to the interior of the Revolution as a whole, apart from a few rhetorical exuberances and easily discounted rationalizations. Where he ceases to be a historian and becomes simply a pamphleteer is in his dealing with the enemies, especially the external enemies, of the Revolution. "On no point," writes Professor Geyl with dangerous and deceptive mildness, "is Michelet's historical writing technically weaker." The truth is that Michelet's concept of international relations is hardly more historical than a Punch-and-Judy show. England is the enemy of France and of the Revolution, and therefore of Civilization and of Justice. About such a country Michelet wished to know no more than an English squire wished to know about Boney or an American Legionnaire about Russia—just enough, in fact, to aim an insult to the satisfaction of his own fellow-countrymen. On England's reactions to the horrors of revolution, the *tu quoque* was useful: "Sitting at your ease on the corpse of Ireland . . . be good enough to tell us: did your revolutions of interests not cost more blood than our revolutions of ideas?" Anglo-Saxon hypocrisy was the main standby: "The Middle Ages knew but one hypocrisy; we are cursed with two: hypocrisy of authority, hypocrisy of freedom; that is to say, the *Priest* and the *Englishman,* the two shapes of Tartuffe. The priest influences the women mainly, the Englishman the middle class." Burke, who was "a pupil of the Jesuits of St. Omer," (Michelet may here be confusing him with Daniel O'Connell) "delivered a furious diatribe against France, for which he was paid cash down by his adversary Pitt." Pitt himself was "a rabid clerk," who encouraged the rising in the Vendée but let it down out of mere gratuitous hypocrisy: "They spent their time asking 'whether such-and-such a band of partisans had respectable leaders,' and other English questions." The general picture of England's role in the counter-revolution was as follows:

England "that knight of human liberty," as Madame de Stael called her, leaning on her fleets and bales of cotton, looked to the Continent for something to fight with, looked for the sword and the dagger. The sword was Germany, poor and warlike, always stretching out her hand for English gold. The dagger was ancient Catholicism, priests and monks, a rusty weapon but good for a stab in the back. The English, to rid themselves of such people, made several revolutions. They hanged them in their own country and encouraged them in ours.

Apart from such polemics, more or less brilliant and more or less suggestive, there is hardly anything on international relations. "The vultures of Germany and the white bear of Russia" come in for a mention, and Poland, like Ireland, receives the tribute of a not wholly disinterested tear. There were conveniently enough two Belgiums, a true and a false one: the "true Belgium" called on France for help, the "false Belgium," which was unfortunately larger, rejected her. The intransigent internal enemies of the Revolution—royalists and refractory priests—fare a little better, both because, being French, they have the honour to exist, and because their bravery at least belongs to the French heritage. But even so, the lack of sympathy is so marked as to be at times ludicrous: "The attitude of the royalists was extraordinarily provocative. One could not pass by the walls of the prisons without hearing them singing."

Certainly this burlesque treatment of the forces opposed to the Revolution is a grave defect, and one which Michelet's critics have not spared. They have in fact insisted on it rather too much. Hardly anyone—certainly no one outside France—is likely to take Michelet's account of international reactions and motives very seriously. Few, except anti-clericals of strict observance, will follow uncritically his analysis of the religious resistance (*Le Prêtre et la femme*). He does not, after all, conceal his point of view, like the perfidious English Gibbon. Michelet's achievement should surely be considered mainly in terms of what he really worked on, what takes up the bulk of his three thousand pages: the Revolution itself, seen from Paris. Like the revolutionaries with whom he identified himself, he did not have much time for studying the psychology, or even considering the point of view, of the enemies of the Revolution. He was too busy considering the conflicting points of view, and the complex psychology, of the revolutionaries themselves. It would be hard to deny that he does this with great skill and concern for justice. He avoids—as subsequent French historians have not done—identifying himself with any single leader or tendency. He sees all the leading revolutionaries, the whole Convention, as engaged not just in an elemental struggle for power—the anti-revolutionary picture—and not just in a series of clashes between patriots and agents of Pitt—the official version—but in a confused, slippery, wily, panic-stricken struggle for individual and collective survival. They all, or almost all, believed in the Revolution, at least in its minimum sense of the destruction of aristocratic privilege and the kind of monarchy associated with it, the so-called absolutism. Some of them, like Carnot and Cambon and Prieur de la Marne, managed to do an astonishing amount of constructive work. Much of the great legal and educational structure which is often vaguely attributed to Napoleon was in fact the work of the Convention—great work accomplished amid fantastic difficulties and dangers. Most of the revolutionaries—including Marat as well as Danton and Robespierre—feared the Scylla of social revolution as much as the Charybdis of counter-revolution. But the importance of the two threats fluctuated bewilderingly, and fatally for many. As it fluctuated the revolutionary vocabulary went through wide changes of meaning, and the political leaders through corresponding arcs of attitude. The term *indulgents* covered originally those who feared counter-revolution—at the moment—less than social revolution; the term *exagérés* covered those with the contrary valuation. The distinction was not unlike that between *revisionist* and *dogmatist* in current communist terminology, but the labels switched faster and more dangerously. You could be an *exagéré* one year and an *indulgent* the next; both Marat and Danton were. Or, like the more politic Robespierre, you could follow an *exagéré* speech immediately with an *indulgent* one or dress an *indulgent* (anti–social-revolution) policy in the language and methods of *exagération*. Indeed the methods of *exagération*—including conspicuous human sacrifice, mass offerings to the guillotine—could be the tactics of those who most feared social revolution, the so-called *indulgents*. The Girondins were arrested (June 2, 1793) as *indulgents,* covering royalist elements who did in fact at that time support them. When they were executed (October 1793) it was for a quite different reason: in order to deceive and hold in check the social-revolutionary movement in Lyons. They themselves had ceased to be of any political significance—"They were exhumed in order to be killed," says Michelet—but to kill them was a useful gesture for people who were themselves beginning to be accused of *indulgence*. At the time of the executions immediately before Thermidor, in the summer of 1794, a time when fifty-four people went to the guillotine in one batch, clad in the red shirt of the parricide, for alleged complicity in an attempt against Robespierre's life, Robespierre was still suspect of *indulgence,* of a desire to go "through clemency to a dictatorship." And the leading group among those who brought him down in Thermidor were not *indulgents* but *exagérés*, terrorists who feared above all the retreat into *indulgence* which they thought Robespierre was likely to make at their expense. It was because they suspected him of being a potential Thermidorian that the Thermidorians guillotined Robespierre.

Michelet can hardly be accused of leaving out the warts. His picture of "inside the Revolution" has been substantially taken over by modern historians, with of course numerous and varied modifications, changes of emphasis and a wider field. And French historians—those who are not royalists—have tended to follow him also, as both Aulard and Mathiez did and as Ollivier did in his recent life of Saint-Just, in accepting at least some of those bloodstained heroes as necessary to the greatness of France. Michelet accepts most of the leaders and many others: "these great citizens who died so young and who, whatever they may have done, died in preparing for us this France." Professor Geyl will have none of this: "sentimentality about the bloody maniacs of 1793–94 . . . positively repulsive." No doubt this is a healthy human reaction and yet Professor Geyl is being hardly less sentimental than Michelet. Bloody maniacs? Marat probably was one in literal truth; Michelet at least depicts him so and does not number him among "the great citizens." He also rejects the Hebertists and those who like Tallien and Fouché were busy butchers in 1793–94 and became respectable *indulgents* by way of Thermidor. Vergniaud, Brissot, Danton, Desmoulins, all these were "great citizens" for Michelet but none can be classed as a "bloody maniac," least of all for 1793-94. It comes down then to Robespierre and Saint-Just. They were cruel and vindictive men certainly, like Cromwell, Sherman, Stalin and many national heroes, or like one "great citizen," still living and respected by all, who killed in a few seconds many more people than were killed in the whole course of the French Revolution. (He did not murder them personally, and neither did Robespierre murder people personally.) But when a professor of history, who is, after all, professionally accustomed both to measuring his words and to the idea of bloodshed, breaks out with "bloody maniacs" about these particular cruel and vindictive men, one may suspect that he has in mind not only the blood but also the great achievement for which Michelet, in spite of everything, admired them: the successful defence of the Revolution. It is precisely because Michelet is torn by conflicting emotions about Robespierre that he can give a more vivid and convincing impression of him than do the productions of the "bloody maniac" school.* Here is his picture of Robespierre at the apparent zenith of his power—and in fact just beginning to slip—at the procession of the Feast of the Supreme Being, Prairial 22 of the Year II (June 10, 1794):

> Robespierre, the President of the Convention, naturally walked in front. He appeared radiant. David painted him as he looked that day, I believe, in the Saint-Albin portrait. Nowhere is he more terrible. That smile hurts. Passion seems to have drunk his blood and dried his bones, leaving only the nervous system. He is like a drowned cat resuscitated by a galvanic battery, or like a reptile stiffening and rearing up, with an unspeakable expression of frightening affability.
> But let there be no mistake. The impression is not one of hatred. What you feel is a painful pity mingling with terror. You cry out, without hesitation—that of all men this was the one who suffered most.
> Robespierre was in the habit of walking with a tense, quick step. That was not the pace of the Convention. The first row of the Convention in the procession remained—by malice perhaps, and with a perfidious show of respect—well behind him, leaving him isolated. From time to time he looked round and saw that he was alone.

---

* In any case, why maniacs? If anything, Robespierre and Saint-Just were bloody depressives.

The passage is very characteristic of Michelet; the extravagant emotional ejaculation in the second paragraph interrupts, but does not disturb, a brilliant exposition of what has been keenly observed. He is like a spectator at a ball game who cheers immoderately and in a partisan fashion but does not miss a detail of the play. There are other historical writers who, in their own case, mistake for keen and dispassionate observation what is in fact just an incapacity to cheer.

In an enthusiastic but not very illuminating essay Mr. Edmund Wilson put Michelet (why not Hegel?) at the start of the line that led to the Finland Station and the Bolshevik Revolution. It is however easier to see Michelet's *French Revolution* as a station on a French line than as an international junction. Here Professor Geyl is a better guide: "Nothing has contributed more to the survival of the work in France—I believe that its popularity is largely confined to the French reading public—than the fact that the ideas (or should I say the sentiments and aspirations) which it proclaims still evoke a response there." It is now nearly a hundred years since the envious Sainte-Beuve told the Goncourts about Michelet: "He omits all verbs. But he has become a church —he has his believers." And he has his believers still, even among those who do not read him, for he has entered the bloodstream of French thought.

It would be idle to enquire whether the French are like that because Michelet wrote in the way he did—a view to which Professor Geyl seems to incline—or whether Michelet wrote in the way he did because he was so French. One could perhaps say that the essence of certain French qualities, distilled by him, went to make later generations more intoxicatingly and dangerously French; like the effect of Calvados in draught cider. What is certain is that his chief qualities and limitations are French characteristics pushed to extremes. The undisguised passion which informs his historical writings and is a source of his greatness, seems rather shocking in an English translation, apparently also in Dutch, and probably in other languages. But in French it comes easily and is acceptable. It has always been recognized that the French are more indulgent to displays of emotion in their social life than are their neighbours; the same is to some extent true of their intellectual life also. This is not exclusively to the disadvantage of French intellectual life, as is sometimes supposed.

"Emotionalism," sniffs the Nordic critic. *"Et alors?"* a Frenchman might reply. "Is an intellectual not human? Does he not have emotions? And if he does, what is to be gained by his concealing them and pretending to be a machine? A historian for example cannot be objective. He is himself part of the historical process; the passions and the interests of the people he is writing about are his too, to the extent that he can find out what they are. An archaeologist does not need to be altogether human—there are some quite good English archaeologists—and a mediaeval historian may be God knows what. But a modern historian, dealing with wars and revolutions which are still vibrating around us, cannot possibly be impartial. We French admit that. Our modern historians conduct themselves accordingly, after the glorious example of Michelet. As for the modern historian who sets out to be impartial, he may be honest and have opinions, in which case he will be prevented, by his commitment to impartiality, from writing anything at all; or he may be honest and have no opinions, in which case he is an idiot, both in the classical sense and in the ordinary sense, and his writings will correspond to his condition; he may be dishonest and have no opinions, in which case more lucrative careers than historiography are open to him, and he has no moral or intellectual reason to refuse them; or finally he may be dishonest and have opinions, in which case he is certain to put across his opinions under the disguise of 'impartial history' with all the prestige which the fog-bound populations accord to such idols. People who believe in fabulous creatures, such as 'impartial historians,' readily become the prey of confidence tricksters."

The normal Anglo-Saxon reply would, I think, be that these are sophistries, turning on the false unstated premise that opinions are immutable, whereas in fact the honest historian is one who has opinions which he is prepared to modify in accordance with the evidence. That is certainly the ideal of the historian-as-scientist. But in practice the man who believes himself to be prepared to modify his opinions in accordance with the evidence cannot help interpreting the evidence in accordance with his opinions. If he is scrupulous this dilemma will paralyse him. Acton's knowledge was certainly not inferior to Michelet's but his production was vastly inferior. From an insular point of view it is the classical contrast between an honest Englishman, tongue-tied by his inhibitions, and a voluble, unscrupulous Frenchman.

Let us assume that the conventions of the objective manner are not necessarily identical with historiographic virtue. The opposing convention, that of Michelet—"the most prejudiced historian that ever lived" according to Lewis Galantière—can claim, in France, the honour due to an art, as opposed to a pseudo-science. Michelet was a great artist, with the respect for his material that that implies. "Michelet's imagination did not work in a void"—it is Professor Geyl himself who is speaking—"he had a sense of the fact, his imagination throve on the truth and genuineness of archive documents." It is one of the misfortunes of Anglo-French communication that the Michelet style, and the idea of history-as-an-art, became discredited in England through the intermediary of Belloc, who wrote good prose—the only good prose some of his academic critics probably ever read—but unlike Michelet could not be bothered with (or afford) the drudgery of prolonged and detailed research. From this derived the famous equation: Good prose *equals* bad history; with its obvious and gratifying corollary: Bad prose *equals* good history.

As in so many other fields the French tendency made towards individual excellence, the English towards collective success. History-as-science, if taken really seriously,* is a sedative, leading to the resignations of agnosticism, one of the artificial paradises. History-as-art on the contrary is a stimulant, enriching and embittering contemporary conflicts. History-as-science could work for UNESCO (Revision of National History Textbooks Project), under the slogan: Fragmentation is the Mother of Amnesia. History-as-art on the other hand—which is history acting on history—is a rough business like history itself—like the Eumenides in Barrault's production of the *Oresteia*, snufflers and diggers-up of bones. In the case of France undoubtedly the history-as-art tradition is part of the long blood-feud, which runs from the Great Revolution and 1848 through the Commune to the collaborations and liberations of the last struggle. A passage in Edgar Morin's recent book, *l'Autocritique,* shows how deeply this tradition—essentially *l'histoire engagée*—has penetrated into the French mind:

The lectures which excited me most were those of Georges Lefebvre on 1789. From the start, Lefebvre showed us how the significance of

---

* This excludes Russian Marxism, a healthy open-air game, in which all are invited to join.

the French Revolution had been continually altered as a result of subsequent historical developments. Lamartine, Aulard, Jaurès, Mathiez—the historians themselves were historicized. It was a fine lesson in relativity which taught me, much better than dialectics did, that there are no pure observers, but there is a constant complex relation between present history and past history, the observer and what he observes.

Michelet's cult of the Revolution, negligible though its influence on world communism may be, has probably helped to form the intellectual background of French communism. Some objective historians have blamed him for this, with one of those lapses into "judgments from the standpoint of today" to which even they are liable. This seems to be a misunderstanding. We may be reasonably sure that the French Communist party would be a force even if Michelet had never existed; the Italian Communist party after all manages to get along without him. Granted he supplies French Communists with much of their intellectual background, is it necessarily the worst part? Would they be better people or less dangerous to France if they derived their intellectual background wholly from German precept and Russian practice? If they really read Michelet, as distinct from hearing about him, they are learning some disconcerting things about how revolutions work, and they are in contact with what is, within definite limits, a very humane and generous mind.

Within definite limits . . . The really harmful capacity of Micheletism—the effect of which is not confined to the Communists—derives, not from what he admires, but from what he lacks. His ruling vice is chauvinism, rooted in an arrogant lack of interest in anything outside the boundaries—the natural boundaries, of course—of France. It is not a malevolent lack of interest, in principle. Far from it: France, which is civilization, is open and accessible to foreigners. They can come and learn; they can even become French. For those who do—like Clootz and Tom Paine—he has a special, paternal affection. But those who opposed Revolutionary France, like the famous "false Belgians," were opposing both civilization and liberty; they are literally "voting themselves out of the human race" as far as Michelet is concerned. The same indeed is true of French provincials who oppose Paris, for "The Commune is everything. Paris is the world."

Many Frenchmen are by nature only too ready to accept this

kind of doctrine. It is, after all, more generous than other national myths, because it is proselytizing rather than exclusive. But, perhaps for that reason, it is also more resentful. If you offer to receive an unfortunate fellow human being into your society, the most gifted and polite society in the world, and he declines that honour, you will begin to regard him as a very low and perverse fellow indeed, with whom you will be justified in dealing severely.

Michelet if alive today would certainly have supported the repression of the rebellion in Algeria. Is it not the same as La Vendée or the Chouans? "They wanted to fight France! Poor fellows, they were French and they did not know it." The Algerian rebels would have been for Michelet, as for many Frenchmen today, no more than primitive fanatics fighting not for liberty—since France is offering them true liberty, the liberty to be French—but for the forces of the dark past, religious intolerance, economic stagnation, backward social customs. The policy of integration would have been Michelet's policy on Algeria, although it must be added that, for him, unlike some of the present advocates of that policy, integration would have involved genuinely equal status for Moslem Frenchmen. As for foreign protests about France's methods of repressing the rebellion, Michelet would have reacted—as he did to those who protested against the atrocities of the French Revolution: *"Ce grand concert de pleureurs qui pleurent tous contre la France."*

With these opinions, Michelet would have been in accord with the great majority of contemporary Frenchmen. That is not to say, however, that he would be at home in contemporary France. He would—again like many Frenchmen—have wished the war, without being able fully to accept its consequences. The Fifth Republic is not a republic in Michelet's sense: it is, as Mauriac has said, a consulate. The charisma attaching to the head of the state, and the privileged status of the army, would have seemed to him not republican but quasi-monarchical, Bonapartist, and therefore detestable. His dislike of Napoleon was so great that he even went so far as to sympathize with those whose countries were invaded, although these were foreigners fighting against—no, not against France; against the Empire. This line of thought, or pattern of feeling, could lead him, in contemporary terms, to reverse his position about Algeria.

Questions about what Michelet would think if he were alive

today are not, I believe, idle or sentimental. Because both of his greatness as an artist, and of the *Français moyen* character of many of his feelings, his picture of the Revolution—and to a great extent, of France itself—is present in the contemporary French consciousness. In that sense Michelet is alive today. With his narrow and intense lucidity and his unguarded felicity of language he can tell us a great deal about the state of mind of the people whom he loved and taught and to whose glories he belongs.

THE PEOPLE'S VICTOR

———◆◆———

How came it that this prudent, economical man was also generous? That this chaste adolescent, this model father, grew to be, in his last years, an ageing faun? That this legitimist changed, first into a Bonapartist, only, later still, to be hailed as the grandfather of the Republic? That this pacifist could sing, better than anybody, of the glories of the flags of Wagram? That this bourgeois in the eyes of other bourgeois came to assume the stature of a rebel? These are the questions that every biographer of Victor Hugo must answer.

—ANDRÉ MAUROIS

Monsieur Maurois, luckily, does not seriously attempt to answer any of them; his book* is very much better than this little collection of paradoxes *à l'Américaine* would suggest. This is a lucid, well-constructed biography, solidly based on wide and deep research, and making discriminating and efficient use of vast materials. M. Maurois's narrative, although fairly long—about five hundred pages—is compact and extremely readable: it has the momentum and the sweep necessary for a subject which demands greater-than-life-size treatment. The work is, the author tells us, "the largest in scale and the most difficult that I have undertaken." Much as it surpasses his earlier biographies—particularly his rather skimpy exercises on English subjects—it could only have been written by a man with long experience of the possibilities and problems of biography—by, in short, a master craftsman. A craftsman, too, not burdened by excessive subtlety or overmuch fastidiousness, or irony—and therefore at home with his subject. Hugo was the concentrated essence of a century of *Français moyens* and it is fitting that he has found a *Français moyen* to write his biography.

"We have so rich a native field of romantic poetry," says the dust jacket, "that Hugo's somewhat rhetorical verse leaves us cold." No doubt you have; perhaps it does. It could also be that you know less French than you think you do, and that you have

---
* *Olympio: The Life of Victor Hugo.*

a taste for misleading comparisons, flattering to yourselves. There is nothing at all like Hugo in the English field of romantic poetry. Nor was Hugo's verse just "somewhat rhetorical," with the implication of poor taste and unwarranted excitement that that conveys. It was a majestic roll of rhetoric sustained for fifty years, with a marvellous variety of expression and an always deepening resonance. Hugo was a public man. He felt the events of his own life—the birth of a child, a bereavement—as public events, archetypes of human destiny. He felt the great historical events of his day as events in his personal emotional life. And always words, millions of words, gushed out of him, scalding hot and at high pressure, like steam out of his boiling century. He said so much that in the end he had said something for everybody. A section of his public followed his body from the Étoile to the Panthéon. There were two million of them.

The corresponding contemporary figure in England was not Tennyson—nothing is more misleading than to think of Hugo as in some sense the Poet Laureate of France—and obviously not Browning or Arnold.

The English Victor Hugo, the prophet and the incarnation of the century, was not a poet but a politician: Gladstone. It is not just that both became respected old men who had uttered more emotive words than any of their contemporary fellow-countrymen. Nor was it that they shared a power for expressing and arousing moral indignation, answering to a great need of the age. It was not even that each was a medium, through whom inarticulate masses found a voice. The essential was that both were artists, and artists of the same kind: If love of liberty, that ambiguous and powerful emotion, was the force that drew their great audiences to them, those audiences desired that liberty to appear in an acceptable form, not inchoate and anarchic, but ordered, rich and beautiful. Gladstone and Hugo had the *souffle*, the mastery of language, and the legend-focussing personality that could confer a formal order on a general release of emotion. In the case of the orator, it has been held that this faculty was daemonic and annunciatory of disasters to come. The road to Nuremberg, on this view, begins at Midlothian. It might be truer to say that it was the nation which had no Midlothians that found itself a voice at Nuremberg. The relevant metaphor, for the age, is still that of "letting off steam": that was, in part, the function for their nations, and in their very different ways, of Hugo and of Gladstone. It is hardly wise to regard the process with suspicion because another nation, in a later day, blew up the boiler.

Frenchmen, on the very rare occasions when they think of Gladstone at all, think of him as a symbol of English hypocrisy. Did he not veil his face in affected horror at the discovery of Parnell's adultery, about which he had already known for years? And did he not indulge in a life of vice with the pretext that he was reforming prostitutes? (It is of no use to reply that in reality he did neither of these things.) The proper comparison, in the French view, would be with Tartuffe and Félix Faure, certainly not with France's greatest poet: how compare the fustian of a politician with verses that are among the glories of the French language? The argument has weight when one places the works of Hugo beside the collected speeches of Gladstone; it has very much less weight when one thinks of the two men, living, in relation to their communities. It is probable that many of the two million who followed the *corbillard des pauvres* to the Panthéon were there because Hugo had written:

> *Je ne fais point fléchir les mots auxquels je crois:*
> *Raison, progrès, honneur, loyauté, devoirs, droits,*
> *On ne va point au vrai par une route oblique.*
> *Sois juste; c'est ainsi qu'on sert la république;*
> *Le devoir envers elle est l'équité pour tous;*
> *Pas de colère; et nul n'est juste s'il n'est doux.*

It is possible to regard these lines as less successful poetry, but more successful politics than: "That cloud in the West! That coming storm! God's minister of vengeance upon ancient and inveterate and still but half-atoned injustice!" For Hugo, in pleading in very flat verse for mercy for the Communards, knew that his words would find an echo in hundreds of thousands of French hearts. Gladstone could have felt no corresponding confidence; the accent of his words, as the first intuition of his Irish task comes on him, is genuinely tragic, in marked contrast to the hollow and perfunctory eloquence of Hugo on the Commune. The poet and the tribune are here in the wrong places.

If we think of the two men of genius as being of the same prophetic race, both poet-tribunes, then we may also think it no accident that in France the prophet turned his face to literature, in England to politics. Gladstone was an engine in which great forces at a high temperature were concentrated to make changes in English life, for good or ill. Hugo changed nothing, except the personal lives of those around him, and his style. And, since a human being who becomes an engine becomes less as well as more than human, Hugo's personality remained the richer and his life the more exemplary—although certainly not in the vulgar moral application of the last term. It is not a question of contrasting M. Maurois's ageing faun, seducer of servant-girls, with the self-dedicated redeemer of fallen women, but of seeing how, in Gladstone, all emotion tends to turn to controversy, to engage in public *work;* while with Hugo, a series of magnificent emotions, in a life filled with drama, found, within and without the limits of his art, free and spectacular *play.* The two men seem almost like complementary colossal figures—not devoid of cliché—designed to express the contrasting genius of the two peoples, art governing and art living. Prodigious creatures, concentrating and revealing the essential character of the life around them, one feels, before their force and mystery, something of what Hugo felt, seeing comparable portents, at the zoo:

> *Moi, je n'exige pas que Dieu toujours s'observe,*
> *Il faut bien tolérer quelque excès de verve,*
> *Chez un si grand poète, et ne point se fâcher*
> *Si Celui qui nuance une fleur de pêcher*
> *Et courbe l'arc-en-ciel sur l'Océan qu'il dompte,*
> *Après un colibri, nous donne un mastodonte!*
> *C'est son humeur à lui d'être de mauvais goût,*
> *D'ajouter l'hydre au gouffre et le ver à l'égout,*
> *D'avoir, en toute chose, une stature étrange*
> *Et d'être un Rabelais d'où sort un Michel-Ange.*
> *C'est Dieu; moi, je l'accepte . . .*

MONSIEUR CAMUS CHANGES HIS CLIMATE

———◆◆———

Monsieur Camus's earlier novels—*L'Étranger, La Peste*—were set in his native North Africa. The sun shone brightly and pitilessly, and underneath it the Latin logic too was as bright and pitiless as M. Camus's generous temperament would allow. His new book marks, in more than one way, a change of climate. It is set in Holland, land of clouds and doves and omnipresent water; there is a slower tempo, a new distrust, not of society or destiny, but of the corrupted heart of man. Have we met something like this evolution before? A similar eclipse, surely, occurred in M. Mauriac's development, when the burning pagan sun of *Thérèse Desqueyroux* and *Destins* began to disappear behind the penitent mists of *Les Chemins de la mer*. The analogy is far from perfect. M. Mauriac had never quite ceased to be a Christian: M. Camus has not quite begun to be one. M. Mauriac, as he became more deeply Christian, lost in imaginative intensity and in precision. M. Camus, on the other hand, has never written better than he does in this magnificent monologue, in which every sentence has the inflection of a living voice, in which the printed word can convey the resonance of a quayside or a sickroom, and can respond to the specific melancholy lyricism of Dutch gin. No one can deny to *La Chute* the character, at least, of a *tour de force*: many will think it, as I do, a small masterpiece. But some serious people, among M. Camus's former friends, will regard it as a betrayal. In this darkest hour of the Algerian struggle it is to M. Camus, lonely eminence among the French of Algeria, that many look, not so much for a polemical lead—that M. Mauriac has given with much more enthusiasm than M. Camus—but for an imaginative expression of colonial reality. On their theory, which was once M. Camus's theory also, this expression would not need to be propagandist, but it would of necessity be revolutionary. This theory is of course very similar to the favourite defence of the Christian novelist, that "all truth is of God," and therefore—unstated corollary—what I write is Christian since I believe it to be true. It was a little hard to extract the necessary implications from M. Camus's previous novels. A not very bright disciple could read *L'Étranger* as a satire on bourgeois justice: one slightly more intelligent could take it as depicting the tragic isolation of the individual in capitalist society. The friendly but patronizing Marxist read it as a significant expression of the simultaneous bankruptcy of bourgeois social relations and bourgeois thought. *La Peste* was easier if one didn't look too closely: the plague was fascism. M. Camus helped this on by the dramatized version, which was localized in Spain. This was clear enough and if M. Camus's metaphysical and historical speculations rather confused the picture—especially in *L'Homme révolté* —it was easy to tidy up. "Camus is no philosopher" has become an article of faith on the Left Bank. Therefore everything Camus says in treatise form can be ignored. *Le cas est classé*. But his "creative" work was another matter; there, according to the theory, his artistic integrity was a guarantee that his work would be *objectively* revolutionary. The critic could bring into action the convenient principle: "I know what he thinks; it doesn't matter what he thinks he thinks!"

Critics of this sort will find *La Chute* hard going. What are they to make of this half-anguished, half-ironic confession of a French lawyer, self-exiled in Amsterdam—why Amsterdam?— and calling himself a penitent judge? Jean-Baptiste Clamance, protagonist and narrator of *La Chute,* had been a pretty decent sort of fellow, as people go. He was never at any time a judge by profession, but a lawyer specializing in defence in criminal cases. He even mentions that he found it hard to conceive how one could be a judge, although he concedes the existence of judges "as one concedes the existence of grasshoppers." In his work he is a champion of the oppressed, an enemy of a vicious legal system; in his private life he is kind and generous; in his opinions progressive—he asserts that property is murder. Apart from that, witty, eloquent, amorous, successful: a favourable and attractive example of a left-wing intellectual. The trouble is that under his own self-criticism, as he walks along the canal banks of Amsterdam with his unrecorded listener, the whole lighting of the picture changes. His acts of kindness and his love affairs, his progressive words and gestures, everything in his life fits into a new picture, that of a man carrying on, as he says, a long love affair with himself. It is to his own conception of himself that he pays tribute when he defends a case, when he makes love, when he helps a blind old man across the street. And it is when he is humiliated, when he can no longer admire himself wholeheartedly, that he sees what he has been doing and takes flight to Holland. (Why Holland? We shall see.) The crisis of his humiliation is a double one. Crossing one of the Seine bridges one night, he sees a girl throwing herself into the river; he hears a cry from the water, then another cry, further off and fainter: he makes no move to save her, telling himself that it is too late. A little time later, again crossing a bridge, he hears a laugh, *un bon rire,* a not unfriendly laugh: looking round he sees no one, no one on the bridge or the bank, no passing boat; then he hears the same laugh again, off down the river, and fainter.

The laugh that strips Clamance of his moral comfort may be thought of as a hallucination, or an image by the narrator, or as a reality: the point is left open. We are reminded, at any rate, of the conception, dear to some French Catholic writers, of laughter as *par excellence* the Satanic means of expression. Such a comparison may seem surprising: we are accustomed to thinking of the world of Bernanos or Bloy as being a very long way from that of Camus. It certainly is from the Camus of, say, *L'Homme révolté.* But the Camus of *La Chute* is quite a different matter. The very title of the book is theological; it refers not only to a particular fall—that of a conceited lawyer—but to the fall of man, whose corrupt condition is exemplified in Clamance. This is not a mere conjecture—Clamance in his confession makes it clear (for some of M. Camus's admirers it will be painfully clear) that original sin is his subject. Again the name which the narrator has chosen for himself has an obvious significance; Jean-Baptiste Clamance —*vox clamantis in deserto*—the name and description of *the* forerunner. Irony? Perhaps. Clamance himself warns his listener that he will find it hard, in this confession, to distinguish the true from the false. But the tutelary presence of John the Baptist, with whatever degree of seriousness we take it, is appropriate, for the frame of mind of the book is in important ways not so much Christian as immediately pre-Christian. There is a deep conviction of the weight and universality of sin, a deep desire for forgiveness and redemption. And there, for the moment at least, it ends. "God" is a word which is sometimes on Clamance's lips, after his fall, in order, as he explains, to mock his humanist friends. He confesses that he can attach no particular meaning to the word. As for the redemption, Clamance can see only the crucifixion, of which he speaks near the end of his narrative. Above all, he hears the words of abandonment spoken from the cross and of these he has his personal interpretation. Christ, as he imagines, although perfect in his life, experienced the sense of guilt because the very fact of his existing had been the cause of the massacre of the Innocents. The conception is a strange one, and it is perhaps better to relate it to Clamance's biography, and his particular obsession, than to M. Camus's system of thought. Yet it does recall another and perhaps a nobler interpretation of these same words by a French writer who long thought himself, like M. Camus, to be in love with justice, and who long hesitated before becoming a Catholic. Charles Péguy in *Le Mystère de la Charité de Jeanne d'Arc* took the words from the cross as expressing despair at the fact that even this sacrifice was not enough to save the damned. This divine despair was in itself to be the means of reconciling saints, racked by a similar horror:

> *Clameur qui sonne au coeur de toute chrétienté*
> *O Clameur culminante, éternelle et valable.*

Clamance has not reached this conception—which for Péguy was the hinge of conversion—but he seems to be groping for something similar, for something in short that would make the Messiah less remote from sinning men. We are all, he tells his listener, looking for "grace, that is to say irresponsibility." And it is this wry and mocking thirst for grace that has made Holland his elected residence. True, following the convention in which he has been brought up, he speaks of Holland as "a soft hell"—Voltaire called it "a phlegmatic hell"—and he compares the concentric canals of Amsterdam to the circles of the Inferno. And certainly if with his guilty memory he has come to this city of water and bridges, it is in part to punish himself. Yet it is not really an Inferno but a sort of *Purgatorio*; there is hope here, however muffled by irony and dandyism. "The newspaper-readers and fornicators"—as he calls our contemporaries—"cannot go any further than this place. They come from all over Europe and they stop around the inner sea, on the colourless beaches. They listen to the sirens, they try in vain to make out the shapes of boats in the fog, then they go back across the canals and go home in the rain." This is not very exhilarating, but it is not a description of hell. Its reference surely is to metaphysical anguish, which implies hope. Elsewhere hope, though grey-haired and in mourning, is more plainly visible. "I am sure you have noticed," says Clamance to his silent companion, "that the sky of Holland is full of millions of doves, so high up that they can't be seen, rising and falling in a single movement, filling the heavens with thick waves of greyish feathers carried to and fro by the wind. The doves wait up there. They turn above the earth, watch, would like to come down. But there's nothing, only the sea and the canals, roofs covered with advertisements, and no head to settle on." This Holland clearly is the frontier of the natural world, the barrier, perhaps impassable, beyond which grace perhaps is waiting. Curiously enough Claudel has had exactly the same thought —naturally more positively expressed—about the same country and even the same city. Amsterdam, he has told us, is "the border of two worlds," the visible and the invisible. In the reflections of its canals he saw "that beseeching of the full by the empty, that continual ambiguity of permanence and contingence, that delicate echo in which all that exists becomes the thought of that which exists."

Bernanos, Péguy, Claudel . . . Some listeners will cock a suspicious ear. Are these comparisons really necessary, or is this an attempt to annex a great humanist writer to the Catholic camp? The comparisons are, I think, necessary: we know that Camus has read these writers—he cites them elsewhere—and here he shows, in several instances, their kind of feeling and of apprehension and in certain passages even their style. The passage, for instance, which begins *"La Hollande est un songe, monsieur, un songe d'or et de fumée, plus fumeux le jour, plus doré la nuit . . ."* is straight Claudel—and Bols. It is necessary to insist on the direct literary relationship, because it probably gives us a truer idea of what *La Chute* actually represents. We cannot affirm, on the strength of *La Chute,* that M. Camus's conversion is imminent or even vaguely probable. What we can safely affirm is that he has moved closer in style and feeling to a certain tradition of French writing, rich in insight and in eloquence, peremptory in form and contemptuous of all that is schematic. This tradition is identified with the names of men who were or are Catholics, but whether or not by attaching oneself to it one moves in the direction of Catholicism is another matter.

What M. Camus is moving away from is clearer than his goal. What he leaves behind is the possibility of moral indignation "in the name of humanity": that moral indignation with which he was once lavish, and which still occasionally flashes from him in *L'Express*. For if humanity, even moralizing and generous humanity, is itself corrupt, how then can you denounce corruption in the name of humanity? Either, it seems, you must stop denouncing, or you must find something outside humanity in the name of which to denounce. It is true that Clamance himself finds a third way: that of unsparing and exhaustive *self*-denunciation, with the growing implication that, vile as he is, his listener in his heart knows that he is just as vile. This technique, here described as that of the repentant judge, is older than Rousseau and need not here be taken very seriously. The clearest thing about it, and about the implications of *La Chute* generally, is that this is not in modern conditions a revolutionary doctrine. The *bonne conscience* that it insidiously destroys is not the *bonne conscience* of the possessing class—the section of that class which reads people like M. Camus has long since ceased to number among its possessions an easy conscience. No, what is ruined here is the *morale* of the progressives: most of the capital of the intellectual left has long been rewardingly invested in moral indignation, and now M. Camus, having transferred his own capital to an unspecified destination, engages in inflationary manoeuvres. The shareholders are justifiably incensed.

If we can discern in *La Chute* any specific reference to what we like to pride ourselves on as "the problems of our time," it would be, I think, in a salutary disgust and in a kind of quietism. To a man living in Algeria it is perhaps more apparent than it is to us that the logical outcome of moral indignation is murder. M. Camus, standing between two proud and bitter communities, whose pride and bitterness he cannot in either case fully share, turns his mind in the direction of humility and peace and therefore, with the culture which is his, to a certain style of Christian conscience. As he is not in fact a Christian it follows that his quietism has at its core a whirl of conflicts. To this we may attribute the richness of *La Chute* and also the difficulty of following its real thought: particularly the difficulty of being quite sure where irony ends and grim earnest begins. In English literature and particularly in Anglo-Irish literature, we are used to the idea of this boundary being badly marked. But in France, like all other boundaries it has been well defined; an ironic intrusion into a serious passage must be provided with front and rear lights. M. Camus has infringed this article of the code, as well as that which lays down a continuous uncrossable line between left and right. "I am losing the thread of my discourse," says Clamance, "I have no longer that clarity of mind to which my friends used to be good enough to pay tribute." Most of M. Camus's friends will probably agree, but some will count that particular clarity well lost for the cryptic twilight of *La Chute*.

SARTRE AS A CRITIC

Most critics are neither philosophers nor practising novelists. M. Sartre, who is a professional philosopher as well as an eminent novelist and dramatist, is unusually well equipped, according to formal categories, to be a critic also. And not according to formal categories only, for he has an exceptionally penetrating and energetic mind. The rhythm of his thought is disconcertingly rapid; the density of ideas per square foot of twelve-point text seems higher than in all but the most strenuous of American critics. The very rich are different from us, as Scott Fitzgerald reminded Hemingway. M. Sartre makes us sadly conscious that the very clever, also, are different from us.

We may cheer up, however—as the stupid have always cheered up on observing the silliness of the clever—when we realize that M. Sartre, for all his formidable equipment and natural gifts, makes a rather poor critic. His tendency is, in considering the work of an author—Mauriac, Dos Passos, Giraudoux, Faulkner, Blanchot, Kafka—to make a kind of incision by means of a single acute observation, whether technical or philosophical or both, and then to develop the "consequences" of that observation by carving the work into an independent structure of which the segments correspond to his own preoccupations rather than to the natural grain of the work itself. His is an imperialist criticism which, after an initial daring raid, annexes to itself a spiritual territory and imposes its own laws without regard to the wishes or the customs of the original inhabitants, or the coherence of their society. So, in his essay "François Mauriac and Freedom"—which deals not with M. Mauriac's work as a whole, but with one unsuccessful novel, *La Fin de la nuit,* presented as typical—he attacks by demonstrating the sleight of hand which M. Mauriac practises by his use of the third person, in gliding almost imperceptibly from a "Thérèse-subject" (to the interior of whose mind we are admitted) to a "Thérèse-object" on whom the author passes judgment from time to time. This analysis, which is clearly and effectively conducted, is followed by the dogmatic statement:

Fictional beings have their laws, the most rigorous of which is the following: the novelist may be either their witness or their accomplice, but never both at the same time.

From this the conclusion that M. Mauriac is not a novelist follows logically. But it is the second premise which remains questionable. Is there, in fact, a "law" which always forces the novelist to choose between being a witness and an accomplice? Are there not many other distinguished writers who, like Mauriac, have broken this "law" and who must therefore be rejected as pseudo-novelists? Do not most novelists, including M. Sartre, find ways, no doubt often much less crude than those of *La Fin de la nuit,* of moving in and out of their characters' minds and also of implying the existence and the judgment of a privileged observer, God, history or the right-thinking man? Such questions are not considered, and we are left with the impression that M. Sartre took intellectual advantage of an opening in a sententious work of M. Mauriac's decline, in order to upset the elder writer's authority over the young and to establish as "law" a theory of his own.

The same critic who considers that M. Mauriac is not a novelist at all regards Mr. John Dos Passos as "the greatest writer of our time." M. Sartre writes with obvious excitement about Mr. Dos Passos—whom, significantly, he compares with French writers, Zola, Proust, Nizan, but never with Joyce—but his excitement is in part the romantic excitement at a discovery useful to him in his own work. He writes of Dos Passos' characters as existing "behind the looking-glass" but it is apparent that this condition is not always so much the product of the American novelist's consummate art as of the French critic's over-ingenious efforts at comprehension. He quotes, for example, a passage from *1919:*

Miss Teazle said he showed real feeling for English composition. One Christmas he sent her a little rhyme he made up about the Christ Child and the Three Kings and she declared he had a gift.

On which M. Sartre's gloss follows:

The narration takes on a slightly stilted manner, and everything that is reported about the hero assumes the solemn quality of a public pronouncement: . . . "she declared he had a gift." The sentence is not accompanied by any comment, but acquires a sort of collective resonance. It is a *declaration*.

Well, I declare! M. Sartre would be scathing indeed about an American critic who might be rash enough to "explain," on the basis of a misunderstood inflection, a point of style in French. But in general, and not only in dealing with the English language, M. Sartre's ear seems to be bad; in particular the whole range of effects which we cover with the term "sense of humour" seems to be closed to him, although he handles the weapon of irony efficiently enough. Amateurs of misunderstood pleasantries will delight in his chapter "Jean Giraudoux and the Philosophy of Aristotle," which presents the spectacle of a playful pedant being pursued, very rightly, by a solemn pedant.

The present collection* contains, as well as critical essays, a number of travel pieces on America and three philosophical essays. The travel pieces resemble the critical essays in their range from the brilliantly perceptive to the merely bumptious. There is a notable picture of a Frenchman turning into an American ("I felt as if I were witnessing an Ovidian metamorphosis. The man's face was still too expressive. It had retained the slightly irritating mimicry of intelligence which makes a French face recognizable anywhere. But he will soon be a tree or a rock.") And then, a little later, we have some Pooter-like reflections on the American economy:

> The war has certainly taught the Americans that their country was the greatest power in the world. But the period of easy living is over; many economists fear a new depression. Thus, no more skyscrapers are being built. It seems they are too hard to rent [1946].

To philosophers the most interesting essay in the book will no doubt be that on "Cartesian freedom" (here undated). M. Sartre's tendency to "annex" takes a rather startling form in this essay, since he actually takes over, for his own variety of "humanism," the Cartesian "freedom of God":

> If he [Descartes] conceived divine freedom as being quite like his own freedom, then it is of his own freedom, such as he would have conceived it without the fetters of Catholicism and dogmatism, that

---

* *Literary and Philosophical Essays.*

he speaks when he describes the freedom of God. We have here an obvious phenomenon of sublimation and transposition.

Of the final essay, "Materialism and Revolution" (1946), it is necessary to say that it by no means represents M. Sartre's full thought on these subjects. His rejection of Marxist philosophy is shown here, but his philosophical acceptance—indeed virtual deification—of the Communist party (*Les Communistes et la paix*) is not included. M. Sartre's very complicated thinking on this matter has been well analysed in M. Merleau-Ponty's recent work *Les Aventures de la dialectique.*

A VOCATION

Fiction begets fiction; the novelist is a disgruntled ex-character from a bad novel. There once was a curly-headed little boy, adored by his grandfather and his mother—his father was dead. He was regarded by his elders as "Nature the Redeemer," as an inspired oracle, a "young knight," even—in a blue muslin dress, with stars in his hair and wings—a *real* angel; he played the parts assigned to him, and when he grew up he wrote *La Nausée*.

The "great event of my life," Sartre tells us in the first volume of his autobiography,* was his father's death; "it returned my mother to her chains"—i.e. her parents' house—"and it gave me my freedom." One can see why the problems of "freedom" have especially preoccupied Sartre, both as novelist and as philosopher, for the freedom which he feels himself to have been given was a singular one: he had lost a father, but gained a grandfather. Charles Schweitzer—Sartre's maternal grandfather and uncle of Albert Schweitzer, Sartre's improbable cousin—was "a nineteenth-century man who, like so many others, including Victor Hugo himself, thought he was Victor Hugo." He "looked so much like God the Father that he was often taken for Him." His grandfather sees him in retrospect as "forever between two melodramatic effects, like an alcoholic between two drinks, as the victim of two recently discovered techniques: the art of photography and 'the art of being a grandfather.'" This second art, as taught by Victor Hugo, was one of indulgence—Sartre's narrative shows how exacting such indulgence can be. He and his grandfather acted out

> a play of a hundred different sketches: flirtations, speedily resolved misunderstandings, good-natured teasings and gentle scoldings, loving resentments, affectionate secrets and passion . . . I found my part so becoming that I could not drop it.

* *The Words.*

A Vocation

Grandfather and grandson became "the God of Love with the Father's beard and the Son's Sacred Heart."

Sartre congratulates himself on not having had a father who would have crushed him: an eminent psychoanalyst, he says, found him to have no super-ego. He contrasts his own freedom, travelling alone, with that of his father-burdened contemporaries—"the Aeneases each carrying his Anchises on his shoulders." It may be doubted whether Aeneas would have found the burden lighter if he had had to carry, instead of his father, his maternal grandfather, Olympian Zeus.

It was Charles Schweitzer, speaking like a father, like "the absentee who had begotten me," who confirmed the boy Sartre in his choice of writing as a profession, what he calls "the dedicated career of a minor writer."

Even today when I am in a bad mood I ask myself if I have not used up so many days and nights, covered so many sheets of paper with my ink, dumped onto the market so many books that no one wanted, in the sole and mad hope of pleasing my grandfather. That would be a joke.

The joke is even more uproarious than that, for this atheist has been writing to please God. His family was conformist rather than religious. His grandmother was brought up a Catholic and "only her scepticism kept her from being an atheist." His grandfather, of a Protestant family, "was too much of a performer not to need a Great Spectator but he hardly ever thought about God except at peak moments." The family as a whole—including apparently Sartre's mother, whom he loved and whom he does not depict very clearly—was "affected by the slow de-Christianisation which was born in the Voltaire-influenced *haute bourgeoisie* and took a century to spread to every stratum of society." This process left strange sediments and these the autobiographer Sartre probes and stirs.

"There might," he says about God, "have been something between us"; if, for example, Sartre had won the gold medal for his French essay on the Passion, there might have been something. But it was only the silver one, and relations were broken off. It is, he says ironically, "the story of a missed vocation." Yet he is conscious that irony does not altogether cover the situation, and not at all sure that the vocation was really missed: "I grew up, a rank weed, on the compost-heap of Catholicity; my roots sucked up its juices and from them I made my sap." He describes how, and in what sense, he lost his faith. One day in 1917, on the way to the *lycée,* waiting for some friends who were late, he could think of nothing better to do than to think about the Almighty:

He at once tumbled down into the blue sky and vanished without explanation. He does not exist, I said to myself, in polite astonishment, and I thought the matter was settled. In one sense it was, because I have never since had the least temptation to revive him. But the other, the Invisible, the Holy Ghost, he who guaranteed my mandate and dominated my life through great anonymous and sacred forces, he remained.

For much of his life—perhaps for thirty years—the manipulation of words remained for him a mystical, quasi-sacramental activity. If he was writing to please that grandfather who so resembled the God the Father who had vanished without explanation, he was also engaged in an enterprise which had its own magical value. Words—"the little swift black mercenaries"—trapped and held reality for him, the signs caught the object, names took the place of things: "that is belief." Literature, as he says, was for him a form of prayer; it was also penance: he was writing "in order to be forgiven for being alive." Writing, in fact, was all the sacraments, all forms of communion, mediation and atonement: the writer was the only true priest.

"Squalid nonsense," he says now. He insists he has got over it and will explain how, in the later volumes of his autobiography.

My retrospective illusions are in pieces. Martyrdom, salvation, immortality: all are crumbling; the building is falling in ruins. I have caught the Holy Ghost in the cellars and have flung him out of them. Atheism is a cruel, long-term business: I believe I have gone through it to the end. I see clearly, I am free from illusions.

And finally: "I have renounced my vocation, but I have not unfrocked myself. I still write. What else can I do?"

Writing about his childhood Sartre is more penetrating, more alert, more lucid, more honest, and somehow better informed, than most of us would be: that is not, perhaps, saying very much. *Words* is surprising, neat and witty; we recognize in the Sartre family structure and the child's illusions about it, one of those odd contraptions, haunted machines, which do produce writers. Yet a feeling of dissatisfaction remains. There is something wrong about the smiling irony, the "detachment," with which the middle-aged writer analyses the mental processes of the child, and of those around him. It is all a little too jaunty; one is reminded rather often that this autobiographer is after all a writer of fiction. His father, he says, "tried to take refuge in death." All that seems to be known is that he took some time dying of a tropical fever; that he was *trying* to die is a novelist's gloss—it has an autobiographical value but an oblique and probably unintended one. Mother, remaining blank, makes one doubt the writer's claim that he has succeeded in the formidable task of "deciphering" his early years "beneath the crossings out." He is "happy"— all too happy—"to subscribe to the judgment" of that "eminent psychoanalyst: I have no Super-Ego." A man who can claim that he is "free from illusions" is surely too young at heart, too happily involved in the absurdities of living, to achieve the real, unearthly detachment, that state of ceasing to care about anything except remembering and telling, in which Proust gave up the ghost.

Sartre, in short, like the good novelist he is, is lying: brilliantly and to our great entertainment and instruction, and with many touches of truth, but lying. Among all these intricately placed, pivoting mirrors which the novelist turns so dexterously for our amusement, the bloody business of childhood has managed to get itself left out. For all the mannerisms and gestures of "ruthless penetration" in which the book abounds, the writer is tender enough with himself, and penetrates—deeply, then—only where he wishes to penetrate. For the rest he follows, more consistently than he seems to know, the valuable advice which his grandmother liked to repeat: *"Glissez, mortels, n'appuyez pas."* That is why he explains how Sartre became a writer, but not the kind of writer Sartre became.

The truths which *Words* contains are the *general* truths of a writer in the tradition of the French aphorists. This is how, in a French middle-class household of the early twentieth century, a boy could come to think that writing was supremely important; this is how the deposit of faith was smuggled on. The process has never, I think, been so well analysed before and Sartre, in analysing it, is helping to clarify the thought of more people than his contemporaries and compatriots. The strange idea that the young Sartre shared with the ageing Yeats, the idea that "Words alone are certain good," is probably a common heritage of the peoples of the Book, in the widest sense: that is to say of all for whom religious writings have been represented to be of supreme importance. The fading of these quasi-magical ideas, and the diversion elsewhere of talents and energies which would in an earlier period have "entered the priesthood" of literature—like those of Yeats and Joyce—may account for what seems to be a real, and perhaps a permanent, diminution in the scale of literary achievement in our generation. It is several centuries since Maurice Scève asked the pertinent question (I quote from memory):

> *Mais que me sert de m'être tant voué*
> *Au monument de Thrace et de Samos*
> *Y murmurant maints magiciens mots?*

Our generation cannot give any clearly reassuring answer. Those of us who still retain at least some interest in the question may be grateful that a writer who, like Sartre, hails from the literary Age of Faith has not really been able to rid himself fully of his illusions. He goes on writing: the Holy Ghost is still in his cellar.

COMMUNISTS AND *COMMUNISANTS*

It has been a fashion for some years for writers, in England and especially in America, to treat of the appeal of communism to intellectuals as belonging somewhere on the fringes between religion and psychopathology. This is a region to which—curiously —the best guides are supposed to be the ex-Communists: those who, having lost their faith, are thereby deemed to have recovered their reason.

Mr. Caute, to whom great praise is due, will have nothing to do with hocus-pocus of this or any other kind. In this richly documented and lucid book* he writes, about those French intellectuals who are his subject, in a manner refreshingly free from condescension and from sentimentality. He shows us what reasons—not merely "inner compulsions"—drew them to the party, at given times, and what reasons repelled them at other times. He has no need of the hypothesis whereby the *communisant* is either madder or more ignoble than the rest of us. True, the *communisant* intellectual swallows quite a lot, but other intellectuals —the *capitalisants,* shall we say—have swallowed quite a lot too, as Mr. Caute effectively reminds us:

> The French intellectual, in accepting broadly the Third or Fourth Republic, has had to do so *despite* Versailles, the domestic policy of the Bloc National, Morocco, Syria, Indo-China, the regime of Chiappe, unemployment, parliamentary corruption, the abandonment of Republican Spain, Munich, McCarthyism, Suez, Algeria. The intellectual may have opposed all these things and he may have openly criticized them. But when weighing up his final allegiance between the Communist party and those parties which defend the *status quo* (in its most general sense), when deciding whether or not to approve France's commitment to a power bloc, to the western alliance, to one of the two great opposing systems, he will, if he finally opts for the western system, have to do so *despite* its defects. This is an elementary point but one often ignored.

* *Communism and French Intellectuals.*

Mr. Caute might well, I think, have illustrated this by reference to the Sartre-Camus controversy. Sartre, with his tendency to toe the party line, whenever it is at all toeable, is often contrasted unfavourably with Camus, seen as a writer of unblemished integrity. This contrast seemed to hold when, in 1948, Camus wrote that Soviet forced-labour camps were no more acceptable than Nazi ones, while Sartre maintained, for over a year, a teleologically suspended silence on this delicate subject. But when it came to something much nearer home—the Algerian War—it was Sartre who spoke out, while Camus's silence on that subject was broken only by humanitarian utterances of an apolitical character. Moral indignation, and plain political condemnation, he reserved for Soviet imperialism in Hungary. On the whole, if a contrast in integrity has to be made, Sartre comes out of it better than Camus. Sartre after all did eventually (January 1950) recognize and condemn the existence of the Soviet camps. A writer's integrity, in political matters, does not necessarily vary directly with the square of his distance from the Communist party.

Mr. Caute's refusal to indulge in anti-communist cant does not mean that he accepts or ignores communist cant. On the contrary the nature of his subject obliges him to provide a veritable anthology of prose and verse in this kind, oscillating between the sinister and the farcical:

Aragon (1937) on the Moscow trials: "How silent are the scandalous advocates of Trotsky and his accomplices! They knew very well that to claim innocence for these men is to adopt the Hitlerian thesis on all points. By doubting this point or that point they imply at the same time . . . that it was not Hitler who burned the Reichstag . . . in fact they are the advocates of Hitler and the Gestapo."

Wurmser (1949) on the Rajk and Kostov trials: ". . . if Dreyfus had confessed there would have been no Dreyfus affair" ("which," as Mr. Caute says, "could scarcely be denied").

Aragon (1953) on Thorez's return from Russia:

> *Il revient Je redis ces deux mots-là sans cesse*
> *Tout se colore d'eux après ces deux années*
> *Il revient il revient il vient il va venir* . . .

André Stil (1949) on a favourite theme: "It is true, they think, it is well known that everyone has a little of *Stalin* at the bottom of him, which watches us from inside, smiling and serious, giving confidence. It is our consciences as communists, this internal presence of *Stalin*."

The people who wrote this sort of thing belonged to the inner circle of party intellectuals determined—in the words of their most gifted and most brazen member, Louis Aragon—"to write the Stalinist truth." The trouble was that the more Stalinist truth they turned out the more they repelled the very people whom it was their business to attract: that considerable number of French intellectuals who were and are generally sympathetic to the Communist party (as the party of the French working class) but are seldom prepared to push sympathy to the point of real or feigned intellectual abdication. Among certain "principles of utility" (of intellectuals to the party) distinguished by Mr. Caute, two are perpetually in conflict. These are the second principle and the fourth. The second principle is as follows: "professional excellence, if possible within the framework of a Marxist-communist philosophy, with the primary object of influencing politically other intellectuals and the educated community in general."

The fourth principle is shorter: "political journalism."

Mr. Caute shows us the two principles in conflict in many fields and during many phases of the party's life. One good example is the Lysenko controversy in which party scientists generally either criticized Lysenko or kept silent, while the non-scientists denounced Lysenko, one of them proclaiming that, for a Communist, "Stalin is the highest scientific authority in the world." Mr. Caute comments: "By shouting in chorus that a new theory about which they knew little or nothing was correct (*a*) because it would be useful if it were correct and (*b*) because Stalin said it was, the intellectuals could only devalue their own currency and help to make of their party an object of deep suspicion and even contempt."

Yet Mr. Caute's narrative also illustrates the vitality of the party and its sustained ability to acquire, from each new intellectual generation, at least some of the support lost in the last one. R. H. S. Crossman's assertion that "the Communist machine has winnowed out the grain and retained only the chaff of Western culture" is, as Mr. Caute shows, "no more than a half-truth." It is safe to predict that as long as the French Communist party remains the principal working-class party it will continue to attract the sympathy of many French intellectuals, people whose teeth are set on edge by the lies and platitudes of so many Communist leaders and spokesmen, but who are determined not to be driven by these distressing phenomena into an anti-communist, and ultimately anti-working class, position. A man like Sartre, whom Communist leaders have accused at different times of being in the pay of the Nazis and of Wall Street, has retaliated as little as possible, reserving most of his ammunition for use against the richer and more plausible mendacities of the Free World.

From about 1924 to about 1956 there was, as Mr. Caute points out, between the intellectuals and the workers, "the Stalinist filter." It was "no more possible for the intellectual to remain true to his vocation as a Communist with a capital 'C' than it was for him to desert the ideal of communism with a small 'c.' Here," Mr. Caute concludes, "was the dilemma."

The Twentieth Party Congress of the C.P.S.U. in 1956 threw down the Russian image of Stalin, but does not seem to have entirely removed "the Stalinist filter" from the French party. Yet the type of the Stalinist intellectual hatchet-man—sycophant, bully and hack—has inevitably lost authority and, to some extent, voice. All Mr. Caute's more Byzantine quotations come from before 1956: most of them are no later than 1953. In present circumstances no foreign Communist party—neither that of Khrushchev nor that of Mao—is in a position to dictate to the French Communist party. Is it possible that that party will shake off the vestiges of Stalinism, and come to speak with a distinctively French accent, thereby solving the particular dilemma on which Mr. Caute ends the present volume?

The answer can only come in a successor volume: *The French Communist Party, 1960-2000.* Mr. Caute is still young enough for it to be within the bounds of possibility that he should write that book.

IV

IRELAND

1891-1916

In the summary historical retrospect which we all acquire at school and probably never quite lose, this period, 1891 to 1916, forms, I think, a sort of crease in time, a featureless valley between the commanding chain of the Rising and the solitary enigmatic peak of Parnell. It was a time in which nothing happened; nothing except (as we find when we look into it) a revolution in land ownership, the beginning of a national quest for a lost language and culture, and the preparation of the two successful rebellions which were, among other things, to tear Ireland in two. Yet despite these momentous events it is not only to us with our memories of school history that the period seems empty: it seemed so to many contemporaries. For James Joyce, as we know, the seething Dublin of 1904 was "the centre of paralysis," a place in which the maudlin mumbled helplessly about "poor oul' Parnell." From its own very different point of view the Ascendancy saw things in a rather similar light: the native Irish and especially the *Babus* were squabbling interminably among themselves, showing their unfitness for self-government. If England held firm by Lord Salisbury's doctrine of resolute government—as she did in effect until almost the end of the period—then the essentials of the Cromwellian settlement could be preserved. *Jam redit et Virgo,* as the Public Orator reminded Arthur Balfour, *redeunt Saturnia regna*: it was a golden age, a return to order after the hideous Time of Troubles of the Land League, the Gladstonian convulsion and the Plan of Campaign. It was easy—as in the stories, though not in the novels, of Somerville and Ross—to see Irish affairs as comic and therefore essentially static. Indeed one could argue that the most characteristically Irish thing about the old landlord class was its inability to take Irish affairs wholly seriously: just as the caricatures of Somerville and Ross resemble the brilliant frozen social scenes of *Ulysses* through their intimations of a world both futile and changeless. Somerville and Joyce—if we may sketch the possibility of such a collaboration—saw through the Gaelic League, the G.A.A., the world of the Citizen and the new crooked County Councillors, but they did not see through them to anything in particular or at least not to anything Irish or anything moving and growing. They could have taken to themselves the majestic words of the English statesman of the day: I was never present while a revolution was going on. In a sense indeed, most of the population was absent while the Revolution was going on. What, for example, did the Gaelic League mean to the working people of Dublin? The eventual alliance of Connolly and Pearse implies that it meant something, but just what that potential something was might have been difficult to discover in the Dublin of the early 1900s. And as for the middle class as a whole, there is some reason to believe that on Easter Monday, 1916, the main focus of its interest was not the G.P.O. but Fairyhouse Racecourse.

If I have stressed the fact that to many contemporaries nothing very important seemed to be going on in Ireland between 1891 and say—for this purpose—1910 or thereabouts, I have done so precisely because many important things *were* going on, and because these important things cannot be understood unless we feel also something of the weight of indifference against which they were working. The backward glance has a tendency to isolate precursors, in the sense of bold and originating historic figures. It is well to remember that the ordinary men and women of a given time are precursors also—precursors of the ordinary men and women of today. We are heirs not only of the traditions of 1916 but also of other traditions and of that more continuous indifference which flows round all traditions. Those of us who were born since 1916 have almost always been taught to think of ourselves as belonging to the revolutionary tradition; this is commonly the case in the aftermath of successful revolutions. It can do us no harm to remember that what we might call the "Fairyhouse Tradition" is not less persistent, although it does not cut such a figure in the history books. With this at the back of our minds, let us turn our attention to the elements of excitement, change and activity that were at work in the period: the elements that we are accustomed to regard as, in a special sense, historic forces. As soon as we turn in this direction we see, of course, that there was an unusual amount of mental activity, an unusual degree of intensity and self-dedication in the minds, certainly not of the people as a whole, but of quite sizeable groups of people.

This excitement and dedicated mood had perhaps something to do with the romantic loyalty which the figure of Parnell, and especially his fall, had evoked in many. In the case of the literary revival, Yeats tells us so specifically. We know that Griffith was a Parnellite and that the Revolutionary movement, rather paradoxically, had Parnell among its heroes. The generation that was young in Ireland when Parnell fought his last tragic campaign, or even when the echoes of that campaign still filled the air, had a peculiar mark upon it: a mark that in many took the form of rebellion and rejection—or that of a cult of the hero and of heroism. We ought not to exaggerate the importance of the cult of the Lost Leader but we should be aware of its presence and of its power to take unexpected forms.

Some of the movements which were now emerging into importance had their beginnings in the Parnellite period itself. One of these, and not the least notable, was the G.A.A., some of whose members, armed with their hurley sticks, formed Parnell's bodyguard in the last tumultuous meetings. In the nineties and early 1900s the G.A.A. built on the ground cleared by the Land League: that is to say that it organized with faith and enthusiasm the replacement, among the young in many parts of the country, of what had been a servile spirit by a spirit of manliness and freedom. It was a new monument and one not erected by a grateful tenantry. More than the Gaelic League, more than Arthur Griffith's Sinn Fein, more even than the Transport and General Workers' Union and of course far more than the movement which created the Abbey Theatre; more than any of these the Gaelic Athletic movement aroused the interest of large numbers of ordinary people throughout Ireland. One of the most successful and original mass movements of its day, its importance has perhaps not even yet been fully recognized. Not that it has not received its full share of conventional praise; that, many friends ensure. But the tribute which it has not received is the more serious one of sustained critical attention; in this context it is perhaps necessary to say that what I mean by "critical" is not hostile but intelligent and, as far as possible, disinterested and dispassionate. I do not know that it has been remarked that the G.A.A., in effect, carried into what might very broadly be called the cultural field the great principle which had brought the Land League victory in the agrarian struggle: the principle of the boycott. It organized the boycott of policemen, soldiers and those who watched or played what the G.A.A. proudly called "Foreign Games." In practice (though certainly not in theory) this last ban meant the exclusion of almost all Protestants, much of the Catholic middle class and (as it worked out) the urban working class. In view of the importance which the G.A.A. came to assume in the life of the countryside these exclusions were of considerable social and even political importance. This is not the place for a detailed discussion of the merits of that famous ban. It is enough to say that if the G.A.A. did a great deal to bring about the freedom of a part of Ireland, its contribution towards the achievement of Irish unity is much more questionable. But then, one of the significant facts about the period we are considering is that while many Irishmen were passionately concerned about freedom, few gave any thought at all to unity—except of course as a technical term meaning party discipline. One is reluctant to invoke the hypothetical reactions of the great dead, yet perhaps may be forgiven for doing so in this instance: Thomas Davis, who was concerned for unity as well as for freedom, might well have felt that here, in the seemingly not very important episode of the G.A.A. Ban, nationalist Ireland first departed from the spirit though not from the letter of his teaching.

There were however other movements of the national spirit around the turn of the century which were more clearly marked by the teaching of Davis. The Gaelic League, under the leadership of Douglas Hyde, relied not on an authoritarian structure of bans and exclusions, but on the love of the Irish language and its literature. It succeeded, probably to a greater degree than any other Irish movement in modern times, in crossing that invisible entanglement of religious and social barriers which later was to take material and geographical form with the partition of our country. The Gaelic League in those days seemed to offer a voyage of discovery which was at the same time an escape from a vicious circle of provincial factions. The hope which it held out was so bright that to this day some thoughtful men, trained in that school and imbued with the principles of Davis, believe that the best way to unite Ireland lies through the revival of the Irish language. Even those of us who believe that the view so stated is illusory must recognize, I think, that it contains this important element of truth: such a generosity of spirit as prevailed to a remarkable extent in the early days of the League is the one essential element in any real movement towards Irish unity.

In this series of talks, in which we are, as it were, interrogating the works and days of a past generation and thinking inevitably of their relevance to our own times, we shall be confronted under various guises with the workings of considerable minorities which were more positive, more sanguine, bolder and more ardent in temperament than any sizeable group which has so far revealed itself in our own generation. The Gaelic League was on the whole the happiest and fairest expression of the mind of such a minority.

The period we are considering was one of combat and preparation for combat, and there is no cause for surprise that many of its manifestations should have had a very different temper from that of the founders of the Gaelic League. Sometimes there may be no particular cause to regret this. The industrial clash between Jim Larkin and William Martin Murphy—to present it in personal terms—produced by its very bitterness and by the fright and shock which it gave to middle-class public opinion a different and, we are likely to think, a better relation between capital and labour. It may have been better, from Murphy's point of view if not from Larkin's, that the shock should have been administered in 1913 rather than in, shall we say, 1917 or 1922. But there was another kind of bitterness, partly political, partly social, partly what is loosely called religious, which was no doubt equally explicable but certainly more ominous. This was the bitterness behind the propaganda for what was known as Irish Ireland. It was, I think, that master of invective and above all of slogans, D. P. Moran of *The Leader,* who first made nationalist Ireland think of itself as Irish Ireland. In Moran's language, which is often still heard, if you were not an Irish Irelander you were either a West Briton, if of Anglo-Irish descent, or a shoneen if of Gaelic ancestry. If you were a shoneen then you possessed "a slave mind." If you were a West Briton you were probably also a "sourface," a term used by Moran with curious religious and racial implications. This polemic was extremely effective, for Moran was a brilliant journalist with a keen sense of the ridiculous and Viceregal Dublin kept him well supplied with targets. But a price has to be paid for all polemics and Irish Ireland never accurately reckoned the cost of its attitudes. We cannot afford, said Parnell, to give up a single Irishman. Moran and his friends, including many Sinn Feiners and even an increasing number of Gaelic Leaguers, acted as if they could afford to lose a million

Irishmen—if those Irishmen did not conform to their idea of what an Irishman ought to be. For many Irish Irelanders—though not, I like to think, for so intelligent a man as Moran himself— Horace Plunkett was a West Briton; Lady Gregory a sourface; Tom Kettle, perhaps, a shoneen. Irish Ireland in its narrower manifestations felt rich enough to lose such men and women; we may feel that there was something wrong with its accountancy. When Moran and his friends talked of West Britons they had in mind, I imagine, some archetype of a dentist's wife who collected crests, ate kedgeree for breakfast and displayed on her mantelpiece a portrait of the Dear Queen. This was of course, like many of the views of Irish Ireland, a Dublin-centred view. Dublin Castle was the seat of British rule. Britain's friends in Ireland, therefore, were Castle hangers-on. It was easy to forget that the particular West Britons with whom the final reckoning would be were the industrial workers of Belfast who collected no crests, ate no kedgeree, hung on to no Castle. Irish Ireland wrote and talked as if it assumed that the battle would be over once Dublin with its garrison of dentists' wives had surrendered. Belfast would bluster a little but would toe the line: was it not a provincial city? So that one could already, even before the victory, use a tone which implied that in the new Ireland the minority had better keep a civil tongue in its head. This assumption and this tone may have had something to do with the shape which modern Ireland eventually took.

It would however be unfair to Moran and his friends, and also historically misleading, to leave out of account the general tone of the Irish upper classes: a tone of sovereign contempt for what they regarded as "The new Nationalist Ireland." Here again a certain amount of misunderstanding was at work. As a class—although there were many exceptions—the Ascendancy and especially its urban fringes, our symbolic dentists' wives, knew little or nothing of Irish history. They even lacked the concept of Irish history as a separate entity. As colonists have always done, and do to this day, they regarded the native tendency to revolt as something essentially modern, artificial and stirred up by foreigners— in this case by "the American money" which had floated the Land League and its successors. They saw the incipient revolt, also, as a social rather than a national phenomenon: the attempted self-inflation of people who were all very well if they kept in their own place. The true inflections of this Ascendancy arrogance remain for us in certain dialogues of the Somerville and Ross novels; we can hear a coarser, louder echo of the same tone if we turn to the Unionist Press of the time, the *Dublin Daily Express,* for example, or in a more good-humoured key, the *Dublin Evening Mail.* And it was of course in the main the coarser and cruder echo which reached the ears of contemporary Nationalists. It was an old complaint. *Ni h-é an bochtanas is measa dhúinn,* a poet of the previous century had written, *ach an tarcuisne leanann é.* But now contempt could be answered in very effective English; all the more easily because Nationalist Ireland genuinely could not understand what the Ascendancy had to be arrogant about. To the Ascendancy itself, thinking in global terms, its contribution to the Empire in generals, admirals and pro-consuls seemed a sufficient answer. But to the Nationalists, thinking solely in Irish terms, it seemed with equal reason that the record of the Ascendancy was one of conceited incompetence and shortsighted selfishness, and that its only monuments were of that stony and trunkless kind bequeathed by Ozymandias, King of Kings. For both sides contempt was a costly indulgence; the cost to the Ascendancy is obvious, the cost to the Nationalists and to Ireland is only now beginning to be assessed. Dublin and rural Ireland, the early Sinn Feiners, the Leader group, the theoreticians of the G.A.A., were too apt to forget that there existed in Ireland another kind of colonist besides the Ascendancy and that these other colonists had built and meant to hold a very non-Ozymandian monument in the shape of Ireland's only modern city. They forgot, as we sometimes forget today, that men like Pirrie, in building up heavy industry in Belfast, were doing as much as anyone to shape modern Ireland. More, indeed, if we stress the *modern.* Ulstermen have argued that the really modern part of Ireland is confined to the Lagan Valley.

That of course raises the question: does Ireland as a whole need or want the kind of modernity that prevails in the Lagan Valley? This question was potentially present, though not expressed in those words, in the period we are considering. It cuts across the ordinary political, religious and social divisions in some curious and perhaps revealing ways. Very roughly we can say that a Lagan Valley solution, in the sense of industrialization and dense population, attracted or repelled people, somewhat as follows: the tendency of Sinn Fein was in favour of it, so was that of Progressive Unionism; William Martin Murphy favoured it, so did Larkin and Connolly; the Gaelic League was against it in feeling if not in theory; the Irish-Irelanders who read *The Leader* were supposed to be militantly for it; the G.A.A., which never caught on in the cities, was against it by nature, as also were most of the Ascendancy. And finally, most explicitly and consciously against it was the remarkable reactionary movement known as the Irish Literary Revival. I do not use the word reactionary in a hostile sense; reaction is often a healthy thing and may well have been so here. As Yeats wrote:

> *John Synge, I and Augusta Gregory thought*
> *All that we did, all that we said or sang*
> *Must come from contact with the soil, from that*
> *Contact everything Antaeus-like grew strong.*
> *We three alone in modern times had brought*
> *Everything down to that sole test again*
> *Dream of the noble and the beggarman.*

The revivalists sought in Ireland the kind of dignity and the kind of health that the industrialized world, the modern world, had lost; the Ireland they loved had an enormous West Coast and no Northeast corner. They belonged with variations of emphasis to the Ascendancy and their thought for good and ill was in the perspective of the Ascendancy, the rural-to-universal perspective. A Griffith or a Moran or a Murphy thought of what Ireland lacked, which as they saw it was industry. A Yeats or a Synge thought of what industrialized Europe lacked, which was contact with the soil. Their message—they certainly had one—was formally destined for Ireland but its ultimate addressees were, one feels, the cultivated European public: "See what can be done here, with this storehouse of legends, in contact with this soil and with this unspoiled people," they seemed to say. And much was done; a great theatre was founded, great plays and poems were written, the memories of great lives were left. But as for the effect of the message, literally understood, upon the first Abbey audiences, those guinea pigs of archaism, that is not so clear. We can hardly be surprised if the poor creatures occasionally, maddened by confusing signals, turned and bit the fingers of the demonstrator.

Confusion is the condition in which history exists, as distinct from the way in which we try to tidy it up afterwards. The ideas which we have separated as those of the Gaelic Leaguer, the Literary Revivalist, the Sinn Feiner and so on were often and perhaps usually found together, in different forms of association, in the same people. One could believe simultaneously that Ireland had peculiar virtues springing from its rural way of life *and also* that it ought to be industrialized. Or one could in Ulster pride oneself on one's loyalty to Britain and the King *and also* on one's readiness in certain circumstances to revolt against His Majesty's Government. The confusion of the time was rich and explosive. And it was the man of action rather than the man of prudence who flourished in it. The caution of an Archbishop Walsh, the constructiveness of a Horace Plunkett, the moderation and inclusive view of a John Redmond, came to seem irrelevant or even tarnished virtues. Through the mouths of Carson and of Pearse all Ireland heard ancestral voices prophesying war. Different ancestors and a different war.

This is not the place to discuss the merits of what was shaped; our view of these, whatever it may be, cannot but be present to our minds—much as certain serious historians deplore the fact—when we are trying to look at the shaping process. But one point it is necessary to make, and that is that modern Ireland did not take the shape that any of its shapers desired. It was not only Redmond that was defeated. The union of Great Britain and Ireland, the cause for which alone Carson had struggled, was wrecked, and Carson was left with a despised fragment in his hands. The Republic of All Ireland for which the precursors, Stephens and Devoy, toiled and suffered, and for which Clarke, Pearse and Connolly died, has not emerged. These facts must prevent us from looking at the men and events of the time from one point of view only, as some have done—the point of view of "those who turned out to be right." Nobody turned out to be right as far as the politics were concerned.

Yeats building his theatre, Pirrie building his ships, Plunkett and AE building their co-operatives, Murphy his business, Larkin his Union: these turned out to be right but were also prisoners, in their thought as in their activities, of the ambiguous historical process. So are we; and the thought should remind us that "Modern Ireland" is not, and cannot be, finally "shaped" and that therefore we cannot be too sure of who its "shapers" at a given time really were. From the standpoint of ten or twenty years hence the "true precursors" who are seen to have flourished in the 1900s may be quite different people. It follows that our best rule in choosing subjects is not to be guided solely by the canon of success—acknowledged posthumous influence—but to look at those who had in fact an influence on their contemporaries.

IRISHNESS

Irish Strategy, 1014-1945: The campaigns and actions of Brian Boru, Owen Roe O'Neill, Marshal Browne, Commodore Barry, Wellington, Admiral Browne, General Sheridan, Field Marshals Alexander and Montgomery, and many others.

Such a compilation would in some ways be less odd than a collection of Irish verse in the English language which includes, as does the new Oxford Book, poems by Goldsmith and Sheridan, Emily Brontë, Edward Fitzgerald and Oscar Wilde, Louis MacNeice and Cecil Day Lewis. For the language of war is an international one, possessing at least no essentially *non*-Irish characteristic, whereas in the case of these poets, not only their language but their culture is English—the language and culture which ousted the Irish language and culture. There exist, therefore, difficulties about an *Oxford Book of Irish Verse** which do not arise for the other Oxford Books, of French or Russian or Portuguese Verse. Many Irish people are by now thoroughly tired of these difficulties and the recriminations which flow from them: they hold that it would be better for Irish writers to get on with their writing, in whatever language they choose, rather than argue interminably about what Irish writing is; whatever it is, there is less and less of it. It may be because Mr. Donagh MacDonagh, very understandably, shares this point of view that he is rather summary in his treatment of the difficulty. He states in his introduction: "A question that will be asked is: What constitutes an Irish poet? In its simplest form the answer is easy, but there are exceptions. By our definition a poet may be Irish in three ways: by birth, by descent, by adoption." Birth? The Duke of Wellington—who would no doubt be represented in this anthology if he had written verse—dealt adequately with this criterion in his celebrated remark about not necessarily being a horse if you were

* *Edited by Donagh MacDonagh and Lennox Robinson.*

born in a stable. Descent? This can lead, as it does here, to the absurdity that a family, originating in England or Scotland and returning to its native country after a few generations in the northeast of Ireland, is to be treated as having become indelibly "Irish." Adoption? A very exceptional case. Swift was perhaps "adopted," much against his will, by Ireland; one or two other poets "adopted" Ireland, but she turned out badly for them.

In practice, the inadequacy of these criteria shows itself in a certain incoherence in the anthology. Nahum Tate's "While Shepherds Watched," Wolfe's "Burial of Sir John Moore," and a piece of the *Rubaiyat* have no serious reason for being in the same volume with Callanan's "The Convict of Clonmel," Ferguson's "Dear Dark Head" and Fanny Parnell's "After Death," nor is there anything relevant in common between Mr. Cecil Day Lewis's "Do Not Expect Again a Phoenix Hour" and Mr. Patrick Kavanagh's "Shancoduff." The total effect, for anyone who reads right through the anthology, is rather like listening to a Radio Éireann program from abroad: faint but distinctive accents continually interrupted by snatches of a program from a nearby and more powerful station. Such, it might be argued, is the nature of Irish life; yet surely one of the functions of an anthology of Irish verse ought to be to pick up the Irish accents with a minimum of interference.

How can this be done? "To demand a recognizably Irish voice as a rigid test of Irish poetry," says Mr. MacDonagh, "would be absurd, and would exclude many fine poets." One could reply that the editor of a book of Irish verse must exclude many fine poets—Homer and Dante, for example—and that one of the troubles here is that the editors have not excluded enough fine poets. Yet Mr. MacDonagh's wariness about the "recognizably Irish voice" is in itself respectable: there are sirens with that voice, whitened bones of bards have been found in alehouses. The problem is: avoiding "national rhythm," the "descent into the ancient blood" and popular concepts of genetically transmitted theology, can we form an idea of Irishness which will be adequate, at least, to permit the making of a reasonably homogeneous anthology, *in English?*

The thing can be done, I believe, if we adopt a historical rather than a geographical point of view. Irishness is not primarily a question of birth or blood or language: it is the condition of being involved in the Irish situation, and usually of being mauled by it. On that definition Swift is more Irish than Goldsmith or Sheridan, although by the usual tests they are Irish and he is pure English. The Irishness of Moore is in part a reflection, in part a nostalgia, in part a schism: a spiritual involvement of wistfulness and guilt, less painful probably than the physical and administrative involvement of Dublin's English Dean. Mangan and Ferguson injected Gaelic poetry into English, and with it toxins of the Irish past, ultimately fatal to that English political settlement of Ireland which seemed so sure a thing a hundred years ago. The movement of Yeats and Lady Gregory was in the same tradition; it was not deliberately political, but Irish life, mauling it and them, made it Irish in a sense which they had not chosen, the sense of political nationalism. Today, political nationalism has ceased to sing—its elegy is here in Denis Devlin's sad and noble "Tomb of Michael Collins." The Ireland in which contemporary writers are involved—or from which they disengage themselves—is very different from the Ireland of literary tradition. The writers are mostly individualists who would curse at the mention of Irishness, or indeed of almost anything else. Yet what they have in common, whether they care to assess it or not, is still their involvement in a country of which one of them, Mr. Patrick Kavanagh, has vividly illuminated an important part. The rest remains to be discovered by others.

In arguing for "historical involvement" as the criterion, I should not like to be taken as abounding in that sense, pleading for a rhapsodical hodgepodge of dirges and war-cries. The only value of the criterion is to make possible some degree of homogeneity in selection. By giving a more precise meaning to the term "Irish writer" we can avoid the indignity of pursuing English literary men with Irish birth certificates. Even there, once the principle is established, much flexibility is needed. Borderline cases, like Louis MacNeice and W. R. Rodgers, might as well be annexed. And even in so English an "Irish writer" as Robert Graves one can sometimes find, or think one finds, an Irish note, as in "Love Without Hope," which Mr. MacDonagh rightly includes here. Perhaps there is a tradition—that of the four-line epigram—for Irish poets; or perhaps it is only the uneconomic nature of the operation described in "Love Without Hope" that seems to produce an Irish note. In any case, let us claim it:

> *Love without hope, as when the young bird-catcher*
> *Swept off his tall hat to the Squire's own daughter,*
> *So let the imprisoned larks escape and fly*
> *Singing about her head, as she rode by.*

OUR WITS ABOUT US

The Irish Comic Tradition* is an original and important book which combines much lightly carried learning with ingenious and entertaining speculation and a vein of shrewd informal comment unusual in criticism. Its originality is its most striking feature. As Dr. Mercier characteristically says in the opening words of his preface: "This book makes no claim to be the last word on its subject; it is much closer to being the first one." He is justified in the claim that in undertaking to write it he was

> compelled to attempt almost single-handed a synoptic view of a subject matter ranging over eleven centuries and two languages: that is, if we agree to call Old, Middle, and Modern Irish—which differ at least as much as Old, Middle, and Modern English—one language.

The Irish Comic Tradition is therefore the work of a pioneer and deserves, at the hands of even critics who disagree with its main thesis—as I do—some of the respect and gratitude which we accord to pioneers in other fields of scholarship. Some Irish scholars and critics, themselves not much noted for breaking new ground, have denounced this particular pioneer, with a suspect vehemence. The cause of their vituperation does not, I think, lie in the vein of malevolence and destructiveness which Dr. Mercier discerns—as Joyce did—in the Irish comic tradition itself. Joyce saw that:

> *'Twas Irish humour, wet and dry,*
> *Flung quicklime into Parnell's eye.*

The hostile reaction to *The Irish Comic Tradition* springs not from Irish humour, but from the humourlessness of some Irishmen. There are Irish people who feel that the words "a witty Irishman" are pejorative: a device whereby the Anglo-Saxon contrives simultaneously to depreciate the importance of wit and circumscribe the possibilities of Irishmen. In fact, for one Irish-

* By Vivian Mercier.

man who might hope to pass for a wit, there must be ten who very sensibly have no such pretension, and another one or two who have attained the condition diagnosed by Myles na gCopaleen as "Paddy Solemn."

Paddy Solemn shudders at the thought, and cringes at the sight or sound, of Brendan Behan; Paddy Solemn likes to use precise-sounding terminology in a vague way, and derives from this a bracing sense of intellectual rigour; Paddy Solemn likes to be thought of as a Thomist, and knows—for he is no fool, despite appearances—that this will do him no harm at all in an academic career bounded on all sides by bishops; Paddy Solemn is not anti-British—for that is a lower-middle-class attitude—but he shakes his head at the sorry intellectual level, and lax moral standards, of English life today. Paddy Solemn has, however, a secret fear. It is that Ireland Will Let Him Down. Of what avail his personal respectability if he is dragged down by a national entity which refuses to be respectable?

Irish history, after that very remote—and even then somewhat eccentric—Golden Age, becomes a monotonous tale of poverty and rebellion: the antithesis of respectability. And Irish literature? Was it not the learned Atkinson who refused to teach Modern Gaelic on the ground that "All Gaelic is folklore and all folklore is at bottom obscene"? This history and this literature are not quite what one would wish, yet one must make the best of them, or accept one's meagre share of a largely alien heritage. The late Donal McNaughton—no Paddy Solemn—played on such fears:

> *We have no ships to bring the Negroes Yeats*
> *Or put Paul Henry in the No-Paul-Henry Places.*
> *With "Made in England" on our very braces,*
> *What are we but a dresserful of plates?*

In this situation Paddy Solemn needs a national heritage: he does not care to look too closely at the one he is actually stuck with. The trouble with *The Irish Comic Tradition* from this point of view is that it lays stress precisely on those elements, richly present in the national literary heritage, which are not respectable: the ribald, the dangerously satirical, the grotesque, the obscene. From the point of view of Paddy Solemn *The Irish Comic Tradition* is a veritable *danse macabre* of the skeletons in the family cupboard. Paddy Solemn's predictable reaction was to slam the book and with it the cupboard door.

It is true that the central theory of Dr. Mercier's book—as of many other valuable books—is open to question. He sets out—and even, rather unguardedly, declares that he is setting out—"to show that an unbroken comic tradition may be traced in Irish literature from approximately the ninth century down to the present day." Having read the book I am in some doubt whether this has really been established.

Irish history from the ninth to the nineteenth century left few things unbroken: not the organization of society, nor ownership, nor even language. Did the literary tradition of the Gaelic aristocracy survive the total destruction both of that aristocracy and of the language which it spoke and wrote? Or is there a more tenacious underlying folk tradition which captures the imagination of Irish writers, even those whose language, family origin and religion have nothing in common with those of the folk in question? Dr. Mercier wavers between, or simultaneously entertains, both hypotheses, under the general and ambiguous heading of "cultural continuity." He finds it reasonable "to attribute cultural phenomena in the first place to cultural causes." If "cultural causes" include war and conquest, fire and famine, I agree with him, but would not expect to find much continuity between pre-Conquest Ireland and the land of Ireland's conquerors and their rebellious serfs. You might not expect to find it, Dr. Mercier says in effect, and yet here is the evidence for it. The evidence is copious, often fascinating and always interesting, but I cannot find it altogether convincing, because too much is left out of account.

The ambiguous word "cultural" in "cultural continuity" seems to fluctuate between its anthropological and its aesthetic use. The common background of mediaeval literature generally, the common characteristics of comic literature generally, are (at least partially) lost to sight in an insistence on the peculiarities of Irishness. Both national history—especially the history of small nations—and literary history—especially the history of peripheral literatures—tend to distort. They distort because of their inherent need to eliminate what is apparently irrelevant to the continuity of the subject. A large part of the eliminated area is the context that affected all the various phases of the subject's existence: the general political, economic and military situation of (in this case) Western Europe at any given moment. A history of a particular current in the literature of a peripheral country is particularly exposed to this danger of distortion; that does not mean that such a history is not worth undertaking.

The idea that there is "an Irish mind," continuing with its own peculiar quirks, not shared even by other Europeans, from mediaeval times to the days of Samuel Beckett, seems to me implausible. Dr. Mercier, although not consistently a victim of this idea, gives it rather more credit than it deserves. Thus he accepts the notion, dear to so many Irish intellectuals, that "hatred of life" is a permanent and distinctive element in the Irish character. The main foundation on which this belief rests is that people in the Irish countryside now marry very late. But before the Great Famine they were noted for marrying very early and having enormous families. The phenomenon of late rural marriage—and the ills and eccentricities which go with it—has definite economic and historical roots, and it is unrewarding to seek for symptoms of the same troubles in an earlier age whose real troubles were different. One can, of course, find such symptoms if one looks for them: disgust and fear seem to be constant and universal elements in human existence, and in all "comic" traditions. The very ancient and beautiful Gaelic nature poetry, and the later and more "European" Gaelic love poetry, testify to the fact that in the Irish tradition, as in others, disgust and fear do not exclude all other emotions.

There is probably no continuous and distinctive "Irish mind," but there has been since the seventeenth century at least an Irish predicament: a predicament which has produced common characteristics in a number of those who have been involved in it. Probably the most striking of these characteristics among intelligent Irish people (whether educated or not) is a propensity to an ironical mode of expression, sometimes achieving wit. In literature, this is the vein common to Swift, Wilde, Shaw and Joyce, and it tends to distinguish the writing of Irishmen from most other writing in English. Why?

Part of the answer, but only part, may be that words are the weapon of the disarmed. "You have your bayonets," said Tim

Healy, "do not grudge us our Billingsgate." A larger part of the answer is, I believe, that the general Irish predicament, especially in the eighteenth and nineteenth centuries, was congenial to the nature of irony, if to little else. Hypocrisy, the permanent and universal element in the ideologies of ruling classes, seeks to mask the gap between profession and action, to cover the realities of social and political struggle with the illusion of harmony. Irony uses the language of hypocrisy—as Swift did in "A Modest Proposal"—with a calculated excess, so that, as the realities show through, the pretences come to seem ghastly. In Ireland, the gaps between ruler and ruled, and between the pretence of benevolence and the realities of exploitation, were, from about 1690 to about 1900, significantly wider than is customary. For some Irishmen, including some who were not themselves directly oppressed, the masks of power and the paradoxes of oppression were lessons in drama and in wit. Easily, too easily, irony became a way of life and the witty Irishman was born.

SOMERVILLE AND ROSS

The protest attending on an alien Ascendancy's callous caperings is of course always most active in a period of national revival.

This opinion is, of course, that of Professor Daniel Corkery and he makes it clear, in that interesting and curious work, *Synge and Anglo-Irish Literature,* that he would apply the description "an alien Ascendancy's callous caperings" to at least a great part of the work of Edith Somerville and her cousin Violet Martin who wrote as Martin Ross.

It would be pleasant in some ways, although perhaps a little dull, to bypass these formidable social, political and moral categories of Professor Corkery's, to dismiss them as "extra-literary considerations" and get down to a purely aesthetic discussion of the artistic merit of the novels and short stories of Somerville and Ross. But the novels and the stories themselves are full of extra-literary considerations and the Irish reader approaches them with his head buzzing with controversial bees. Anti-Irish . . . ? Stage-Irish . . . ? Snobs? These are stock responses—to use the language of Professor I. A. Richards—and therefore not particularly useful in literary criticism. But they cannot be ignored in any discussion of this body of work; they have to be confirmed, to the extent that they are true, or dismantled, to the extent that they are prejudices, before we can be heard saying something relevant about the merits of the books themselves.

On one of Professor Corkery's counts at least we must find a true bill. They were certainly ascendancy. They belonged to old established landed families, the Somervilles in West Cork and the Martins in Galway, and they flourished in a time when such families did in fact constitute an ascendancy. Most of their best work, indeed, was done or at least conceived in what might be called the Indian Summer of the Ascendancy, between the fall of Parnell in 1890 and the outbreak of the World War in 1914. The terrible eighties were behind, and the more terrible twenties undreamed of. There was honey still for tea, and there was hunting, plenty of hunting—and, of course, for the callous, capers. If there was a hint of future trouble in the air—a whiff of the acrid journalism of D. P. Moran, poison laid on certain lands, barbed wire across the path of the hunt—it was no more than lent tang and tension and distinction to the lives of high-spirited people like Edith Somerville and her cousin.

That they were snobs—in one sense of that word—followed naturally from the fact that they belonged to the Irish landed gentry. They had to look down on other people in order to see them. Or so they sincerely felt. And they wanted to see them clearly, to place them socially: "Catholic middle-class moving up"; "Protestant lower-middle-class, stuck"; "Gentleman run wild, with touch of brogue." They wrote on these matters with an almost pedantic care for accuracy, within social conventions which they thoroughly understood and thoroughly approved. Their approval is, to profane ears, often excessive, and one cannot help feeling that the ability to detach themselves from the conventional values of their class would have enriched their work. But their snobbery, as I think we must call it, was at least a live and intelligent system of social apprehension, strictly contemporary and even brisk. It is confusing to have to describe it by the same name as we must apply to the dreary and indiscriminate archaism of certain modern writers, or the vicarious nostalgia of Mr. Evelyn Waugh.

Were they then aliens, colonial writers—to use, again, some of Professor Corkery's terminology—who exploited Ireland in their work for the amusement of the foreigner? This can only be tested by attention to the work itself. The work to which the reproach is most directed is the popular and comic *Irish R.M.* series of short stories—*Some Experiences of an Irish R.M., Further Experiences of an Irish R.M.* and *In Mr. Knox's Country*. From among these I have selected—and have had to abridge—the extract which you are about to hear read. It is from a story called "Lisheen Races, Second-hand." A character called Slipper is describing to a crowd, including the R. M. and a pompous Englishman, a trick he played at the races on one Driscoll:

'Twas within in the same whisky tint meself was, with the bandmasther and a few of the lads, an' we buyin' a ha'porth o' crackers, when I seen me brave Driscoll landin' into the tint, and a pair o' thim long boots on him; him that hadn't a shoe nor a stocking to his foot when your honour had him picking grass out o' the stones behind in your yard. "Well," says I to meself, "we'll knock some spoort out of Driscoll!"

"Come here to me, acushla!" says I to him; "I suppose it's some way wake in the legs y'are," says I, "an' the docthor put them on ye the way the people wouldn't thrample ye!"

"May the divil choke ye!" says he, pleasant enough, but I knew by the blush he had he was vexed.

"Then I suppose 'tis a left-tenant colonel y'are," says I; "yer mother must be proud out o' ye!" says I, "an' maybe ye'll lend her a loan o' thim waders when she's rinsin' yer bauneen in the river!" says I.

"There'll be work out o' this!" says he, lookin' at me both sour and bitther.

"Well indeed, I was thinkin' you were blue moulded for want of a batin'," says I. He was for fightin' us then, but afther we had him pacificated with about a quarther of a naggin' o' sperrits, he told us he was goin' ridin' in a race.

"An' what'll ye ride?" says I.

"Owld Bocock's mare," says he.

"Knipes!" says I, sayin' a great curse; "is it that little staggeen from the mountains; sure she's somethin' about the one age with meself," says I. "Many's the time Jamesy Geoghegan and meself used to be dhrivin' her to Macroom with pigs an' all soorts," says I; "an' is it leppin' stone walls ye want her to go now?"

"Faith, there's walls and every vari'ty of obstackle in it," says he.

"It'll be the best o' your play, so," says I, "to leg it away home out o' this."

"An' who'll ride her, so?" says he.

"Let the divil ride her," says I.

There was no great delay afther that till they said there was a race startin' and the dickens a one at all was goin' to ride only two, Driscoll, and one Clancy.

"Stand aisy now by the plantation," says I; "if they get to come as far as this, believe me ye'll see spoort," says I, "an' 'twill be a convanient spot to encourage the mare if she's anyway wake in herself," says I, cuttin' somethin' about five feet of an ash sapling out o' the plantation.

Well, I hadn't barely thrimmed the ash plant when I heard the people screechin', an' I seen Driscoll an' Clancy comin' on, leppin' all before them, an' owld Bocock's mare bellusin' and powdherin' along, an' bedad! whatever obstackle wouldn't throw *her* down, faith, she'd throw *it* down, an' there's the thraffic they had in it.

"I declare to me sowl," says I, "if they continue on this way there's a great chance some one o' thim'll win," says I.

"Ye lie!" says the bandmasther, bein' a thrifle fulsome after his luncheon.

Well, when I seen them comin' to me, and Driscoll about the length of the plantation behind Clancy, I let a couple of bawls.

I declare to ye when owld Bocock's mare heard them roars she sthretched out her neck like a gandher, and when she passed me out she give a couple of grunts, and looked at me as ugly as a Christian.

"Hah!" says I, givin' her a couple o' dhraws o' th' ash plant across the butt o' the tail, the way I wouldn't blind her; "I'll make ye grunt!" says I, "I'll nourish ye!"

Well whether it was over-anxious he was, turnin' around the way I'd hear him cursin', or whether it was some slither or slide came to owld Bocock's mare, I dunno, but she was bet up agin the last obstackle but two, and before ye could say "shnipes," she was standin' on her two ears beyond in th' other field! I declare to ye, on the vartue of me oath, she stood that way till she reconnoithered what side would Driscoll fall, an' she turned about then and rolled on him as cosy as if he was meadow grass!

The blood was dhruv out through his nose and ears and you'd hear his bones crackin' on the ground! You'd have pitied the poor boy.

"Was he hurt, Slipper?"

"Hurt is it? Killed on the spot! Oh, divil so pleasant an afthernoon ever you seen; and indeed, Mr. Flurry, it's what we were all sayin', it was a great pity your honour was not there for the likin' you had for Driscoll."

That is callous enough, if you take it literally, and I suppose it could be called capering to amuse the foreigner. Certainly the *Irish R.M.* books must have been read by more English people than Irish: after all, there are more of the English and I am afraid they read more books. But I suggest that it is time, in this matter of literary criticism, that we should apply the essential principle of Sinn Fein. I mean by that that we should judge a book not by how we think it may affect a hypothetical foreigner, but solely by how it actually does affect ourselves. In short, if Slipper's story and the *Irish R.M.* books in general do seem funny to us, they need no other justification. They will not, of course, seem funny if we feel, for instance, that their idiom is divorced from any living Irish speech or that the scenes and traits of character that they describe have no roots in Irish life. But this is not the case with Somerville and Ross; they exaggerate, obviously, as every comic writer does, but their exaggeration is firmly based on Irish ground which they knew well and which in their own way they loved deeply. They lived in Ireland for almost all their writing lives and they had, as a writing team, a sensitive ear and a penetrating, humorous eye. If their writing is not part of the literature of Ireland, then Ireland is a poorer place than many of us believe it to be.

Let us get back to Driscoll, for a moment, whom we left for dead under his horse. The end of that story is that Driscoll appears, at the climax of Slipper's story, with a face like "a red-hot potato in a bandage" and thirsting for vengeance on Slipper. Does that remind you of any other scene in our literature? It seems to me to resemble rather strikingly the return of the supposedly murdered da in Synge's *Playboy of the Western World*. There is something of the same rodomontade, there is the same macabre relish for violent death, the same vengeful return from the dead. I do not know whether the parallel has been pointed out before—such writers on Synge as I have consulted do not mention it. In any case the *Irish R.M.* was published in 1899, and *The Playboy* was written in 1905-6, so it is at least possible—I think myself it is probable—that "Lisheen Races, Second-hand" was at the back of Synge's mind as he wrote. The world of Somerville and Ross may not be quite as remote from the world of the Literary Revival as we sometimes suppose. I make a present of the point to Professor Corkery; it suits his thesis; indeed I cannot think why he missed it. Could it be that he has never read the *Irish R.M.*?

Martin Ross died in 1915, and in 1915 also the last collection of *Irish R.M.* stories appeared. Edith Somerville continued to write as Somerville and Ross—and in fact maintained that the collaboration extended beyond the grave—but Slipper and Flurry Knox appeared no more. Probably the survivor in the partnership, which was also a close friendship and affinity, felt she could no longer maintain the lighthearted mood of the *R.M.* stories; also the grimmer climate which set in in 1914 might have been less kind to Slipper and his friends. But there had from the beginning been a tragic side to the work of Somerville and Ross. This had predominated in such early novels as *An Irish Cousin; Naboth's Vineyard,* which contains one of the best descriptions of boycott that have been left to us; *The Real Charlotte,* which is generally regarded as their masterpiece; and *The Silver Fox,* to which we shall return. All of these novels were published before 1899, the year in which the first *Irish R.M.* scored its immense success with, as Professor Corkery would wish me to point out, the English public. From that date until the death of Martin Ross in 1915 the tragic vein almost disappears from their writing, although signs of it may occasionally be glimpsed even in the *R.M.* series. After that date it reappears in two important novels, *Mount Music* in 1919 and *The Big House of Inver* in 1925, and in the less successful but interesting *An Enthusiast* (1921), which deals with "the troubles." *The Big House of Inver* is their last important work, although there were many occasional publications, and one rather slight novel, *French Leave,* between then and Edith Somerville's death in 1949, in her ninetieth year. Those who are interested in her long life and remarkable character and in the nature of her literary partnership with Martin Ross should read Miss Geraldine Cummins's valuable biography, published in 1952.

Three novels are more important than the rest—*The Real Charlotte, Mount Music,* and *The Big House of Inver.* Mr. Stephen Gwynn, speaking out of his wide knowledge of the subject, has said that *The Real Charlotte* is one of the most powerful novels of Irish life ever written. Its central figure, Miss Charlotte Mullen, is certainly a massive and formidable concentration of evil intent working in commonplace detail, without any thunderclaps or blue flame. Evil has often been more dramatically exhibited, but I do not think it has ever been more convincingly worked out in humdrum action, or brought home with such a terrible cumulative effect as an element in everyday life. The people on whom she brings ruin—the common, pretty Francie Fitzpatrick, and common, swaggering Lambert the agent —are satisfactory enough as experiments in ruin, but somehow the class convention—which is particularly hard and disdainful in this book—comes between them and our pity, and between the book as a whole and complete success. Francie and Lambert are not wellbred, not therefore quite human. Charlotte Mullen is of course of the same class, but one feels her to have attained a certain aristocracy of evil like Satan in Pandemonium:

> *by merit rais'd*
> *To that bad eminence.*

The middle class—which is, by the way, here a Protestant middle class—occupies the centre of attention—a circumstance which is unique in the work of Somerville and Ross. Above is a highly idealized Ascendancy family, the Dysarts; below are the peasants, who are in this book a collection of grotesques envisaged bleakly and without sympathy. For the rest, the book is exceedingly well and sparely written and more carefully constructed than any of their other novels—although the pace at the finish is, as is usual with them, recklessly forced. *The Real Charlotte* is generally considered the best of their novels, and I think it is so. It is also, unfortunately, the one most marred by evidence of lack of sympathy with outsiders. Professor Corkery, in a striking phrase, denounces the presence in our literature of "an alien ascendancy streaked with the vulgarity of insensibility." The verdict itself has a little streak of the same, and its harshness is unjust, as far as most of the work of Somerville and Ross is concerned. But in *The Real Charlotte* the streak is noticeable and it harms an otherwise splendid achievement. That does not mean, however, that I think *The Real Charlotte* is un-Irish. There is nothing un-Irish about aristocratic pride; a great part of our Gaelic literature throbs with a full and blue-blooded contempt for the lowborn.

The two other main novels, *Mount Music* and *The Big House of Inver,* are much more loosely written, but with more generous feeling. The ice has melted—there are twenty-five years after all between *The Real Charlotte* and *Mount Music*—and the style has lost some of its edge, the edge that I think Martin Ross put on it, for good and ill. The central theme of *Mount Music* is one of which Irish writers have in general tended to fight rather shy, that of religious intolerance, on the part of both Protestants and Catholics. Miss Somerville calls it, cheerfully enough, the Spirit of the Nation and follows its devious workings and its double language with remarkable detachment. The whole subject is of course now utterly out of date, and such a spirit can scarcely be conceived by the modern Irish reader, who positively drips with tolerance. Nonetheless the book may be read for its antiquarian interest.

Although both *Mount Music* and *The Big House of Inver* lack style as compared with *The Real Charlotte,* they have not lost the power of generating a daemonic force in a credible character. Such is Dr. Francis Mangan in *Mount Music;* such, in *The Big House of Inver,* is Shibby Pindy, the illegitimate greathearted daughter of a gentle family, who has had a peasant upbringing, but whose passion is to restore, through her half-brother, the glories of *The Big House,* which stands empty at the beginning of the novel and is in flames at the end. *The Big House of Inver,* were it not for something a little blurred and loose in the writing, would surpass *The Real Charlotte.* I am not indeed quite sure that it does not surpass it as it is, for if there is a blur in the writing, there is no such smudge of meaningless character as in the Dysart family group in the earlier novel.

What we regret, then, among so much that we admire, is that, as imaginative sympathy deepened, style declined. The youthful arrogance which somewhat blunted the moral perception yet carried itself extremely well. The quality of unwavering intelligence was in the writing—an intelligence not worried by clichés, but never allowing a cliché to come between it and the reality of the given moment. This alertness flags in the later works, which have wider vision but a less precise one. Perhaps had it not been for the success of the *R.M.* stories, which diverted them for so many and such important years from their vein of tragedy, Somerville and Ross might have given us a work of their maturity which would have been as alert as it was humane.

You have heard, near the beginning of this talk, a passage from the *Irish R.M.* illustrating the comic side, which is the better-known side, of Somerville and Ross. I want you to hear, before the talk ends, a passage in their tragic vein. The passage I have selected is from one of the less-known works, a short novel called *The Silver Fox,* which appeared in 1897, three years after *The Real Charlotte,* and two years before the first of the *R.M.* books. It was the last novel of tragic temper published in the lifetime of Martin Ross. As a story it is not fully thought out—probably the minds of the two writers were already beginning to turn towards the *Irish R.M.*—but it has certain scenes where we glimpse that balance of alertness and humanity which is never quite sustained in any of their major novels. The passage which you are going in a few moments to hear Miss Lynch read is one of these rare scenes, or so it seems to me. *The Silver Fox* is about hunting and about the supernatural; the fox itself is an unearthly creature, of which the peasantry stand in terror and which the hunt vainly and ruinously pursues. Maria Quin belongs to a peasant family and she has lost her brother and her father because, she believes, of the fox and of the hunt. As the hunt passes near the house in which her brother lies dead she rushes out "full of a blind indignation against those who, for their own amusement, had wrecked the fortunes of a family, and now came to gallop past the house of death, guided by that grey and ill-omened thing." She finds that a horse and rider, having cleared a high bank, have fallen deep into an unsuspected cleft. She manages to rescue the rider, an Englishwoman, Lady Susan French, who had on the previous day seen her brother Tom Quin's body lifted from the river.

"Is the horse killed?" [Lady Susan] said hoarsely, scrambling on to her feet and looking down through the naked branches that fringed the long cleft.

Even the first glance could certify that Solomon had met his death in an instant. He lay in a heap in the obscurity forty feet below, on loose rocks among dark water; his head was doubled under his chest at an impossible angle that told the tale of a broken neck. The uttermost effort of a good horse had not been enough to save him, when he had tried to jump out from the top of the high bank across a chasm nearly twenty feet wide. That endeavour and all his simple and gallant life seemed expressed in the wreck of strength and intelligence that lay below, with the water washing over the flap of the saddle, over the shapely brown fetlocks, over the thin and glossy mane.

It was mysterious water, an underground stream that slid out of the dumb and sightless caverns of the rock, and passed away into them again with a swirl, a stealthy swift thing, escaping always from the eye of day, and eating the foundations of the limestone walls that sheltered it.

Lady Susan still held the hand that had rescued her; it led her through the brushwood to open ground, till the short wet grass was under her foot and the mist blew in her face. She turned her head away, and the sobs broke from her. Any one who has loved horse or dog will know how and where they touch the heart and command the tear. Let us trust that in some degree it is known to them also, that the confiding spirit may understand that its god can grieve for it.

Maria Quin looked at Lady Susan with eyes that were as dry as glass. The Irish peasant regards the sorrow for a mere animal as a childishness that is almost sinful, a tempting of ill fate in its parody of the grief rightly due only to what is described as "a Christhian"; and Maria's heart glowed with the unwept wrongs of her brother.

"What happened him?" she asked, and the knot of pain and outrage was tight in her voice.

"I tried to pull him back when I saw what was coming," said Lady Susan, with difficulty. "I couldn't stop him; he had too much way on. I only did harm. I think he would have got across only for that." She stopped and gulped down the sob. It was dreadful to her to cry before an inferior. "He all but got over, but he dropped his hind legs into it and fell back. I somehow caught those branches just as he was going, and he dropped away from under me, and I hung there. I couldn't climb up. Then you came." She recovered herself a little, and turned towards her rescuer. "I haven't thanked you yet. It was awfully good and plucky of you."

Their eyes met, and it seemed as if till then Lady Susan had not recognized Maria Quin. She visibly flinched, and her flushed face became a deeper red, while the hand that had begun to feel for her purse came out of her pocket empty.

"Little ye cried yesterday whin ye seen my brother thrown out on the ground by the pool," said Maria, with irrepressible savageness, "you that's breakin' yer heart afther yer horse."

Lady Susan, you remember, is an Englishwoman, and the dialogue between her and Maria is, in the full sense, an Anglo-Irish dialogue; a dialogue also in the writers' hearts, torn by irreconcilable things. As long as England and Ireland are neighbours I think that dialogue must continue in some form, and the work of Somerville and Ross will not easily go out of date.

THE FALL OF PARNELL

This book* is the first thorough investigation of the period of Irish history between the O'Shea divorce case (November 1890) and the death of Parnell (October 1891). It covers the stormy interregnum between Parnell's years of power and the deceptive years of "collective leadership," already dealt with in Dr. Lyons's *The Irish Parliamentary Party, 1890–1910*. This interregnum is a crucial period which probably determined much in the subsequent pattern of Irish political history. Such hope as there was of a peaceful evolution of Anglo-Irish relations, on something like "Canadian" lines, succumbed at this time. The political influence of the Church, publicly displayed, suffered hidden diminution. Parnell and the Catholic Hierarchy working together—as they did in a broad political sense during most of Parnell's time of leadership—brought to bear a powerful moderating influence on the development of Irish nationalism. When Parnell and the Bishops bitterly clashed, that influence was weakened in a number of ways. Parnell took up an "extremist" posture. The Bishops, while being drawn deep into politics, were inhibited from taking up any clear political position at all, since their ground for intervention was "the moral issue" and that alone. Difficult ground, for the Bishops had spoken out, not after the divorce-court verdict—which clarified "the moral issue"—but after Gladstone's letter, which shed no further light on morals, but was decisive on an important political issue: the attitude of the Liberal party towards Parnell's continued leadership. The Bishops, with this flank exposed to the most telling propaganda weapon of the Parnellites—"sacrificing the greatest of Irish leaders at the bidding of an Englishman"—were forced to accept a loss of real political influence, in the long-term sense, at the very moment when the hollow "victory" over Parnell seemed to show that influence at its height. The effects of the sordid, scurrilous struggle on the spec-

---

* F. S. L. Lyons, *The Fall of Parnell*.

tators were also destructive of the hopes of moderate men. Among the young in Ireland the spectacle engendered contempt for constitutional politicians; among the English it fostered contempt for the Irish. The contempts converged in the ruin of the Irish party and the rise of Sinn Fein.

Short as it is, the period discussed by Dr. Lyons in *The Fall of Parnell* is therefore eminently worthy of the detailed attention he gives it. *The Fall of Parnell* is a work of most exacting scholarship, bringing a clear, steady light to bear on a time darkened by a multitude of controversial reminiscences. His cool and lucid narrative, with its scrupulous fairness to all the contestants, is a more moving record of this tragic time than all the eloquent and embattled pages that have been devoted to it before now. In following what might be called the "diplomatic history" of the Parnell split—the attempts of the "moderates," John Dillon and William O'Brien, to find some firm basis for compromise—Dr. Lyons has explored, with tact and thoroughness, a set of situations which were of great importance for Ireland's future, and were indeed perhaps of wider significance. "Violence," William O'Brien had said much earlier, "is a way of securing a hearing for moderation." This is a tenable argument but, as O'Brien was himself to experience in repeated political failures, it has its counterpart; if moderation, having secured a hearing, does not achieve a quick solution, the violence resumes and the moderates are doomed. Psychologically, the Parnell split marked the resumption of violence. In that climate of denunciation, no compromise was possible. Parnell had to win or die. Parnellism in its old form was dead already, once the leader's personal authority was turned against the policy of accommodation with Britain—the "liberal alliance"—which he had made his own. The men who had been most identified with the spirit of the old Parnellism came to seem irrelevant in the new conditions.

In his conclusion, Dr. Lyons comes down, very reasonably, against Parnell's decision to refuse to retire after the divorce-court verdict. I cannot follow him, however, when he suggests that all might have been well if Parnell's relations with Mrs. O'Shea had been made public at an earlier date. "No doubt, even if the relationship had been made public in 1881 or 1882 there would still have been criticism," writes Dr. Lyons without overstatement, "and there might still have been pressure on him to retire. But if he *had* retired then, the retirement might possibly only have been temporary . . . and would surely have been less damaging both for him and for his party than what actually happened in 1890." Parnell's prestige was considerably less great in 1881 or 1882 than it was in 1890—he had accomplished much less—and if his relations with Mrs. O'Shea had been made public in one of the earlier years he would certainly have been obliged either to retire or to split his following. If he had retired, his retirement would almost certainly have been definitive. None of those who urged "temporary retirement" at the time of the split ever seriously tried to show how such a retirement could be ended. And if Parnell had retired, peacefully, in 1882, can we be sure that a united Irish party (under what leader?) would have won the elections of 1886, or that Gladstone and the Liberal party would have become converted to the cause of Home Rule for Ireland? Just as it was impossible for O'Brien and Dillon to "tidy up" the Parnell situation in 1891, so it is impossible for the historian to construct a tidy hypothetical order in retrospect. Living and dead, Parnell defies rearrangement.

It is unfortunate—and yet an index of Parnell's importance—that one or two Irish critics have taken the appearance of Dr. Lyons's sober, well-balanced book as the signal for the renewal of intemperate anti-Parnell polemics. Criticism of Parnell's last disastrous actions should surely, by this time, be kept within bounds by a recognition of his unique services, if not by any glimmerings of a sense of tragedy. The tragic import of Parnell's last year is admirably brought out by Dr. Lyons, both in the whole story which he has to tell and in those just words: "The very things that had served him so well in the past now led him over the precipice."

The god Hercules
Deserted Antony whom he had loved so long.

THE GREAT CONGER

There are three Yeatses in these two books.* There is the young man who wrote down and embroidered, richly or with careful plainness, the stories of the Sligo countryside: this in *The Celtic Twilight, The Secret Rose* and *Stories of Red Hanrahan*, which form the bulk of *Mythologies*. Then there is the aesthete-*illuminé* of *Rosa Alchemica, Per Amica Silentia Lunae* and other reveries, also in *Mythologies*. Finally, Mr. Monk Gibbon considers the Yeats he knew, the great bonze, the Senator, the literary boss who controlled the world of anthologies and poetry prizes as absolutely and as arbitrarily as Ed Flynn controlled public works contracts in the Bronx. "Every great man's door crowded with petitioners and everywhere, in the State, in the family, an inequality made law."

None of these three Yeatses is indispensable; all of them are of some interest. *The Celtic Twilight* is that part of Irish folklore that Yeats knew, through English; less strange in itself than the archives of the Irish Folklore Commission, yet a mine for those who like to look for the ore of imagery. The tone of this very early work (1893) does not yet exclude humour, humour which was not grand enough for Yeats's middle period, not harsh enough for his old age. The best is the story of the giant eel's advice:

> I began a tale of an immense conger, three times larger than the one I carried, that had broken my line and escaped. "That was him," said the fisherman. "Did you ever hear how he made my brother emigrate? My brother was a diver, as you know, and grubbed stones for the Harbour Board. One day the beast comes up to him and says, 'What are you after?' 'Stones, sur,' says he. 'Don't you think you had better be going?' 'Yes, sur,' says he. And that's why my brother emigrated."

* William Butler Yeats, *Mythologies*; Monk Gibbon, *The Masterpiece and the Man: Yeats as I Knew Him.*

After this it is hard not to regret the change to *Rosa Alchemica* and all that ("as I joined the alembic to the athanor and laid the *lavacrum maris* at their side"). How much was it a publicity device—high stilts to catch the eye—how much an effort to translate into the idiom of the nineties the mental world of the Sligo boy, native superstition disguised as sophisticated superstition? The native superstition seems to have been on the whole kinder, and certainly less hysterical, than the incense and peacocks. The difference is in part that between pre-Christian and anti-Christian. For most of the "mystical" works "anti-Christian" would be too much to say; there is here and there a timid and muffled wish to blaspheme without any great interest either in what is blasphemed against or that in whose interest the blasphemy is supposed to be intended. Yet there is something, a hardening, a discovery of the need for hardness, which gives an underlying seriousness to the nonsense of *Rosa Alchemica* and *The Tables of the Law*. The narrator, arguing with Michael Robartes,

> could find nothing better to say than: "It is not necessary to judge every one by the law, for we have also Christ's commandment of love."
> He turned and said, looking at me with shining eyes:
> "Jonathan Swift made a soul for the gentlemen of this city by hating his neighbour as himself."

That last great sentence—it flashes out among the tarnished stage jewellery—could receive a Christian interpretation; perhaps someone is working on it. In its context, both the immediate context of the words and that of Yeats's life, it suggests a discovery: that cruelty, to yourself and others alike, is the condition of power.

> *All neighbourly content and easy talk are gone*
> *He that's mounting up must on his neighbour mount . . .*

Having taken the giant conger's advice to emigrate, you become the giant conger.

The great conger, very much later, larger and more slippery, was what the unfortunate Mr. Gibbon encountered. Mr. Gibbon had legitimate and honourable literary ambitions. The conger inquired whether it was not time for him to be going. Mr. Gibbon had the courage to refuse to emigrate and the further courage to write a book about the subsequent events.

MOTHER'S TONGUE

When Synge died, in 1909, he left behind him, as well as his published work, a considerable quantity of manuscript material—diaries, notebooks and letters—of importance not only for his own biography but for the history of the Abbey Theatre and the Anglo-Irish literary movement. These documents passed to Synge's nephew, Edward M. Stephens, who made use of them in preparing a vast work, which has not been published, on Synge and the Synge family. On Stephens's death a few years ago his widow entrusted all these papers to an American scholar, Mr. David H. Greene, who has now produced what is likely to remain the standard biography of Synge.* As befits a biography which, to a great extent, breaks entirely new ground, it is straightforward, economical, free from theorizing and uses important new material copiously and with a minimum of comment. These, gentlemen, are the facts, Mr. Greene seems to tell us, and leaves us to make what we can of them.

The main facts were, it seems, mother and the Irish language. Mother was evangelical, ultra-loyalist (for her the Unionist *Irish Times* was pro-Fenian) and prim even by the standards of Victorian Dublin. She was disappointed with her son from both a worldly and an other-worldly point of view—not that she would have distinguished the two very sharply—and her yearnings and naggings, with the latter predominating, were the background of his boyhood. In later life his own unhappy relations with various women tended to fall into the ominous pattern of yearning, nagging and religious controversy: this pattern may, of course, have been socially as well as psychologically hard to avoid. He went, understandably enough, abroad—to Germany, then to France—studied languages, wrote some conventional verse, drifted and looked of little account. Then—it seems, on Yeats's advice—he went to the Aran Islands. He had already—unlike any of the other prominent figures of what was to be called the Irish Literary

* David H. Greene and Edward M. Stephens, *J. M. Synge, 1871–1909*.

Revival—studied the Irish language seriously. This visit to Aran was the decisive event in his life. Not only did it give him a style—an English that could make direct and creative use of Irish rhythms and idioms—but it also seems to have liberated a suppressed part of his personality. One of the most revealing anecdotes in the book, the significance of which Mr. Greene brings out very well, tells how towards the end, after an operation, Synge exclaimed as he came out from under the anaesthetic: "God damn the bloody Anglo-Saxon language that a man can't swear in without being vulgar." Mr. Greene rightly stresses the double impoverishment—social and doctrinal—of the language which he learned, in Yeats's phrase, "at his mother's knee."

Irish was for him a language that a man could swear in without being vulgar, but he found that when he brought some part of the frankness of spoken Irish back into English he himself was denounced for vulgarity by the very people who claimed that they wished to revive Irish—and was therefore promptly defended by those other people against whose "refinement" he was reacting: his mother's class. The *Playboy* controversy was an intellectual blindman's buff, but neither it nor the *Playboy* riots did much harm. The real tragedy for the Abbey Theatre was Synge's early death, which deprived the Abbey not only of its first great dramatist but also—as a memorandum printed here for the first time shows—of one who was prepared to argue about what the function of such a theatre should be and to admit that that function might change with time.

SOME LETTERS
OF JAMES JOYCE

―――――◆●◆―――――

I want that information about the star of the Sea Church, has it ivy on its seafront, are there trees in Leahy's terrace at the side or near, if so, what are these steps leading down to the beach? (p. 136.)

I started to write down this passage as an example of the *practical* nature of almost all the letters in this collection. I was pulled up by the obviously corrupt text. The last words as they stand are meaningless: one can easily surmise that they should read ". . . if so what, are there steps leading down to the beach?" Pursuing his own concept of art, or exploiting dream-language, Joyce could perhaps have written more or less what is printed here; asking his aunt for information he would have written good plain prose; his editor has got lost somewhere in between. Mr. Stuart Gilbert, as all interested know, was a friend of Joyce's for years and knows a great deal about him. It is all the more surprising that the present volume* is edited in a relatively perfunctory way—a way which Joyce himself, pedant that he was, might have thought decidedly unbecoming. If it is worth while publishing letters at all it is surely worth while identifying the people named in them, but that is not attempted consistently here. It is true that when Joyce writes (p. 314):

I never met Rops.

Mr. Gilbert conscientiously notes: "M. Daniel Rops, well-known Catholic scholar and writer." But how many readers will be able to identify, say, the *"Dail Éireann* Minister of Propaganda" (p. 181) who wished to propose Joyce for the Nobel Prize? Mr. Gilbert does not identify him, although a note on Desmond Fitzgerald (?) would be at least as interesting as one on a French

* *Letters of James Joyce,* edited by Stuart Gilbert.

writer whom Joyce had not met. Similarly, how many non-Irish readers will guess who "Hiber and Hairyman" (p. 295) are supposed to be? These points are not, I think, capriciously selected. I looked myself for references to three people in whom, for personal reasons, I was interested. Of these, one is referred to in two letters, noted in the index, and not identified in a footnote; the second, the subject of an entire letter, is noted in the index and vaguely and indirectly identified in a footnote; the third, the subject of a long and rather important passage in a letter, is neither noted in the index nor identified. In all three cases (Mrs. Skeffington, Thomas Kettle, Richard Sheehy) the required information was easily available from sources which, as elsewhere appears, are known to Mr. Gilbert. Similarly, a glance through the index reveals many surnames unsupported by Christian name or initial. Nor is such information given or withheld on any very clear principle. The names of "d'Annunzio, Gabriel," "Claudel, Paul," "Eliot, T. S." and "Shaw, G. B." abide our question, but the names of "Adams," "Bence," "Buss" and "Dunn" are free, together with those of "Einstein," "Hemingway" and "Goethe."

The collection edited in this rather quietistic manner consists of 426 letters, ranging in time from 1901 to 1940, with relatively few letters for the earlier years. Some letters available to the editor have been omitted because they "relate to private matters," others "for reasons of space"; cuts have been made in some letters at the request of their recipients and in others by the editor. One can easily understand these omissions in a collection published during the lifetime of some of Joyce's immediate family and many of the recipients of the letters. But the mere fact that a deliberate process of selection has been at work, under the control of a dedicated admirer of Joyce, forces one to treat with reserve the publishers' claim that their book constitutes "a revelation of personality" and that "the character of an astonishing genius is revealed." Most of the letters printed here reveal nothing more than that Joyce was keenly interested in practical details relating to the composition and publication of his own works and the critical reaction to them; and that he was, for good reasons, worried about his health, especially his eyesight. A few letters reveal his affection for his father, his son and—more anxiously—his daughter. Here and there we have flashes of humour, of superstition or irritation.

But those who are interested in "the character of an astonishing genius" would do better to turn to the genius's work than to these letters, usually hastily scribbled on urgent business. When a man is working sixteen hours a day—as Joyce did on *Ulysses*—his letters are unlikely to rival those of Madame de Sévigné. The student of Joyce needs these letters, of course; or rather what he needs is the *full* text of *all* Joyce's letters which have been preserved. If these were made available by degrees, on microfilm, in, say, a dozen libraries, and quotable by consent of the recipients (where living), the needs of our generation in this matter would probably be adequately met. At a later time the collected letters might be edited and published.

The present volume contains an agreeable introduction by the editor, with some interesting first-hand information about Joyce and his family, and also a handy chronology of the life of James Joyce by Mr. Richard Ellmann.

QUEER WORLD

Brendan Behan was arrested in Liverpool late in 1939, at the age of sixteen, for participating in the IRA bombing campaign in England. After two months or so on remand in Walton Prison he was sentenced to three years Borstal detention. The judge at his trial expressed regret at being prevented, by the law and Behan's age, from sentencing him to fourteen years penal servitude. He thought that the law should make allowances for people like Behan, and he did not mean indulgent allowances.

Borstal Boy is the story of Behan's time, first in Walton Prison and then in Hollesley Bay Borstal. Mr. Behan is a violent but fair-minded man and, as might be expected, he has written a very good book in very good bad language. *Borstal Boy* is free from bitterness and self-pity, and free also from any affectation of objectivity. He has some old scores to pay off and he pays them gaily. The prison doctor:

> Afterwards I heard the screws talk about the doctor and what a good man he was, and overworked, and he did go round looking like Lionel Barrymore, and sighing like the doctor in *The Citadel,* but I never heard of him actually doing anything for anyone. The prisoners said that he gave a man two aspirins for a broken leg, but that it was not really viciousness, only stupidity, and anyway, if he wasn't a prison doctor he'd have to go in the Forces.

A prisoner:

> . . . a real cup-of-tea Englishman with a mind the width of his back garden that'd skin a black man, providing he'd get another to hold him, and send the skin 'ome to mum. . . .

The last quotation suggests Anglophobia, and there are several passages in the book from which the casual reader might infer that Mr. Behan likes nothing about the Anglo-Saxons except their monosyllables. Anyone who reads the whole book will retain the impression as regards the monosyllables, but will realize that the author is far too good-humoured and intelligent to be any kind of xenophobe. The clue to his humanism is to be found in a remark about his Liverpool landlady:

> The landlady was a mean woman from the [Irish] Midlands. I don't mean that coming from the Midlands caused her meanness. You'll get good people from there, or from any airt or part of the world, but if Cockneys or a Siamese are mean or decent, they'll be mean or decent in a Cockney or a Siamese way.

Like much else in *Borstal Boy* that judgment recalls the kindness and curiosity of Huckleberry Finn. Mr. Behan's indignation when it occurs is always vehement and picturesque, but discriminating. Unlike many prison books *Borstal Boy* never settles into a groove of "exposure-for-reform." He hated Walton Prison and most of the officials there, but even there he tells how, after he was brutally beaten up by two warders, the librarian called him "Paddy" (kindly) and offered him a book about Ireland. His only general comment on this sequence of events is: "It's a queer world, God knows, but the best we have to be going on with."

About Borstal itself, on the other hand, he has nothing, or almost nothing, but good to say. This part of his book is indeed a striking vindication of the Borstal system, and highly creditable to the people who ran Hollesley Bay. It is remarkable that in the atmosphere of wartime a youth who had committed Behan's offence could have been as decently treated as he was, once he was out of the hands of the Liverpool warders. The present-day Mr. Behan, who is unreconstructed in his political views, freely recognizes that the activities for which he was sentenced were not such as to evoke the warmhearted approbation of the British people.

> The first day he was in Liverpool [he writes about a comrade] an incendiary primer exploded in his pocket and, with half his face burned off, he was savaged and nearly lynched by the populace, who apparently disapproved of having the kip burned about their ears.

Against that kind of background the record of how Borstal treated Brendan Behan is something remarkable and something of which Englishmen have every right to be proud, provided they are ashamed of a few other things.

TIMOTHY MICHAEL HEALY

A hundred years ago last year Tim Healy was born in Bantry, County Cork. The centenary, as far as I know, went completely unmarked. Ireland has forgotten, or remembers only with a faint aversion, one of the most remarkable and gifted of her sons. It is true, of course, that more historical figures are more forgotten than we like to think—one hears of university graduates who have difficulty in identifying Henry Grattan. True also that Healy's generation more than others has suffered from what Sir Thomas Browne denounced—"the iniquity of oblivion blindly scattering her poppy." The poppies that were scattered in 1918 in that anti-khaki election when Ireland chose her present destinies, obliterated from the nation's memory the most prominent of Healy's contemporaries—John Dillon, William O'Brien, John Redmond. Yet Healy himself, although he had been the ablest parliamentarian of them all, was not one of those who went down with the parliamentarian ship. He had already broken with the Irish party—or it with him; he had clearly foreseen its downfall and the rise of Sinn Fein; he was on sufficiently good terms with the new Ireland to become the first Governor-General of the Irish Free State—an ambiguous eminence but still an eminence whence he could contemplate the waste of waters which had engulfed the companions of his political life. We may be sure the spectacle agreed with him; he was no inconsolable survivor. The sardonic side of his character may have been pleased at the reflection that thirty years before he had buried his leader "in the name of the party" and that he had now succeeded in burying the party as well. Yet the reflection would not have afforded him amusement for very long. The book he wrote in these last years, *Letters and Leaders of My Day,* is to a great extent a justification of the part he played in Parnell's downfall. Many years after his own death his daughter, Mrs. Maev Sullivan, wrote another book, *No Man's Man,* which is, in entirety, a defence of her father's memory through a denunciation of Parnell. When that last book was written Parnell had been more than fifty years in the grave. His ghost, it seems, is hard to lay. And Healy, impressionable and imaginative behind his cruel public mask, was an excellent subject for haunting.

In this series of talks we have been concerned mainly, by definition, with the period from the death of Parnell to the rising of 1916. The peculiarity of Healy's life is precisely that its most positive periods came *before* the death of Parnell and to a less extent *after* the rising of 1916. As Parnell's helper or, in the end, Parnell's hunter he had cut a great figure; in the new Ireland of after the treaty he becomes, again, at least imposing. In the three decades between—the years which would normally be those of the maturity and fulfilment of a public life—he is as active as ever, but squalidly in a sort of wilderness within a wilderness, spraying his deadly invective impartially on all his political associates—except those who could trace their origin to Bantry, County Cork. It would be meaningless, in discussing his strange career, to confine ourselves to this period which, in his case, can only be understood as a postscript to a relationship: the relationship of Healy to Parnell.

Parnell, during the divorce crisis, claimed that he had discovered Healy and put him on the road to success. Healy himself preferred to imply that his success was solely due to his own talent. Both claims were slightly misleading. It is true that Healy's beginnings in life were modest: his father was a workhouse clerk, first at Bantry, then at Lismore, County Waterford. He himself, as he tells us in *Letters and Leaders,* finished his education at thirteen years of age after some schooling in Fermoy with the Christian Brothers. His first regular job, at seventeen, was as a railway clerk in Newcastle-on-Tyne. It was an unpromising start for the great parliamentarian, the Queen's Counsel, the Governor-General to come. Healy's worst enemy—a title for which there was always acute competition—never denied his remarkable innate ability: but ability alone, without the aid of luck or influence, might never have carried him out of earshot of the Newcastle goods yard. But fortunately Healy was well-connected —not certainly as contemporary England or Ireland interpreted that expression—but in terms of the historical realities of the day.

A semi-revolutionary period, characterized by a particularly intense parliamentary action, was opening before Healy's generation in Ireland. Healy had the advantage, over other bright young men of his day, that relatives of his, men of talent also, were placed where they could help him most. T. D. Sullivan, who had married his aunt, was a well-known member of parliament on the popular side; his patriotic songs, like *God Save Ireland,* were loved by nationalists throughout the country. A. M. Sullivan, T.D.'s brother, was a parliamentarian of great ability, and a gifted writer: one of his books, *The Story of Ireland,* converted Winston Churchill, for a time, to Irish nationalism. Even more important, the brothers Sullivan controlled the weekly *Nation,* then the organ of what might be called the "advanced constitutional" section, the section which had, then, a great future before it. And a more distant connection of Healy's, John Barry, with whom he lived for a time in Manchester, was the leader of the same section among the Irish in England—the same Barry who was very soon to precipitate the downfall of Isaac Butt, and who, thirteen years later, was the most resolute of the enemies of Parnell. With such a background it is not surprising that the young Healy was a patriot, and honourably ambitious, and that a career was open to his talents. His first political job, which brought him to London in 1878, at the age of twenty-three, was that of parliamentary correspondent to *The Nation.* The salary was one pound a week but the post was a key one. It was from *The Nation* that Nationalist Ireland liked to hear about Parnell, and it was Healy who was telling them. Just at this time the obstructive tactics of Westminster of the so-called active section of Home Rulers led by Parnell and Biggar were beginning to achieve fame in Ireland and notoriety in England. The only newspaper that praised them was *The Nation,* in Healy's articles. This was good for Parnell, for *The Nation,* and for Healy. The articles themselves were very well written, with shrewd observation, by a man mad about politics, and they were not weakened by any excess either of deference or of charity. To his brother Maurice he complained in surprise of the "sensitivity" and "childish resentment of criticism" of many members. These were phenomena that he was destined to encounter again and again, always with surprise, throughout his long and turbulent life.

Inevitably the parliamentary correspondent of *The Nation* was taken to a great extent into Parnell's political confidence. Healy, closer to the people than Parnell could be, and brimming over with intelligence, was a man whose advice was worth having and for three years he was, in his own words, Parnell's closest counsellor. But even Parnell's closest counsellor was not particularly close: the relation between the two men never seems to have been one of real friendship, merely an association for purposes of political business, useful to both. Of Parnell's feelings towards Healy at the time—if he had any feelings—we know nothing. Healy's feelings towards Parnell as recorded in his letters to his brother Maurice Healy are of much interest. Indeed, if Balzac had been minded to give us the letters of an ambitious young man—his own Rastignac for instance—he might have invented something like the progression of feelings in these letters. For the first few months Healy's letters express uncritical admiration of his protector: then we have a cessation of overt admiration and a number of minor criticisms: in this phase he notes Parnell's shortcomings on certain aspects of politics—electoral organization for example—and implies that he himself is better equipped in these matters. The third phase is that of open admiration for himself and Parnell as a team, with the implication that he himself is the brains of the team. "As I tell Parnell . . ." In the fourth phase the disciple lets it be known that his master is something of a sham. In the grand parliamentary manner which he sometimes affected in his letters to his admiring brother he wrote: "I regard it as almost a calamity that our political interests compel us to idolize this man in public, so insecure do I feel as to the possible protrusion of those 'feet of clay' at any instant before the crowd of worshippers whom it would drive into immediate and unriskable derision." This was in 1879, eleven years before those feet of clay were to crumble to dust under Healy's hammer.

Publicly, this was the period of Healy's closest association with Parnell. He accompanied him on his American tour at the beginning of 1880 and afterwards became his secretary. He acted as organizer on Parnell's behalf, in the General Election of 1880, as a result of which Parnell—who had until then no official title to leadership—became chairman of the Home Rule party in Parliament. Healy, who was not returned at this election, continued as Parnell's secretary until the following year. The incident which brought about his resignation is obscure, as we know of it only through reminiscence which we must suspect as being possibly coloured by later events. From Healy's own account it seems that, in an unexplained absence of his chief's, he handed over some private correspondence to be examined by two of his political colleagues. On the following day, he tells us he resigned his post as Parnell's secretary. The timing of the break is interesting, for Healy had just taken his seat in the House of Commons as member for Wexford. He was now an important person in his own right, not a mere adjunct of Parnell's. Years later Parnell's widow told the young Henry Harrison that Healy's hatred of Parnell had a definite cause. She claimed that Parnell had told her that Healy had been a suitor of one of his sisters and had taken mortal offence when he, Parnell, had dismissed the idea on account of Healy's social origins. This was probably a fantasy: Mrs. O'Shea was a highly imaginative woman and had good reason to detest Healy. But a contemporary fantasy can be revealing and Mrs. O'Shea, in stressing the class factor in the relationship, was surely right. This late Victorian time was the Golden Age of conscious and overt snobbery. It was a thorny, lacerating world for a man making his way up, and Healy, who was less thick-skinned than he liked to claim, got his share of cuts and scratches. In this world of Gentlemen and Players, Healy was a very talented Player; the Captain of the side at the time had to be a Gentleman and Healy resented the fact. He felt himself to be the stuff of which leaders were made; he found himself playing Figaro; he thought of himself as a Grey Eminence. The situation was both irksome and confused, and therefore dangerous.

Meanwhile he continued to rise. In Parliament, at a very troubled time, he was at first intensely unpopular. The policy of the Irish members at this time was to obstruct the business of Parliament; Healy's method of carrying out this policy was characteristic. He did not, like others, read Bluebooks or spin out long and rambling declarations. He spoke briefly and to the point, but with calculated and astonishing violence of language, unerringly directed at vulnerable personalities. The effect of this tactic was, by arousing general indignation, to induce the English to waste their own time. This unusual and effective parliamentary debut naturally made Healy popular overnight in Ireland. More surprisingly it succeeded in gaining for Healy the ear and the unwilling respect of the House. He became in a short time an accomplished parliamentarian: some have held that the day when Gladstone came over to him in his place in the House and congratulated him on a speech was decisive of his future development. Outside Parliament he became widely known as a journalist and pamphleteer and he was called to the Bar in Ireland in 1884. His career as a lawyer does not concern us directly, but a description of his methods at the Bar may shed some light on the personality that shaped important political events which still implicate us all. We are fortunate in having a very good description of Healy as a barrister, by an eminent and not unfriendly authority, Sir James O'Connor, who had experience of him both as a colleague and as an opponent and also from the Bench. Sir James tells us that Healy was no lawyer, and that he was not even a good advocate. "But," he adds, "he has been known to get the truth out of a hostile witness by unscientific and sledgehammer daring which no other advocate would attempt, though I am sure the same methods have often cost him the verdict. By sheer force of personality and perhaps a little stagecraft he often created a favourable atmosphere for his client, which made up for the absence of more regular advocacy. In Ireland the clients rather than the attorneys chose him: he said such good things that they thought all things which he said should be good. Ireland too is full of people who would rather lose a law case gladly—with the salt rubbed into the sore spots of the opponent's carcase—than win it soberly and sombrely!"

Healy's recklessness and his taste for rubbing salt into sore spots may have been more costly to Ireland than to his clients. The first clear sign of his political recklessness came in 1886, at the time when his party, the party led by Parnell, was on the verge of its greatest victory: the so-called conversion of the Liberal party to Home Rule. At this moment, in February 1886, Parnell nominated Captain O'Shea as Nationalist candidate in a by-election in Galway. The candidature was preposterous, and was almost certainly forced on Parnell by a kind of blackmail. But the party as a whole felt obliged to acquiesce because of the need for unity and discipline. Only Healy and Joe Biggar decided to rebel: they went to Galway to oppose O'Shea and there they let the truth be known, that O'Shea was the husband of Parnell's mistress. This was certainly proof of rugged independence on their part—and of no more than that, in Biggar's case. For Biggar had not been, as Healy was, engaged in political conversations with the liberals behind Parnell's back. Healy had conveyed, through Labouchere, to wavering liberals like Joseph Chamberlain, the assurance that Parnell's intransigence need not be feared: the party, according to Healy, was controlled behind the scenes by a small group which included himself; Parnell was a mere figurehead. Now those liberals who disliked Gladstone's Home Rule ideas knew that Gladstone attached a condition to putting these ideas into practice: the condition was that Parnell should be able "to keep his men together." Healy's talk of caucuses and puppets was therefore very interesting to Chamberlain and his friends: Healy's open act of rebellion was even more interesting: if the Irish party were to split, or Parnell's authority be severely shaken, a great deal of inconvenience might be saved. Chamberlain was to be disappointed: Parnell went down to Galway, and Healy crumpled.

For the next five years Parnell was the undisputed leader and Healy, now distrusted by him, became himself something of a figurehead, no longer a political strategist but an orator merely. His chance of independent action, of free play for his great talents, did not come until, at the end of 1890, the O'Shea divorce case threw open the question of Parnell's leadership. In the dislodgment of Parnell from the chairmanship of the party, as distinct from his leadership, Healy's part was not decisive. He began by making a brilliant speech, in Dublin, for the retention of Parnell as leader: then in Committee Room 15, at Westminster after Gladstone had intervened against Parnell, Healy made an even more brilliant speech—it is indeed one of the masterpieces of Irish oratory—urging Parnell to retire from the chair. Then he wavered again, moved to tears by what seemed a conciliatory gesture of Parnell's. It was only towards the end of the debates, when that gesture had proved a feint, that he found the note, the note of cruel mockery, that was to be his original, and perhaps decisive, contribution to the destruction of Parnell. When Redmond said that Gladstone was claiming to be "the master of the Irish party," Healy put in, "And who is to be the mistress of the party?" Parnell had, of course, been re-elected as chairman by his party in full knowledge of the divorce: the party rejected him because of a political circumstance, that Gladstone said he could no longer work with him. Parnell's other opponents—men like Justin McCarthy, William O'Brien, John Dillon—shrank from this kind of thing, but Healy, as we know, liked rubbing salt into wounds. He was probably right in his view that ridicule, the mockery of a detected sexual offender, was the only weapon which could destroy Parnell in the country. In his speeches, and in the new anti-Parnellite paper, *The National Press,* he concentrated on this theme and reaped his reward: the petticoats on poles flourished by youths at Parnell meetings with shouts of "Kitty O'Shea!" In this salty way Parnell's candidates were defeated in three successive by-elections; Parnell collapsed and died. Within a few weeks of his death Healy referred publicly to his widow as "this British prostitute": Mrs. Sullivan admits that on this occasion her father failed, as she puts it, to find the *mot juste.*

I do not propose to follow in any detail Healy's activities in the following years. They were characterized by persistent attempts to find the *mot juste* to describe his colleagues—Sexton, Dillon, O'Brien, later Redmond—and they led Healy, through many tortuous passages, into that rather shabby isolation which ultimately proved the condition of his survival. Yet it was probably in those years—in 1891, the year of the hounding of Parnell, and the years of aimless snapping that followed—that his character impinged most forcibly upon his country's history. It was he more than anyone who brought the Irish party into discredit, and so cleared the way for Sinn Fein. To hear Healy speak, to read what he wrote, must have had the effect on many of disgusting them with cleverness and oratory, of turning them towards self-discipline and the idea of a violence that was cleaner for not being wholly verbal. It was, from the point of view of Sinn Fein, an excellent thing that the Irish party should have carried within itself its own destruction in the shape of a Bantry lawyer experimenting with words. Historically it was fitting that he should have been rewarded with the ceremonial headship of the new state which issued from the insurrection. Symbolically there was a tragic fitness in the fact that the Ireland over which he presided was torn by civil war.

Bricriu, I suppose, is always with us in one form or another;

there will always be among us the descendants of those bards who could raise the three blisters of contempt upon those who displeased them. There is no point in lamenting this national Thersites complex, as one might call it. It has to be accepted as existing and it adds much to the interest and the fun of life, for the non-blistered. But to raise any crop, even a crop of blisters, is a costly business and one of the few questions which a student of Healy's career may ask is: how much is a crop of blisters worth? The Greek Church, I believe, had a word for the practice of a charitable, and often silent, tolerance: it called this practice Economy. In that sense, as perhaps in others, economy is not one of our virtues and Healy was one of the supreme examples of the uneconomic Irishman. We could not afford many more like him.

Lady Gregory tells us that Yeats once wrote formally to Healy, then Governor-General, asking His Excellency for an interview. The old man wrote back, "My dear Boy, come and see me whenever you like in the bee-loud glade" and signed Tim Healy. One thinks of Sir James O'Connor's description of Healy's personality in private life: "He pleases without effort, he is full of fun and sympathy, he has a winning eye, a pleasing and caressing voice." The affection of Healy's family and his intimate friends confirms this picture of a kind and lively man, simple in manner and rich in intelligent reminiscence. Where then have we left the arrogant and vindictive public man, the political scald-crow with his terrible beak? I raise the question here, not to answer it but to show where our survey must stop. We have not attempted in this survey to plumb the mysteries of human personality, but to assess the style and effects of certain personalities in action at a given moment of our country's history.

In that sense one can, if one adopts the historical retrospect of Sinn Fein, regard Healy as a sort of salutary plague, speeding the rot of parliamentarianism: clearing the ground for a new and better Ireland. If on the other hand one feels, as on the whole I do, that the destruction of the movement which Parnell had created maimed Ireland in some important ways, then one is likely to echo the phrase with which Tom Kettle, years ago, saluted Healy: "A Brilliant Disaster."

V

FOUR CRITICS

GENERATION OF SAINTS

Joyce, Proust and Mann being representative writers of "the first generation," the representative writers of "the second generation" chosen by Professor R. W. B. Lewis are Moravia, Camus, Silone, Faulkner, Graham Greene and—in an epilogue, for some reason—André Malraux. The "second generation" writers have their "representative hero," the picaresque saint: "a person who is something of a saint, in the contemporary manner of sainthood, but who is also something of a rogue." Along with this, his unifying theme, Professor Lewis stresses certain other common elements—concern with death, metaphysical sense of loss, human companionship, need to "exist." Sub-themes appear as well:

> If, in the generation-wide struggle to come alive, Moravia represents the erotic motif; if Camus represents human reason in its compassionate workings; if Silone represents the conversion of the political ambition into the charitable urge, and Faulkner the conversion of darkness into light and the old into the new; if Greene represents the interplay of the more than human with the less than human—then Malraux may be said to represent all of these things or versions of them.

As a critic Professor Lewis is always attentive, often perceptive. Taken separately, his essays are never less than intelligent introductions to their subjects and sometimes—as on Silone and Faulkner—considerably more:

> The English regarded Faulkner's verbal eccentricities in somewhat the way Italians of a traditionalist temper regarded the unconventional irregularities of Silone's prose. The irregularities of James Joyce, for the English, remained conventional ones: recognizable deviations from the known center, the only center; but Faulkner's idiom, which came from no center known to them, seemed simply unforgivably bad writing. His hot Southern American Protestant rhetoric fell on deaf Anglican ears; his "ideas" seemed extravagant and intrusive; and his recurrent expression of outrage appeared dubi-

ous to a country which was to wait another decade or so before producing its own race of angry young men.

Without altogether relinquishing the suspicion that "hot Southern American Protestant rhetoric" may sometimes be a synonym for bombast, one must concede that Professor Lewis is here carrying out one of the most important functions of the critic: the exposure of prejudices and complacencies which hinder the understanding of a work of art.

The Picaresque Saint is, however—as its publishers state—"no random collection of literary essays." It is an ambitious attempt to isolate determining characteristics in contemporary writing. The attempt, well worth making, and made with enthusiasm as well as intelligence, has proved, in my opinion, a respectable failure. And I believe that the reasons for its failure are fundamental and identifiable. There are also, of course, preliminary difficulties of definition. "Generations" are not really so easy to sort out: what "generation" did Gide belong to? Professor Lewis puts him firmly in the "first generation," in "a world in which the aesthetic experience was supreme." André Walter fits neatly into such a world, but the mature Gide was not an aesthete at all but mainly an odd kind of moralist—a picaresque saint, in fact, disqualified by the age limit which Professor Lewis, by his terms of reference, has to impose. The idea of "representative writers" is also open to question. Such "representatives" tend to be elected by the critic alone: is Moravia a more "representative writer" than Auden or Brecht?

These difficulties, and even the critic's apparent indifference to their existence, would not necessarily imply the failure of the enterprise. Professor Lewis has chosen an interesting group of contemporary writers, and if he did in fact isolate characteristics present in them, and not in comparable earlier writers, we could accept readily enough phrases like "representative writers" and "second generation." But the characteristics on which he concentrates most of his attention turn out to be as easy to find in earlier writers as in his group *taken as a whole*. Thus what he considers to be the most fertile of his themes, that of the picaresque saint, is not present to any significant extent in several of his "second generation" authors and is to some extent present in many authors of past generations. Only in the work of Silone and Greene are there heroes who are both "saints" and picaresque. As against this rather meagre and doubtfully classified collection, the nineteenth century can show numerous and authentic examples of the picaresque saint, both in life and literature: Tolstoy's Pierre, Dostoevsky and almost any of his heroes, Baudelaire, Rimbaud, Claudel's *Tête d'or*, Léon Bloy and his self-portraits, Lionel Johnson . . . The "picaresque saint" idea, in fact, far from providing an identifying symbol for the "second generation" of twentieth-century writers, could be considered with less difficulty as a nineteenth-century heirloom, somewhat marked down. The way it has been marked down—the journey from Rimbaud to Pinkie Brown—would be worth study, but to treat it as a highly significant contemporary invention is misleading.

When we are asked to consider a group of twentieth-century writers, why should we dwell on themes inherited from the nineteenth century? Is there really nothing distinctive about these writers, marking them off from their predecessors? It is Professor Lewis himself who suggests the answers, when he says that "the form or soul of the modern epoch, its essential plot, is the shape of the experience of political history. Or rather: it is the shape of individual experience during a period when political history affects all experience." If this is so, the critic, in dealing with the writers of this epoch, ought to examine, in every case and as a matter of primary importance, the writer's relation to the political experience of his place and time. This is precisely what Professor Lewis fails to do, or refrains from doing, in the case of all his authors except Silone. (It is no accident that the essay on Silone is much the most solid in the book.) Thus in the case of Camus we are given no clue to the probable political relevance of *La Chute* —the implicit link between the ironic withdrawal of the "penitent judge" and Camus's own withdrawal from judgment on the Algerian War. Indeed Professor Lewis gives no sign of being aware that there is any war in Algeria—a rather strange omission on the part of one who expresses such strong views on the literary relevance of political history. Again in the case of Malraux, where it is even more difficult to ignore politics, Professor Lewis largely succeeds in doing so, mainly by concentrating on *La Voie royale* and *Les Noyers d'Altenburg* and ignoring *La Condition humaine* and *L'Espoir*. In the case of Faulkner, although he does not altogether ignore the relevance of the peculiar institutions of Mississippi, he suggests that Faulkner's central insight is "a sense of the fertile and highly ambiguous possibility of moral freedom in the new world." The critic, like the turtle, is a specialist in fertile ambiguity: it is useful for survival.

In a political age literary criticism which attempts to leave out politics inevitably becomes detached from reality. A literary criticism which brings in politics, however, is obviously open to the dangers of becoming doctrinaire, passion-blinded or corrupt. These are dangers; the unreality which comes from "leaving politics out"—when dealing with writers profoundly affected by politics—is not a danger but a certain calamity. The critic must therefore confront these difficulties, and cope with them as best he can; he will also have to cope with certain pressures—the "reader-over-his-shoulder" will begin to wear a different expression. Like the creative writer, and after the creative writer, he will be drawn or dragged into politics. We rightly condemn those Soviet "politico-literary" critics who are ready to act as gendarmes controlling the writers of Russia. And we applaud those Polish critics—some of them represented in Mr. Lionel Trilling's valuable collection *The Broken Mirror*—who have struggled, often with the aid of "fertile ambiguities," to defend the idea of freedom, both in relation to literature and to their people. What we easily fail to see is that the "non-political" Western critic resembles his Soviet rather than his Polish colleagues by the way in which he acquiesces in the orthodoxy which prevails in his society. Soviet orthodoxy falsely pretends that literature can be produced in conformity with a predetermined political line; Western orthodoxy falsely pretends that literature, being connected with spiritual values, can be kept out of politics, which belongs to a baser, more material sphere. Both of these false doctrines are closely related to political realities in their areas of origin, because they are ways of diverting serious critical attention from these realities. The Soviet effort in this direction, backed as it is by harsh penalties and centralized power, is clearly much more thorough; the Western pressure, vaguer and more diffuse, almost impalpable, is probably more effective than we realize.

The Picaresque Saint is a particularly disturbing symptom of the effects of this pressure, for here we have an intelligent critic explicitly conscious of the importance of politics in relation to literature and yet turning aside, time after time, from political implications clearly present in his subject—indeed, turning aside always except where the implications concern fascism, officially dead, or communism, officially "hell" (his own word). This kind of criticism—acute on small matters and absent-minded on very large ones, inventive of diversions, cosmically concerned and terrestrially calm—is important not in itself but as marking a dangerously close intellectual atmosphere. The canary in the mine shaft is important when its song hesitates and stops.

BEARS

―――◆◆―――

Tolstoy asked Aylmer Maude: "How is it ... that these gentlemen do not understand that, even in the face of death, two and two still make four?" The "gentlemen" in question were members of the Orthodox hierarchy who were endeavouring to bring the novelist back into the fold. But the challenge is addressed even more crucially to the metaphysics of the irrational put forward by Dostoevsky. "What have I to do with the Laws of Nature," demanded the narrator in the Letters *from the Underworld, "or with arithmetic, when all the time those laws and the formula that twice two make four do not meet with my acceptance?"*

Mr. Steiner's "essay in contrast"* contains many fruitful juxtapositions of this kind, and propagates them wisely. Although he himself seems to lean to the view that two and two do *not* make four—and therefore to the side of Dostoevsky—he does not abound in that sense. He has indeed an unusual combination of breadth of sympathy with excitement about his subject. Tolstoy and Dostoevsky are not, for him, fodder for critical "strategies," but living forces with which he as a person, not as a technician, must wrestle. Although he is obviously, and usefully, familiar with the techniques of what is still known, especially in America, as the "new criticism," he rejects its dominant attitudes and openly claims to return to "the old criticism."

The old criticism is engendered by admiration. It sometimes steps back from the text to look upon moral purpose. It thinks of literature as existing not in isolation but as central to the play of historical and political energies. Above all the old criticism is philosophic in range and temper.

The principles of "the old criticism," thus revived and interpreted, could, and probably will, encourage vague and pretentious writing and provide cover for the type of literary propagandist whom the methodological rigours of the "new criticism" so effec-

* *Tolstoy or Dostoevsky.*

tively discouraged. The manifesto part of Mr. Steiner's opening therefore arouses some misgivings. As far as Mr. Steiner's own practice as a critic is concerned, however, these misgivings prove almost entirely unfounded. His tone is modest, his literary judgments precise and shrewd, and adequately insulated from his political opinions, which are quite another matter. The principles of "the old criticism" invoked by him are a way of giving elbow-room to the kind of critic he is; and they are thereby justified, for he is a remarkably good critic.

The area covered by *Tolstoy or Dostoevsky* is vast; Mr. Steiner's arguments are numerous, close in themselves and yet rather loosely connected. The book, therefore, defies summary; it has to be read. In what follows I shall do no more than take up those of his themes that have particularly interested me, and have consequently aroused at least some degree of disagreement.

The fifty years or so before the Revolution of 1905 were, as Mr. Steiner points out, "the *anni mirabiles* of Russian fiction." As he also points out, "the Russian novel"—he might have widened the judgment to include the Russian theatre—"was conceived under a single sign of the historical Zodiac—the sign of approaching upheaval." Underlying most of what Mr. Steiner has to say about Tolstoy and Dostoevsky is the question of their relationship to that "approaching upheaval." On the whole he agrees with Communist criticism in seeing Tolstoy as "for" the Revolution and Dostoevsky as "against." On Tolstoy's Christianity he twice quotes Gorky with approval and with telling effect. On Tolstoy and Christ: "When he speaks about Christ it is always peculiarly poor—no enthusiasm, no feeling in his words, and no spark of real fire. I think he regards Christ as simple and deserving of pity; and although at times he admires him, he hardly loves him." On Tolstoy and God: "With God he has very suspicious relations; they sometimes remind me of the relations of 'two bears in one den.'"

This Tolstoy is essentially a man of the Enlightenment, rationalist, authoritarian, supremely confident in a reasoned program for the improvement of man's life on earth, contemptuous of tradition and rituals—in short the Voltaire of the Russian Revolution. With Tolstoy—who said "I love truth more than anything in the world"—is contrasted Dostoevsky who said that he would remain with Christ even if "someone had proved that Christ is outside the truth." And it was Dostoevsky, with his perception of the dark and tragic in human nature, who, on this view, turned out to be right. "The *univers concentrationnaire*—the world of the death camps—confirms beyond denial," writes Mr. Steiner, "Dostoevsky's insights into the savagery of men" . . . It was Dostoevsky who foreshadowed, and Tolstoy—provisionally and rather shyly identified with Ivan Karamazov's Grand Inquisitor —who is in some degree responsible for the totalitarian regimes and the brutish delight of the masses in the musical and dance-like rituals of the Nuremberg rallies and the Moscow Sports Palace.

Mr. Steiner's reasoning on this matter is not quite as crude as I have had to make it in summary, but I do not think I have distorted his argument significantly. It is because he is a good critic and because his book is important that it seems necessary to challenge him here, on this border of literature and politics, where his argument is weakest and likely to be most influential. For one actual reader, who has considered Mr. Steiner's admirable detailed criticisms of passages in Tolstoy and Dostoevsky, there are likely to be several bystanders who receive indirectly the impression that Dostoevsky was a good man but Tolstoy was a Red. Indeed Mr. Steiner himself very nearly says as much, in a dangerously quotable passage on his last page: "Dostoevsky, pre-eminently the man of God; Tolstoy one of His secret challengers." It is hard to see how this judgment could be sustained by anyone except a committed Dostoevskian: one, that is, who not merely admires Dostoevsky's genius, but also completely and uncritically accepts Dostoevsky's teachings. For Dostoevsky, as Mr. Steiner shows, had his own very peculiar religious notions, hardly more orthodox than Tolstoy's. He, no less than Tolstoy, was co-bear in the divine den. If Tolstoy could be accused of atheism, Dostoevsky could be accused of diabolism. Mr. Steiner, without coming to any conclusion, presents the grounds on which such a charge could be made. Both writers were, in fact, heretics. If the Russian Orthodox Church put up with Dostoevsky and not with Tolstoy, that was not for any abstruse doctrinal reasons but simply because Dostoevsky became a conservative and Tolstoy became a rebel. And that also, I suspect, is what Mr.

Steiner means when he says that Dostoevsky was pre-eminently the man of God and Tolstoy one of His secret challengers. To reverse Péguy, *Tout commence en politique et finit en mystique.*

As regards the relation between the two great Russian writers and the politics of our own time, Mr. Steiner does much less than justice to Tolstoy. Tolstoy was no stranger to the *univers concentrationnaire.* How could any Russian be, then or now? The prisons, the law courts and the exile trains of *Resurrection* form a clear testimony against oppression—all the clearer for being matter-of-fact in tone, detailed and measured. The character of Novodyorov in the same novel proves that Tolstoy was not under the illusion that revolution would automatically bring oppression to an end. Tolstoy is uncompromising not only in *Resurrection* but in all his work about power, about pretence, about cruelty. No tyrant could ever really "make him do." It is useless for any official critic to expound him as criticizing only the cruelty of "the people who were." He makes his meaning too plain, and no power can prevent people from trying that meaning against the life around them. Instead then of exclaiming *"C'est la faute à Tolstoi!"* when we hear that his books are issued in enormous editions in the Soviet Union, we ought surely to be glad and thankful. If Russian history has tended to inculcate callousness and prostration before power, it is surely well that great classics of Russian literature, central texts of the Russian language, work to correct the pressures of history. Since no people is so close to the great age of its literature as are the Russians, and no people reads its own classics so much (they have no thrillers and no telephone directories), it is probable that no other great writer is such a living force in the world now as is Tolstoy. It is hard to see how anyone who—like Mr. Steiner—believes in the moral force of great literature can be indifferent to this.

Lenin, of course—and this is what Mr. Steiner finds it hard to forgive—saw in Tolstoy's works "the mirror of the Russian revolution." Although the responsibility of a "mirror" may be questioned, we may agree to take this as implying that Tolstoy's works, his critique of the Orthodox Church and of aristocratic life, did help to prepare the way to revolution. But in reality the forces of which Dostoevsky made himself the spokesman had a much greater share in preparing the ruin of the old Russia.

Levin's sullen disapproval of the volunteers for the Balkan War was wiser—from a strictly conservative point of view—than the mystical chauvinism of Dostoevsky, with its nonsense about territorial expansion, as part of "the Christ-bearing mission of the Russian people." Mystical chauvinism—extreme nationalism, combined with the inefficiency that flows from a superstitious contempt for reason—led logically to war, defeat in war, and the consequences of defeat: the Japanese War and the Revolution of 1905, the World War and the Revolution of 1917. And the other disasters of our time, even outside Russia, can more naturally be traced to something like the Dostoevskian chauvinism than to Tolstoy's belief in the possibility of moral progress.

If the rather boring proceedings in the Moscow Sports Palace can fairly be traced back to Tolstoy's belief in progress, the quite different goings-on at the Nuremberg rallies can, not less fairly, be traced back to the chauvinism and irrationalism of Dostoevsky, an author in whom Dr. Goebbels showed some interest. In both cases it is well to recollect, more steadily than perhaps Mr. Steiner does, the very limited influence which even the greatest writers have on the course of historical events.

It is true that Dostoevsky's dramatic genius revealed gulfs in the human mind which the twentieth century has further explored, both in practice and in theory. We are apt, therefore, today to think him closer to us, and "more nearly right," than the rational Tolstoy. Mr. Steiner encourages this tendency too much. Auschwitz and Dachau are not the ultimate criteria of reality, and Dostoevsky is not necessarily a wiser guide and teacher because he understood better than Tolstoy the extremes of horror which man can reach. There is a kind of understanding which is a complicity, and Dostoevsky's very deep intuitive understanding of cruelty took the form, in politics, of chauvinism. He was a prophet of disaster who helped his own prophecies towards fulfilment. Dostoevsky's insights have given, we may hope, their full measure; it may be time to give more of our attention to Tolstoy.

RE-ENTER THE HERO

Mr. Colin Wilson, in his new book,* is concerned with Man and Society. He is troubled by the apparent insignificance of the individual and the oppressive power of organized people. He illustrates these themes by examples from a few contemporary American sociologists—principally Riesman and Whyte—and many modern writers, including Herman Wouk, James Jones, Tennessee Williams, Sartre, Camus, Zola, Joyce, Shaw, Yeats and others too numerous to be mentioned (in a book 157 pages long) by anyone other than Mr. Wilson. He makes an attempt to introduce "the sociological evidence" into the consideration of contemporary literature, but in practice this turns out to be little more than a pinning of Riesman's labels "inner-directed" (good) and "other-directed" (bad) on to various writers. The book concludes with a plea for reviving the "inner-directed" Hero, by means of a new existentialism "based upon recognition of the irrational urge that underlies man's conscious reason."

Many middle-aged readers, and no doubt some younger ones, will find *The Age of Defeat* scarcely less irritating than Mr. Wilson's earlier books are said by most of their more intelligent readers to have been. They will resent—as I do—his "classics-in-pictures" summaries of so many books and the disc-jockey commentary: "It was startling that a book of such extraordinary merit [*Room at the Top*] should have been written, not by a widely travelled journalist, but by a Yorkshire librarian." Most of all they will resent his careless pontification ("Marxian materialism and Freudian psychology are excuses for laziness") and—as a last straw—his citation of solemn inanities from like-minded or otherwise dubious sages: "Stuart Holroyd has written: 'in our time, the writer who does not dare to be great cannot hope to be anything.' This penetrates to the heart of the problem." "The writer should not underestimate his possible influence. Alexander

* *The Age of Defeat.*

Werth states that the attitude of *Les Temps modernes* helped to discourage the Americans from launching an anti-Soviet crusade at the time of the witch-hunts."

Yet, trying as he can be, Mr. Wilson is not without importance. He has a real curiosity about life and about books and he can apparently communicate his interest to others. This makes him a medium of communication, a line of approach to various fields of thought for people to whom these fields might otherwise remain closed. His usefulness here is not diminished by his endurance of platitudes. Undue sensitivity to platitude is, after all, the form of arrogance which most effectively blocks communication between intellectuals and others, and it is often unwarrantably assumed. (As a boy I used to cherish an excessive contempt for the philosopher Plato, in the belief that the word platitude was derived from his name.) Nor does Mr. Wilson's prophetic posture lessen his value as a teacher. The successful teacher has to be something of a charlatan and Mr. Wilson possesses this qualification in good measure. It is more fun to read something called *The Age of Defeat*, and feel in the movement, than to read something called, say, *Introductory Notes on Some Modern Writers*, and feel a neophyte.

There is a sense, then, in which Mr. Colin Wilson is a more relevant critic than Mr. William Empson: more relevant because more readable, and more read—although Mr. Empson is so much more perceptive than Mr. Wilson that the word "critic" to cover the two becomes almost empty of meaning. The point is, though, that Mr. Wilson, writing brightly and urgently about valuable ideas, is a great deal better than nothing; and nothing, if we are to believe Mr. Koestler and others, is what large numbers of educated young people now are most inclined to read. If Mr. Wilson can catch their attention, so much the better. It is not exactly a question of "the dark places where his apostolate lies"— to adopt a memorable phrase once used in *The Tablet* by Mr. Waugh about Mr. Greene. What seems to have happened, rather, is that more gifted "apostles" have been too busy discussing abstruse points in undertones for any clear message from them to reach a new generation; and the most lively transmitter of literary culture today therefore is apt to be someone like Mr. Colin Wilson. Those of us who are middle-aged may reflect that *our*

Wilson was Edmund—a teacher-critic, too, but with higher standards and lower pretensions than are now fashionable in that field.

Through Colin Wilson a certain romantic dissatisfaction with the quality of modern life and literature makes itself heard. That this is in some degree healthy no one who has read *The Organization Man* or *The Captive Mind* is likely to doubt. That the protest can be much more deeply felt, and of much higher quality, anyone who reads the work of young Polish writers in the collection *The Broken Mirror* (edited by Lionel Trilling) will easily agree. But Mr. Wilson's protest, too, is real and in its own way moving. His breathless, jerky accounts of so many books are the notes of a man who is looking for something and not finding it. He is genuinely oppressed by the discovery that the sense of the individual's insignificance which pervades modern urban life informs also the literature of that life. *The Age of Defeat* often suggests the state of feeling of the young Chesterton:

> *A cloud was on the minds of man and*
> *wailing went the weather*
> *Yea, a great cloud upon the mind, when*
> *we were boys together.*

Unlike Chesterton, Mr. Wilson hopes the cloud may be dispelled by autonomous human exertion. A criticism renewed by sociology—he seems to imply—can help to renew literature by restoring "the hero," and "the hero" will re-accredit in real life the image of the "inner-directed" man. This theory raises, but does not answer, a number of more or less interesting questions. What can sociology in fact contribute to literary criticism? Can literary criticism have a fundamental effect on literary practice? Is the restoration of "the hero" in literature desirable? If it occurred would it make the "inner-directed" man more acceptable in real life? And to what extent is it desirable to rehabilitate the inner-directed man?

Of these questions, the two most worth discussing are probably the first and last. Sociology, like historiography and other "human" studies, is obviously related both to literature itself and, as a method of investigation, to literary criticism. Literary criticism has long been very conscious of historical and social factors and ought to be able to use the insights and discoveries of recent sociologists. In a serious sense literary critics have surely much to learn from the best examples of sociological method. The appendix "On Intellectual Craftsmanship" in Professor Wright Mills's new book *The Sociological Imagination* is a model for critics as for other workers in the science/art borderland. And certain pairs of sociological concepts, like Mr. David Riesman's "other-directed" and "inner-directed," can stimulate and (within limits) help the literary critic as well as, say, the politician. Yet literary criticism remains a highly specific form, dealing with so complex, filtered and unusual a human activity that it has little enough in common with other social sciences. Ideally, the literary critic should know a great deal about the social sciences and then leave them to one side, forgetting above all their jargon, when he does his proper work. Unfortunately, and naturally, current practice is often very different. "I know the end of the story," said the society lady, interrupting Léon Bloy's account of the Prodigal Son, "the son left the swine and came to his father." "No, madame," said Bloy, "it was the swine who came."

Similar considerations apply to the idea of rehabilitating the inner-directed man. Which inner-directed man? Hitler or Gandhi? The terms "inner-directed" and "other-directed" had useful meaning in Mr. Riesman's critique of American society; they are probably less useful as general categories. There is much, naturally, in Mr. Riesman's analysis that is specifically American: other-directedness, in its malignant form, is the disease of a society which has had to be a melting-pot, a society also with a short history of spectacularly quick development. This is a society in which the opinions of elders—who are both "out-of-date" and often less "American"—are necessarily at a discount. It is in this way that, for lack of anything else, the opinion of contemporaries tends to become the super-ego. To generalize from the American case is difficult and rather dangerous, particularly when the generalization is intended, as in *The Age of Defeat,* to prop up a cult of the hero, as against a supposedly prevailing "cult of the ordinary chap."

Mr. Wilson occasionally shows a rather uneasy awareness that parts of his program—cult of the hero, emphasis on will, recognition of the irrational—were associated with an earlier twentieth-century myth. But what he completely ignores is that his program is being put into practice before his eyes, in one of the three countries he is writing about. Modern French literature is not, as he suggests, exclusively dominated by a "cult of insignificance," inculcated by Sartre and Camus. It has long had a very influential "cult of the hero" school, in which the leading writer was M. André Malraux who now, as Minister for Culture, is giving the watchwords of heroism—*audace, énergie, grandeur*—to the dynamic French youth of today. The Algerian War, as has been rightly said, is a school for heroism. And the cult of the hero is a school for the Algerian War. Some French people seem to feel that "the cult of the ordinary chap" may not, after all, have been entirely a bad thing.

POETRY, INSPIRATION
AND CRITICISM

He was not an omnivorous devourer of sensations; he did not scour the world for them or pick tit-bits from many times and places. When something caught him, he was its devoted and responsive victim, who sought to extract all that he possibly could from it and was by his very devotion hampered from looking at anything else.

This, on Walter Pater as a critic, is typical of Sir Maurice Bowra's sober and clear appraisals. It is also, I think, a self-criticism, for Sir Maurice is the kind of critic that Pater was not. Omnivorous, in his new book of essays, *Inspiration and Poetry,* he scours the world from Dorset to the Caucasus and from Moscow to Nicaragua; "devours sensations" as different from each other as a mediaeval Georgian epic can be from the hymns of Hölderlin; ranges in time for his tit-bits from Augustan Rome to the end of the nineteenth century. Unlike Pater, again, he does not seek to extract everything possible from a chosen subject; perhaps he is too sane for that; "sanity" is a favourite word of his. He writes like one who feels that in criticism also there is a margin beyond which it is unprofitable to cultivate, a point at which it is better to push on and work the surface of new territory, leaving the Paters to scratch in the dust-bowl of unanswerable questions. Not, of course, that he is impatient or American in the vulgar sense; few critics have so even a temper, such catholic sympathies, a mind so open or so quick to fill. Simply, with a restraint which is perhaps classical, he is content to act as the introducer of the poets, the sensible and travelled man who knows the city; an unusually alert chorus, enormously well-read and learned in many languages. This kind of critic is much more obviously useful than the "devoted and responsive victim" of the Pater stamp; but he is a teacher. The devoted and responsive is interested primarily in his own relation to the work; he may be confused, obscure, boring, tortuous, but he is sincere in the sense that he is not interested in deceiving anyone, except perhaps himself. The teacher has already settled accounts with the work; he is interested in the relation between himself and his class, in the act of teaching. If he is to hold the interest of his class he must skim and simplify, therefore to some extent betray. A good example, in the present volume, is Sir Maurice Bowra's analysis of an effect of Thomas Hardy's. He makes the sound point that Hardy "supplements a body of simple spoken English with resonant and unusual words of Latin origin and with Anglo-Saxon words which have passed out of currency and have an archaic air." To illustrate this Sir Maurice quotes the lines from Hardy's poem on the loss of the *Titanic:*

> Steel chambers, late the pyres
> Of her salamandrine fires,
> Cold currents thrid, and turn to rhythmic tidal lyres.
>
> Over the mirrors meant
> To glass the opulent
> The sea worm crawls—grotesque, slimed, dumb, indifferent.

Sir Maurice's comment on this needs to be quoted in full:

> The contrast is between the proud hopes of those who built the great ship or travelled in it and the cold lifelessness of its present state. He uses his Latin words "salamandrine" and "opulent" to stress the first side of the contrast. Each has a touch of irony. The engines which seemed to flourish like salamanders in the flame are quenched for ever; the mirrors on which the sea-worm now crawls were meant for people whom wealth seemed to protect from any stroke of doom. Against these words of pride, turned with irony to express the huge degree of the catastrophe, Hardy sets his humble words like "thrid," and "slimed," of which the first conveys the inhuman, relentless movement of the water, and the second the absolute difference of the *Titanic*'s present inmates from those for whom it was built.

This is interesting and impressive; to an audience—it was part of a Byron lecture delivered at Nottingham University—it would be very impressive indeed. But the reader, who can reconsider the lines themselves, will soon have less faith in the commentary. The contrast in Hardy is surely neither so clear-cut nor of quite the same kind as Sir Maurice Bowra suggests. The Latin words are not really symmetrically disposed: "indifferent" applied to the sea-worm is quite as Latin as "opulent" applied to the voyagers, to take only one of several instances. "Rhythmic tidal lyres" are very far from being "humble words" and very far also from suggesting the "cold lifelessness" which Sir Maurice identifies with the present state of the ship; neither the tide nor the sea-worm is lifeless, and the point is surely that their life is "indifferent"—the keyword—to human life, not that there is, or could be, such a thing as an "absolute difference" between the two sets of inmates. The commentary blurs also the curious use of "salamandrine," applied not to the engines, as Sir Maurice implies, but to the fires themselves: a fact which leaves little room for the supposed irony about the quenched pride of fire-resistant engines. In short, the commentary subtly distorts Hardy's meaning by simplifying his contrasts, both of language and of situation, and by coarsening his irony. This distortion is natural, and may even be necessary, in the lecture room, to convey something like the general sense of a poem, but a criticism which works in such a way can only be loose and approximate: "an approach to" Hardy and others rather than something that actually tries to arrive.

Sir Maurice Bowra rightly reminds us that "there is room in the world for more than one kind of critic, and in general it seems foolish to lay down rigidly what a critic ought to be." His own variety of "approach" criticism makes pleasant reading and has the very considerable merit of introducing us to writers of whom—lacking his formidable linguistic attainments—we should otherwise know nothing. He has the great gift of curiosity, and makes us share something of his pleasure in handling so exotic an object as the mediaeval Georgian epic, Shot'ha Rust'hveli's *The Knight in the Tiger's Skin*—even though, as he so truly says, "we cannot enjoy the many felicities of language which its admirers claim for it." He is at his best, however, in discussing writers, like Hölderlin and like Rubén Darío, who belong to the literary traditions which we know but who are, because of language difficulties, less read than they deserve to be. He quotes freely and aptly and gives a translation; often what he quotes is something which, we know, will always remain in our mind even if we never read another line of the author concerned. Thus he tells us of Rubén Darío's poem, *"Los motivos del lobo,"* the story of the wolf of Gubbio, who was converted by the example and preaching of

Poetry, Inspiration and Criticism

Saint Francis but relapsed after a spell of convent life and, when appealed to by the Saint, made his devastating criticism of humanity:

> Hermanos a hermanos hacían la guerra,
> perdían los débiles, ganaban los malos,
> hembra y macho eran como perro y perra,
> y un buen día todos me dieron de palos.
>
> (Brothers made war on brothers,
> the weak lost, the wicked gained,
> woman and man were like bitch and dog,
> and one fine day they all took sticks to me.)

And the wolf takes leave of the Saint with his own version of "So get you gone, von Hügel, though with blessings on your head":

> Déjame en el monte, déjame en el risco,
> Déjame existir en mi libertad,
> vete a tu convento, hermano Francisco,
> sigue tu camino y tu santidad.
>
> (Leave me on the mountain, leave me on the cliff,
> leave me to live in my liberty,
> go to your convent, brother Francis,
> follow your way and your sanctity.)

The essays on Pushkin and on Lermontov and that on Dante and Arnaut Daniel—the last the most closely reasoned in the book—are rich in both quotations and information; indeed, curious facts come second only to quotations among the attractions of *Inspiration and Poetry*. One feels a wiser and a better man for knowing that Walter Pater was not invited to the unveiling of the Shelley Memorial at Oxford because "he was not thought quite respectable."

The book takes its title from its opening essay, but it is also suggested that the essays collectively form some sort of enquiry into the working of poetic inspiration. "Sir Maurice Bowra starts," say his publishers, "with a chapter on inspiration and its ways of working in poetical creation. He then looks at some of the problems which this raises, and examines them in individual cases, which vary from [Horace to Rust'hveli] and includes [*sic*] matters so different as [Dante and Daniel, Gil Vicente and Samson Agonistes]." That this claim to a unity of conception is quite misleading (as well as unnecessary) immediately appears from

Sir Maurice Bowra's own preface, in which he states that the various essays "have indeed been composed for different purposes, often for special occasions, and they cover very various ground." He hopes that the other pieces "are not too distantly related to the subject treated in the first chapter"; in fact, they are related by being (with one exception) about aspects of poetry. The problems of "inspiration" are hardly discussed except in the opening essay. This is not to be regretted, for Sir Maurice Bowra is not at his best among the foggy generalizations which accumulate round such a subject. "There is no doubt of the fact: what the poets have conceived through inspiration is also what we feel to be their most essential and most authentic poetry, and we are justified in calling it inspired." And on the following page: "when we say that a poem is inspired, we mean that it has an unusual degree of power." The problem is surely to find whether, in fact, the poems or the lines conceived by poets in the "rapturous moments" of "inspiration" are always, or even very often, those which the reader regards as possessing an unusual degree of power. Sir Maurice Bowra assumes that they are, but a critical examination of what evidence we have, from the letters and notebooks of poets, would be more interesting than mere assumptions—even the assumptions of a very learned man who loves poetry. Perhaps he has the noble fault of loving poetry too much; he is certainly very credulous where the assertions of poets are concerned. He tells us, for example, that, for Horace, "poetical inspiration is an occasion for Dionysiac joy," and that Horace takes us "into the secrets of his poetic being" in his lines about the Bacchic frenzy:

> *Euhoe, recenti mens trepidat metu*
> *plenoque Bacchi pectore turbidum*
> *laetatur; Euhoe, parce Liber,*
> *parce gravi metuende thyrso.*

of which he quotes Sir Edward Marsh's translation:

> *Still reels my mind with joy and holy fear,*
> *Still throbs my heart with presence of the God;*
> *I faint, I tremble—mighty Liber, hear!*
> *Spare me the terrors of thy rod.*

With all the great respect which is due to Sir Maurice Bowra in such a matter, it is also possible to feel that Horace was simply putting on some highly traditional airs and that these frigid *vers calculés* are evidence against the very assertion which they make. But Horace is artistically infallible in the eyes of this admirer: "His words, chosen with unfailing care and insight, are always fresh and alluring, and the result never looks laborious."

The criticism which results from "the maximum response which maximum attention can give"—Mr. R. P. Blackmur's well-known words—is often a pretty grim thing. Critics who remind us that the reading of poetry is a civilized pleasure—and not just a gruelling spell of service in the ambiguity-squad—are rare enough today. So are critics who write plainly and modestly and keep their tempers. On these grounds we have reason to be grateful to Sir Maurice Bowra, and to hope for more of his far-flung essays. The "relaxed" school of criticism has its limitations, as the "tense" school has its excesses; in either school we are apt to wish for the methods of the other. Yet the best members of both schools have something in common: the combination of curiosity and taste which finds for us things we should not have found by ourselves.

VI

THE COLD WAR

CRITIC INTO PROPHET

From 1946 to 1955 Edmund Wilson did not file any income-tax returns. 1946 was the year in which "for the first time in my life . . . I was making what was for me a considerable amount of money." He does not tell us how much, although he does tell us that his top earnings up to then had been $7,500, and also that by the time he was married again—still in 1946, month unstated—his financial situation was "no better than it had been in 1936"; he does not tell us what it was in 1936, but he does tell us that in 1935 he had a tax-free Guggenheim Fellowship of $2,000 "which the Foundation generously supplemented when, just as I was leaving Russia, I came down with scarlatina and had to be quarantined." In 1947-51 his income "averaged $2,000 a year" and for some reason this led him to think that "before filing for the years since 1945, it would be better to wait until I was making more money." This happened in 1955—what his income was between 1951 and 1955 he does not tell us—and he then went to a lawyer who gave him good advice: "he thought the best thing I could do was to become a citizen of some other country." Mr. Wilson did not then take this advice, and became heavily involved with the tax authorities who, after various exhausting interviews, settled for "$25,000 plus a collateral agreement for four years": the collateral agreement meant that his future literary work is mortgaged ahead for over $30,000.

Like many another distressed taxpayer, Mr. Wilson has been led by his unpleasant experience to take a closer look at what the state is doing with his money, and to be displeased with what he finds. A man wishing to borrow money from Julius Caesar explained the appalling chaos of his financial position. Caesar replied: "What you need, my friend, is not a loan but a civil war." Mr. Wilson, in a like financial position, can look forward to no such panacea: he actually has to pay "Caesar" for, among other things, keeping a civil war going in Vietnam, at a cost of a million dollars a day. Nuclear weapons, chemical and bacteriological warfare, napalm, detention camps and the protraction of civil war have two things in common: they are horrible, and they cost money. The fact that they cost money—Mr. Wilson's money—has caused him to see and to protest against their horror. And the fact that the protest begins with the money, instead of with the horror, may make it more effective than any display of altruism would be. This pamphlet—as Mr. Wilson rightly describes it—can hardly fail to have a considerable impact inside and outside America.* Mr. Wilson is not only one of the most distinguished of living American writers, he is also one of the most American, with even a touch of old-fashioned Anglophobia. That such a writer, nearing seventy, should come to reject his country is certainly a personal tragedy for him; it also has some disturbing implications about what is happening in, and to, his country. It is not merely that he speaks of the present image of the United States as being "self-intoxicated, homicidal and menacing." He goes further and formally rejects his country in these words:

I have always thought myself patriotic and have been in the habit in the past of favorably contrasting the United States with Europe and the Soviet Union; but our country has become today a huge blundering power unit controlled more and more by bureaucracies whose rule is making it more and more difficult to carry on the tradition of American individualism; and since I can accept neither this power unit's alms nor the methods it employs to finance them, I have finally come to feel that this country, whether or not I continue to live in it, is no longer any place for me.

Pasternak never went quite so far as that.

Would the tax imbroglio, in itself, account for so profound an alienation? As far as one can make out from Mr. Wilson's confused account of his tax situation, he does not seem to have been treated unjustly, and his own suggestion that he may have been in some way penalized for having had four wives, or having been a leftist in the distant past, seems to lack foundation. His tax offence is quite adequate, by itself, to explain what happened to him. Could his resentment at this—real, natural and excessive as it is—be enough to drive him to this strange declaration, resembling a mediaeval "defiance," whereby he severs the bond be-

* Edmund Wilson, *The Cold War and the Income Tax: A Protest*.

tween himself and his sovereign state? If we assume that it *is* enough—as some will do—then we have to regard what he has to say about the arms race and related matters as no more than rationalization of his resentment at a penalty imposed on him personally. I don't think that a reader of *The Cold War and the Income Tax* is likely in good faith to reach quite that conclusion. Rather, he is likely to feel that although it was the income tax which caused Mr. Wilson to look at the cold war, the horror he experienced when he did look at it was genuine, and carried him to his act of "defiance." The horror comes not so much from the means of mass destruction themselves as from the minds concerned with the means. Not just the military minds, and not perhaps even mainly the military minds, but also minds of politicians and of scientists and other intellectuals. James B. Conant was regarded by many as the epitome of the liberal, humanist intellectual. And up to a point, the late James B. Conant lived up to this reputation when he had to advise on the use of the first atom bombs:

James B. Conant foresaw "super-super bombs" delivered by guided missiles and urged Secretary of War Stimson to first demonstrate "Little Boy" and "Fat Man," as the bombs were affectionately known, before unloading them on the Japanese.

Conant's advice on this point was not, however, taken and he then determined—it would appear—to demonstrate that there was nothing "soft" about him. Subsequently we find an extract from the minutes of the Interim Committee which met in the Pentagon on 31, May 1945 and took the critical decisions:

After much discussion concerning various types of targets and the effects to be produced, the Secretary [Stimson] expressed the conclusion, on which there was general agreement, that we could not give the Japanese any warning; that we could not concentrate on a civilian area; but that we could make a profound psychological impression on as many of the inhabitants as possible. At the suggestion of Dr. Conant, the Secretary agreed that the most desirable target would be a vital war plant employing a large number of workers and closely surrounded by workers' houses.

When contemplating the cold war, especially in its present phase of perhaps deceptive mildness, we are apt to comfort ourselves with the thought of a "balance of terror" by which the vast arsenals on both sides somehow harmlessly cancel each other out. The service rendered by a book like Mr. Wilson's—as by a film like *Dr. Strangelove*—is to remind us that no balance is automatic, since all depends on decisions made by people, of whom all are fallible, some are liable to panic, some are bloody-minded, and some are afraid of not seeming bloody-minded enough. The strategists tell us that situations can "escalate" from one level of retaliation to another, but what really escalate of course are human minds, as Conant's escalated from unsuccessfully urging an initial harmless demonstration of the bomb to successfully recommending an initial use against a war plant "closely surrounded by workers' houses." It is uncomfortable to feel that minds more or less like Conant's are now ticking away in all the crucial capitals. We know that there are those in Washington who are now arguing for an extension of the war in Vietnam, and who maintain that military advantage should be taken of China's perhaps temporary estrangement from the Soviet Union. What plans for making "a profound psychological impression" are being made for the event of the predictable "deterioration" of the situation in South Vietnam, and for further, also predictable, deteriorations in Latin America?

Mr. Wilson's cry of indignation and warning is warranted and may be salutary. Its passion may be more telling than much cool analysis, and its defects, like those of *Uncle Tom's Cabin*, may prove irrelevant to its historical significance. Logical defects abound; the critic in Mr. Wilson has been struck dumb and blind by the prophet. The confusion which marks the opening pages on personal finance and taxation lifts somewhat, but never altogether clears, in the rest of the book. A chapter is devoted to Major Claude Eatherly, the Hiroshima pilot, said to have become "unhinged by guilt." It is Mr. Wilson's bad luck that he has here swallowed, whole, claims that—it now seems—were largely false.

Mr. Wilson could not have known this, for the evidence has only very recently been published, but were he not carried away by passion, he would surely not have accepted Eatherly's claims unreservedly. For one thing Eatherly's account of the Hiroshima decision conflicts with the minute of the decisive Pentagon committee meeting which Mr. Wilson cites in a footnote on the same page and which has obviously far higher evidential value than any "reminiscence"; for another, Eatherly's claim, after his petty crimes had been detected, that he committed them, in effect, "to try to discredit the popular myth of the war hero" (Mr. Wilson's words) would hardly be accepted at face value by anyone retaining a normal degree of scepticism about human motivation. Having considered this chapter, one is disposed to suspend judgment about Mr. Wilson's other heroes, such as Dr. A. J. Muste and the Reverend Maurice F. McCrackin, two advocates and practitioners of tax refusal.

The final chapter, "The Strategy of Tax Refusal," is important because it contains the writer's declaration of internal emigration, but it is, logically, a weak and inadequate conclusion. Mr. Wilson, having aroused us to the appalling dangers of our situation, tells us that he intends to "make as little money as possible . . . so keeping below taxable levels." But it is as a writer, not as a taxable unit, that Mr. Wilson is important to us, and as a writer, Mr. Wilson here fails us by leaving out of consideration matters of enormous importance, directly relevant to his theme.

It has been reckoned that the developed countries—that is, the white countries, plus Japan and minus Latin America—with less than one-third of the population of the world have about 80 per cent of the world's income. This gap is widening, and against the voluntary aid given by the developed countries to the underdeveloped—considerably less than 0.5 per cent of the "developed" income—has to be set the "aid" involuntarily given—in the form of cheap labour and low fixed prices for raw materials—by the underdeveloped to the developed: a sum difficult to compute but certainly considerably more significant than the first, and better known, category of aid. The underdeveloped countries are not only the main theatre of the cold war: they are also the area in which cold war is most likely to pass into hot. This being so, it is strange that in such a book as this the question of more serious, and unrequited, aid to the underdeveloped—with the taxes and restrictions it would involve—is not even mentioned. It seems to be assumed that if military expenditure is cut, taxes will automatically fall, ending the "deprivation and coercion" of which Mr. Wilson and his fellow-citizens are at present, in his opinion, victims.

The assumption about military expenditure and taxes may well be true. But it is not true, as Mr. Wilson seems to imagine, that if America reduces her military expenditure and tax levels, the cold war will be at an end. The real cold war—that between the underdeveloped and developed countries—has still a long course to run. Even to mitigate it and reduce its dangers would require the intelligent application of great efforts. Such efforts are not compatible with reducing taxation in order to raise American living standards higher still. That is why *The Cold War and the Income Tax,* helpful by its emotional shock-value, must be considered intellectually frivolous in its conclusions. A severe but just verdict on such reasoning was given, well before this book was written, by Professor J. K. Galbraith in his essay "The Strategy of Peaceful Competition":

Finally they will hope that the bill for doing what we must can somehow be avoided. Let there be no mistake. Most of the things we must do to reveal the quality of our society will cost money—public money. Willingness both to advocate and to pay is the test of whether a man is serious. If we haven't yet learned to mistrust, indeed to ignore, the man who talks about high national purposes and then omits all mention of the price—or perhaps urges strict economy in public outlays as one of his higher purposes—our case could be pretty bad.

JOURNAL DE COMBAT

———•◆•———

> *No one before 1914 or 1917 could possibly have foreseen a situation in which the basic and permanent preoccupation of an important review would be the designs of a great power on the tranquillity and free action of such nations, long immune from outside threats, as Britain and the United States . . .* Encounter *from its foundation has been a* journal de combat. *It has been the organ of protest against the* trahison des clercs *. . . the role of a journal like* Encounter *with its continual concern with reminding us of the realities behind the Iron Curtain is necessarily an ungrateful one . . . There are many people, some of them merely silly, some of them silly and dishonest and some of them dishonest but not silly, who resent, quite rightly, the obsession of* Encounter *with the promulgation of uncomfortable truths.*

We ought to be mildly grateful to Sir Denis Brogan, who makes these statements in his introduction to *Encounters*,* an anthology drawn from the journal's first ten years, for telling us plainly, if a little testily, what *Encounter* is about: what its "basic and permanent preoccupation" is. The editors of *Encounter* have never, so far as I know, explicitly owned to such a preoccupation. In the editorial of the first number (October 1953) we were told that "*Encounter* seeks to promote no 'line,' though its editors have opinions they will not hesitate to express." We were told also that the Congress of Cultural Freedom which sponsors *Encounter* was brought together by "two things: a love of liberty and a respect for that part of human endeavour that goes by the name of culture." Mr. Melvin J. Lasky, co-editor, is even vaguer in his preface to the new anthology:

a review is a way of looking at the world, a record of glimpses and perspectives, concerned with the colour of things, and not only with their meaning, with the visible surface of life as well as with its hidden patterns.

He says not a word about any political intent or "basic preoccupation." It is still part of *Encounter*'s line, as it was in the begin-

* Edited by Stephen Spender, Irving Kristol and Melvin Lasky.

ning, that it "seeks to promote no line." It seeks rather to carry the impression that its anti-communist and pro-capitalist propaganda is not propaganda at all, but the spontaneous and almost uniform reaction of the culturally free, of truly civilized people. And it does this with much success; there is nothing "silly" about *Encounter*. It has been ably edited and never less than interesting; almost every issue contains some work of real merit, almost always non-political—and sometimes by people who are known to be opposed to *Encounter*'s putatively nonexistent "line." Much of this writing is preserved, happily, in the new anthology. Together with this, almost every issue has contained some cleverly written material favourable to the United States and hostile to the Soviet Union.

Is this bad? Is there not in fact much to be said in favour of the United States and against the Soviet Union? There is indeed; it is also a fact that communists have often in speech and writing shown contempt for truth and that it would be a case, as Sir Denis says, of *trahison des clercs* for an intellectual review to ignore or condone this. But clerks can betray in more than one way, and in our culture the communist way is neither the most tempting nor the most rewarding. A clerk who says, for example, that he "seeks to promote no line" and goes on over ten years to promote a most definite and consistent line, may not yet have "betrayed"—for it is possible to argue about definitions—but he would seem, to me at least, to be something of an intellectual security-risk. And the line itself—or "basic preoccupation" if you wish—is not reassuring. There is a significant contradiction in the case for *Encounter* presented by Sir Denis Brogan. *Encounter* cannot be *both* basically and permanently preoccupied with "the designs of a great power"—one great power—and *also* "the organ of protest against the *trahison des clercs*." This would make nonsense of Benda, for it would assert that all intellectual dishonesty is, and must permanently be, an import from the Soviet Union. Reading through the files of *Encounter,* I found little evidence of vigilance against non-Soviet intellectual dishonesty. I did find several examples, in *Encounter*'s own practice, of the intellectual vices against which Benda warned us.

The new anthology—which naturally enough presents a more favourable picture than the files—contains one such example in

Professor Leslie A. Fiedler's "The Middle against Both Ends," a defence of American "comic books." This was written at a time when hostile criticism of these works of art and literature was considered to be causing some damage to America's image in the world. Professor Fiedler's thesis, argued as cleverly as possible in the unpropitious circumstances, was to the effect that anti-comic-book talk was petty-bourgeois and middlebrow; the ordinary man likes these books and real intellectuals, like Professor Fiedler, at least tolerate them. (This same Professor Fiedler shows himself, in a sense, more fastidious in other situations. In an article on the Rosenbergs, published in *Encounter* after their execution, he showed distress at "the pretentious style" of the letters written by Mrs. Rosenberg to her husband while they were both awaiting electrocution.) The case for "comic books" was argued, in the pages of *Encounter*, within a specific political context. The United States (good) produces these books in enormous numbers; the Soviet Union (bad) neither produces nor imports them, but does publish, in addition to much dull propaganda, very large editions of the Russian classics which are read by, among others, people in similar employments to those who, in America, buy comic books. Let us suppose this situation reversed. Suppose that, in America, subway employees are reading Herman Melville, while the presses of the Soviet Union are pouring out crudely produced, sadistic fantasies for the use of the semi-literate. Would Professor Fiedler then have written in the same sense? I doubt if he would, but I am quite sure that if he did, *Encounter* would rightly regard his essay as *trahison des clercs* and reject it without hesitation. Yet the national provenance of these books should not, to a clerk who is loyal in Benda's sense, be a relevant factor at all. It is not necessarily either "silly" or "dishonest" to dislike in *Encounter*, not its "promulgation of uncomfortable truths," but its selection of such truths on cold-war lines. Where the truth in question is uncomfortable for the Soviet Union it is promulgated; where it is uncomfortable for the United States it is mitigated.

One of the basic things about *Encounter* is supposed to be its love of liberty; it was love of liberty that brought together, we are told, the people who, in the Congress of Cultural Freedom, sponsored *Encounter*. Love of whose liberty? This again is conditioned—as it would be for a communist, but in reverse—by the over-all political conflict. Great vigilance is shown about oppression in the communist world; apathy and inconsequence largely prevail where the oppression is non-communist or anti-communist. This generalization needs to be qualified. Silence about oppression has been, if possible, total where the oppressors were believed to be identified with the interests of the United States. Thus the sufferings of Cubans under Batista evoked no comment at the time from the organ of those lovers of liberty, well informed though they undoubtedly are. For Nicaragua, Guatemala, South Vietnam and South Korea the same held good. The Negro problem—that is, the problem of the oppression of Negroes in large areas of the United States today—was consistently played down until quite recently, when the news made it impossible to play it down in the old way.

Last August *Encounter* had a special number, "Negro Crisis," which on the whole put as good a face on things as possible (whites suffering more than blacks, rapid progress, end in sight, and so on). This revealed that "we liberals" had been struggling for civil rights for a long time. Richard Rovere, in the leading contribution, said that:

For as long as I can remember we liberals have been saying how helpful it would be if the sitting President would put the "moral prestige" of his great office behind the Negro drive for justice and equality.

These liberals were not saying this in *Encounter* throughout the reach of any normal adult memory. A check for the first five years (1953–58) shows that at that time they were saying as little as possible about the matter, and giving the impression, in occasional asides that appeared amid the copious comment on the American scene, that it was of no great significance, and in any case well on the way to a solution. (A 1958 book review by Sir Denis Brogan formed an honourable exception to this.)

Where neither the Soviet Union nor the United States was directly involved, love of liberty neither flared up nor was extinguished; it flickered feebly. *Encounter* was moderately anti-Suez, pro-Dulles rather than pro-Eden, as one might expect since *Encounter*'s first loyalty is to America. On South Africa it has presented "both points of view." The first article on the subject which it carried—in its third year of publication—was a debonair little piece by Emily Hahn:

"How do you like it here? Isn't it awful?" she said.

I said it seemed not at all awful. The place was beautiful, the people, if excitable at times, were charming and friendly; what did she mean awful? Impatiently she explained that she meant The Situation, of course. Unlike me she knew exactly what she thought about it, and what the natives thought about it too. She had had several long talks about it with her maid.

The context makes it clear that the terms "the people" and "the natives" are sharply distinct.

Callous flippancy of this kind could not appear in *Encounter* about Poland or Hungary. The fact that it could appear in *Encounter* about South Africa combines with other indications to suggest that what *Encounter* means when it says that it loves liberty is merely that it hates communism. Hatred of something disguised as love of something else is common enough, on all sides of the political fences; special pleading and selective indignation are also common. But it is rash for Sir Denis Brogan to invoke, in tribute to a periodical so prone to these defects, the terminology of Julien Benda. Benda's point was that writers were not to cheat, for any side.

VARIETIES OF ANTI-COMMUNISM

Here are three writers who differ fairly widely in talent and in method but who have a conviction in common: Mr. Fitz Gibbon is a lively, and sometimes witty, journalist; Mr. Howard a strenuous and unconsciously entertaining moralist; Mr. Mander, the most important of the three, a political writer, earnest, able, but factually and otherwise misleading.* The conviction which the three have in common is that anti-communism should be a central element in Britain's foreign policy.

Mr. Constantine Fitz Gibbon is of course no more a fascist than he is a hyena. He is something less exotic and—in our present environment—more harmful than either: an intellectual propagandist with a gift for blurring distinctions. The theme which underlies his new collection of articles is that communism and Nazism are essentially the same. That blessed word "totalitarian" does much of his work for him, but almost anything will serve. Thus, even Auschwitz, the subject of Mr. Fitz Gibbon's first article, puts him in mind of the dangers of communism. It might more pertinently have reminded him of the dangers of anti-communism, since the gentlemen who found and paid Hitler did so because they needed, or thought they needed, an anti-communist demagogue. But for Mr. Fitz Gibbon there is, it seems, no important difference between Khrushchev and Hitler: "in our dealings with the Soviet Union we are once again face to face with a monstrous tyranny, just as we were when dealing with Nazi Germany in the late 1930s." A sombre thought if anyone really thinks it; Mr. Fitz Gibbon seems remarkably cheerful for someone who has to live with a revelation of this order. Some of his other "random thoughts" are even more inflammatory. Thus

---

* Constantine Fitz Gibbon, *Random Thoughts of a Fascist Hyena;* Peter Howard, *Britain and the Beast;* John Mander, *Great Britain or Little England?*

he is able to tell those who live under monstrous tyrannies what their "prime duty" is: "In any European country where democracy has been destroyed or has never existed it is the prime duty of honest men to bring it into existence as soon as possible and with all the means at their disposal, including, if need be, the ultimate means." This, or something like it, was once the gospel of Radio Free Europe to the Hungarians (though not, I think, to the Portuguese). We are not told, except by implication, what the duties of the honest men who offer such advice are to the more exposed honest men who take it. The implication is that—as was the case in Hungary—those who take such advice must fend for themselves, for the conclusion to Mr. Fitz Gibbon's bit about the monstrous-tyranny-just-like-the-Nazis is the surprisingly tame: "we must be prepared, if attacked, to fight and defeat this present enemy." The effect of that "if attacked" after so much breathing of defiance is rather like Saint George announcing that he will defend himself if the dragon tries to bite him.

For Mr. Fitz Gibbon, the Reds are under the bed; for Mr. Peter Howard, they are already in it. We are introduced in his pages to "some astute observers" who have found that "the disturbing increase in homosexuality . . . is the result of a Moscow-directed propaganda, expressly designed to corrode the tissues of capitalist society." How else indeed can one explain the Kremlin's vociferous support for the British public-school system? As one would expect, the relation of sex and left-wing politics is a two-way affair. Communism begets homosexuality, but sexuality itself if "indulged" ("sex indulged becomes an addiction") begets anti-colonialism: "men who exploit someone else's body for their personal pleasure may feel better when they denounce British Imperialism for, as they say, exploiting the body of Africa for national gain." Fortunately, as Miss Rice-Davies could tell us, most exploiters in Class A (sexual) can steel themselves against the craving to denounce exploitation in Class B (political). In any case the remedy for it all is clear: Moral Rearmament. The remedy is, Mr. Howard admits, a drastic one, but there is nothing else for it: "A fool pretends cancer is nothing but collywobbles. A friend reaches for the surgeon's knife." I can see the necessary friendship and daring in Mr. Howard's eye. What I do not see is what might be more reassuring: his qualifications as a surgeon.

To a mind assailed by the committed rhetoric of Mr. Fitz Gibbon and the incisive intent of Mr. Howard, Mr. Mander's calm tone comes as a relief. His tone is indeed calmer than one feels it would be if he were altogether convinced by his own political argument, which is not much less alarmist in content than Mr. Fitz Gibbon's. Despite the title, *Great Britain or Little England?* is not so much another "state of England" book as a survey of international politics, with recommendations about Britain's foreign policy. Britain should, in Mr. Mander's view, be more wary about communist intentions, more responsive to American anti-communist moves and at the same time more Europe-minded. These are the positions we should expect from an assistant editor of *Encounter*, and there may not be very much in the book which will come as a surprise to regular readers of that periodical. One exception, perhaps, is the conclusion, which is to the effect that General de Gaulle might be "bought"—Mr. Mander's own word—with "British nuclear expertise" to permit Britain "to join in shaping the future of Europe." Alternatively—or perhaps simultaneously—West German support could be bought by giving the Germans control over nuclear arms.

It is for Englishmen, and not foreigners like the present reviewer, to say whether these prospects seem inspiring or alluring from an English point of view. To many outsiders they will seem menacing. What exactly is all this concentration of "independent deterrence" required for? To defend Western Europe against the Russians, according to Mr. Mander. The communist will to aggression is unsleeping and America might not use nuclear weapons to defend Europe against Russian attack. This combination of hypotheses does not seem quite plausible enough to supply by itself the motive power for a European nuclear directorium such as is urged here. The demand for "independent deterrents," both in Britain and France, has perhaps had less to do with fear of Russian invasion than with the memory of occasions—Suez and Dien Bien Phu—when partly for lack of "independent" and decisive weapons, independent policies had to be abandoned. A Western Europe with a concerted—or more or less concerted—foreign policy and a nuclear armoury could afford to conduct its business in the Middle East, in southern Africa, in the Far East and perhaps in Eastern Europe with much less deference to

American, Russian or Afro-Asian opinion—and therefore to the United Nations—than the governments of France and Britain have been able to permit themselves in recent years. For some sections of the right—and not only in France, Britain and Germany, but also in South Africa, Portugal and elsewhere—this is understandably an attractive idea, and it is correspondingly alarming both to the newly independent countries and to those who fear that the combination of nuclear weapons and *politique de grandeur* may endanger world peace.

Mr. Mander—who is not himself Suez-minded—does not examine the interesting question of what the independent policies of his West European nuclear-armed "directorium" would be likely to be. On the whole he seems to invite us to assume that the "directorium" will be content just to sit there and deter the communists. He is at pains to stress the need for this because of the "coordinated strategy" for our destruction which international communism has been able to pursue, no less under Khrushchev and Mao than under Stalin. The latest campaign began during the autumn of 1957. At that time

Krushchev removed his last important rival, Zhukov, from the Party Presidium. The success of the sputnik showed that Russia would soon be in a position to threaten America. Centrifugal tendencies in Russia and in Eastern Europe had been checked. "Revisionism" was in retreat. In Poland Gomulka had won a measure of internal autonomy, though at the price of subservience to Moscow abroad. With the affairs of the Communist bloc in reasonable order, and America in the grip of a serious recession, the stage seemed set for another period of advance. There was the Turkish crisis in the autumn of 1957; the Middle Eastern crisis in July, 1958. The Quemoy crisis of August, 1958, led on to the second Berlin crisis in November. Between 1958 and 1961 the guerrilla campaigns in Laos and South Vietnam were renewed; the infiltration and satellisation of Cuba completed. In June, 1961, at Vienna, Krushchev presented Kennedy with a fresh Berlin ultimatum. In August came the Berlin Wall and the virtual annexation of East Berlin.

Looking back, the period 1957-1962 bears all the marks of a coordinated campaign, comparable to the offensive of 1947-1952.

At first sight the accumulation of events and dates seems quite impressive, but closer examination shows some odd flaws. Thus, it is true that both the fall of Zhukov and the so-called Turkish crisis occurred in the autumn of 1957, but it cannot be true, as Mr. Mander suggests, that Khrushchev unleashed the Turkish crisis as soon as Zhukov's fall left him free to begin his "coordinated campaign." It cannot be true, because the "Turkish crisis" —which was a war-of-nerves affair conducted by the Soviets mainly in the press, on the radio and at the United Nations—occurred *before,* and not after, the fall of Zhukov. The fall of Zhukov in fact precipitated not the beginning but the end of the "Turkish crisis." Anyone who was present at the United Nations in those days will recall the tension among Eastern European delegates at the height of the crisis—immediately before the fall of Zhukov—the jubilation with which many of these delegates, especially the Poles, greeted the news of that fall, and the almost contemptuously casual way in which the Soviet Delegation "switched off" the Turkish crisis once Zhukov was out of the way. But one does not need to have been at the United Nations: the *Annual Register* for 1957 shows that the Turkish crisis began in early September, reached a peak in mid-October and was publicly declared at an end by Khrushchev on October 29—three days after Zhukov's dismissal. I am not concerned to prove a relationship—such as some well-informed Poles believed to exist—between Zhukov and a "tough school" in the Kremlin, but what is certain is that Zhukov's fall was not, as Mr. Mander suggests it was, the signal for an offensive—on the contrary, indeed. This has important implications for our view of Khrushchev's Russia and its international policies, and Mr. Mander's misrepresentation of the order of events has its implications for our view of his argument generally.

Again, what evidence is there to show that the Middle Eastern crisis of July 1958 was part of a communist "coordinated campaign"?

The crisis in question consisted of a military putsch in Iraq, followed by landings of American and British troops in Lebanon and Jordan, and by Arab and communist protests against these landings. Are we to believe—and if so on what grounds—that Kassem's revolt against Nuri was planned and precipitated by the Soviet Union and China? Or is the sole fact of propaganda against the Western landings enough to sustain the theory that international communism caused the Middle Eastern crisis of 1958? If the Russians and Chinese had sent their armed forces to the Middle East at that time—as the Western powers did—Mr. Mander's case here would be considerably stronger.

In the same year, the Quemoy crisis, according to Mr. Mander, "led on" to the second Berlin crisis. The words "led on," in Mr. Mander's scheme of things, imply that the two "crises" were part of a planned political offensive. Mao at Quemoy was softening the Westerners up for Khrushchev to squeeze them in Berlin. Were the relations of the two great communist powers as close as this, and of this character, even in 1958? Mr. Mander's "coordinated campaign" theory requires them to have been so, even up to the autumn of 1962 and perhaps beyond. We are asked to believe that this agreed strategy, and not any local needs or initiatives, also determined the renewal of the guerrilla campaigns in Laos and Vietnam. This is unlikely even on Mr. Mander's own showing. Referring to the earlier period (1947–52) he speaks of Stalin, while blockading Berlin and raping Czechoslovakia, also "ordering"—as part of his "strategy"—"the communists of South-East Asia onto the barricades." This was a failure generally, but "in one country"—Vietnam—"the strategy was conspicuously successful." "Ironically," Mr. Mander adds, "the Viet Minh had launched the offensive independently of both Stalin and Mao." Any irony involved would appear to be at Mr. Mander's expense, for what he is saying is that the only part of his much-emphasized "strategy" which came off was not a part of the "strategy" at all.

There is more to this than a breakdown in logic—although that is significant enough. What is more significant is the distortion of political perspective. Mr. Mander is so preoccupied with the great game of international strategy that he fails to consider those realities—movements of peoples, classes, sects—which in any given country so often take the distant "strategists" by surprise. On Berlin, certainly, the communist strategists can create or end crises at will, but in most of the world, in the poor regions, communism spreads—or communisms spread—not because of Stalin's or Khrushchev's skill in pressing buttons, but because of the failure of local parasite ruling classes and because of Western insistence on propping up these ruling classes until their last gasp.

When in answer to a Ho Chi Minh the West pins its faith to a Bao Dai or a Madame Nhu, the Kremlin needs no strategy—just time.

Mr. Mander might well agree with this—there are few to defend the "anti-communist strong men" of Asia and Africa once the public-relations varnish has begun to crack—but his thesis, with its "realistic" emphasis on power, weapons and high strategy, tends to distract attention from people onto objects and remote abstractions. Even on his chosen plane he is hardly, as we have seen, a reliable guide: a serious matter in a field where overconfident advice, insofar as it may influence the thinking of those in power, may bring us all just that much nearer to annihilation. Thus his very shaky account of the international communist "offensive" of 1957-62—an account which, in addition to its other defects, coolly omits mention of the 1959-60 "spirit of Camp David" *rapprochement,* ended by the U2—concludes that "the Cuba debacle of October 1962 seems to have forced a pause, possibly a temporary armistice." The moral suggested is that toughness is the only way to hold in check the communist will to aggression. Corollaries: (1) those in Britain who urged caution over Cuba were in the spirit of Munich (a very odd parallel, considering the positions of Cuba and of Czechoslovakia); (2) the West Germans should have nuclear weapons. If this advice is sound, it can only be so by coincidence, for the chain or argument by which Mr. Mander reaches it is demonstrably defective. If coincidence fails, and "tough" advice is unsound, it could, if taken, prove fatal.

Mr. Mander's book nevertheless deserves to be read carefully, for the ideas he advocates, and the character of his thinking, are bound to attract powerful support. This is in many ways a depressing thought. His "get-tough-with-Russia" advice to Britain is probably a less serious matter than his specifically European ideas, for the kind of Europe which may take shape from such blueprints as his could, with its nostalgias and new-found strength—and France's overseas involvements—be more dangerous to the world than is either of the present Great Powers. Mr. Mander, who admires General de Gaulle and has confidence in German democracy, tells us that there is no cause for alarm.

Probably the most disturbing thing in the books here reviewed is that Mr. Fitz Gibbon and Mr. Mander apparently support Labour. "My sympathies," says Mr. Mander, "are with the Left." "My political adherence, so far as I have any," says Mr. Fitz Gibbon, "is to the Left." Mr. Mander also notes approvingly that a Labour government, "being always under pressure to take a strong British stand," need not be expected, in foreign policy, to be necessarily "softer on communism" than the Tories. Both writers—and Mr. Howard also, if it please God to "change" Harold Wilson—hope that a coming British Labour government will make anti-communism a central plank in its foreign policy. It is perhaps possible that they may get their wish for they have some formidable allies on their right, and some electorally lethal arguments against opponents on the left. It is easy to suggest that those who warn against an anti-communist foreign policy must either wish for a pro-communist one or be dangerously naïve—in short, be either knaves or fools. Faced with this terrible fork, we have seen some left-wing writers begin by grovelling for the second option—"don't mind me, sir, I'm no fellow-traveller, just a decent, muddled idealist"—and then recover their intellectual self-esteem by becoming tough, cynical anti-communists, beady-eyed birds in whose sight the net is spread in vain. If you are not anti-communist, they will tell you, you must be anti-NATO, and if you are anti-NATO, then you are virtually inviting the Russians to take over Britain. This is a telling line, which enables the speakers to "sell" to some socialists a world-wide system of political intervention which has nothing to do either with the defence of Britain or with anything else which a socialist could possibly approve. The "anti-communist" doctrine is designed to blur the vitally important distinction between telling the Russians that you will fight if they attack your allies—a valid and clear-cut non-ideological position—and telling the Vietnamese and others that you will fight to stop them from "going communist"—an outwardly ideological commitment of uncontrollable scope.

An "anti-communist" foreign policy involves an indefinite number of such uncontrollable and therefore potentially explosive commitments. It also involves incessant interference in the affairs of the weaker states, the perpetuation of the system which has become known as neo-colonialism—a term which evokes smiles more readily in Britain than in Africa. These activities do nothing to weaken communism—which thrives wherever it becomes identified with the more potent force of nationalism—but they do increase the dangers of war, and widen the gap between white and non-white. Probably most of those outside Britain who desire a Labour victory hope that a Labour government will not only abandon these practices but will do its best to moderate the ideological and pseudo-ideological zeal of its allies.

Against the realization of such a hope there are at work not only certain foundations, media, periodicals and pamphleteers but also those phenomena whose existence Mr. Mander notes with so much satisfaction: the need not to appear "soft on communism," the "pressure to take a strong British stand." These three books are designed to increase the pressure. Mr. Mander and Mr. Fitz Gibbon do so with some efficiency; we should be grateful to Mr. Howard for breaking the strain by making us laugh.

THE PERJURED SAINT

This collection* of posthumous fragments—notes, letters, articles—is of little importance in itself. The main themes—communism, God, Whittaker Chambers—have already been thoroughly ruminated in the copious pages of *Witness,* and *Cold Friday* offers us no new revelations of any great importance about any of them. What the book does, however, is to raise again the interesting question of the liar as saint: the question of why this veteran liar should become a saint in the eyes of so many intelligent people who dislike lies, or say they do. That is the question I propose to discuss.

In a piece of *Cold Friday* called "The Third Rome," Chambers, who loved to educate his readers, especially about Russia, imparts some information about the Russian feeling for Constantinople:

> On that strange horizon, the Russian eye sees, flaring in imagination, the domes and minarets of the Second Rome—Byzantium (Constantinople, now Istanbul), by which Christendom and culture reached the steppes. It is a legendary vision, and the Russian does not call it Byzantium. He has his own special word for it: Tsargrad—the Imperial City, city of the Tsar (Tsar, the Russian form of Caesar). The depth of the special Russian feeling for Byzantium is perhaps suggested by the fact that Tsargrad alone, or almost alone, among the names of foreign cities is declined through all nine of the inflections of the Russian noun; is treated as a Russian word.

One can imagine the confrontation before the House Committee:

Mr. Nixon: Mr. Chambers, do you know the Russian noun?
Mr. Chambers: I do.
Mr. Nixon: How many inflections does it have?
Mr. Chambers: Nine.

* Whittaker Chambers, *Cold Friday.*

	THE COLD WAR
Mr. Mundt:	Thank you, Mr. Chambers, for that frank testimony, very different from some of the witnesses we have had here today.

. . . .

Mr. Nixon:	Mr. Noun, does Mr. Chambers know you?
Russian Noun:	It depends what you mean by "know."
Mr. Nixon:	That's not a very satisfactory answer. How many inflections do you have?
Russian Noun:	Six—you could call it seven if you include the archaic vocative.
Mr. Stripling:	Make up your mind. What is it? Six or seven?
Russian Noun:	It depends whether you count the vocative. You see . . .
Mr. Mundt:	We're wasting our time. I've had enough of these evasions. Have you a relative called Tsargrad?
Russian Noun:	Yes—as a matter of fact he's considered rather unusual in our family—he's declined fully, in both components. Rather jolly, really.
Mr. Nixon:	You say Mr. Chambers doesn't know you. Yet he has already—quite spontaneously—testified to this Committee about this little detail, which could hardly be known to someone not on intimate terms with your family. How do you account for that, Mr. Noun?
Russian Noun:	Well, you see, I didn't exactly say he didn't know me. We have met on a couple of occasions . . .
Mr. Mundt:	Now we're beginning to get somewhere. Can you still not remember how many inflections you have?

The Committee would undoubtedly have concluded that Chambers had told the truth, and that the Russian noun had nine inflections.

It would remain the fact, universally recognized by grammarians, that the Russian noun has six or (counting the fossil vocative) seven inflections: not nine.

Most didactic mortals find it painful to have discrepancies of this kind brought to their attention. Chambers, for whom this was a frequent experience, never seemed abashed. When one of his stories, in the Hiss case—an alleged trip with the Hisses to New Hampshire—broke down for lack of confirmatory evidence (hotel guest-list signatures) which should have been there if the story had been true, Chambers, in *Witness,* shrugged the matter off in masterly style. "Obviously," he wrote, "if I had been lying, I would have taken care to contrive a better story, since there was no need to invent any story at all."

It would be hard to think of a better all-purpose stretcher for carting away broken-down lies than "obviously if I had been lying I would have taken care to contrive a better story." Titus Oates could have used that. As for the "no need to invent any story at all," that was a lie in itself. What Chambers needed—very badly at the time in question, which was well "pre-pumpkin"—was evidence to support his story of a very close association with Hiss. The New Hampshire trip would have been useful as evidence if it had proved "a better story."

The "nine inflections of the Russian noun" are of course a mistake, not a lie, but the mistake is, I think, a revealing one because—as with the New Hampshire story—there was a "need," a motive, for it. In this case—and I suspect, often though not always elsewhere in Chambers's writings and testimony—the pressure to distort is a rhetorical pressure. "All nine of the inflections of the Russian noun" gives just the reverberation Chambers needed at this point in his boomy incantation. "Nine" is good, both as sound and number. As sound it gives a solemn chime, sonorous corroboration of all those domes and minarets. As number it is mystic and appropriately large: ordinary languages do not have as many as nine inflections of the noun: the number, in its solemn excess, corresponds to the vastness of the Russian land, the ceremonious endurance of the Russian soul ("You too can write like Whittaker Chambers"). "All nine inflections of the Russian noun" is, in its context and to suckers for this kind of thing, impressive, even awesome. ("Fair makes your flesh creep, don't it? Shows you what we're up against!") Six, on the other hand, will hardly do. "Six," as sound, is miserable, thin and unhelpful; as number it is inadequate, too much like other languages, fails to evoke Slavonic mystery. As for "six" or (if you count the archaic vocative) "seven," that is altogether out of the question; if one were to burden oneself to that degree with tedious accuracy one would have to give up rhetoric altogether.

So Whittaker Chambers looked out and saw, flaring in imagination, a legendary vision: the Nine Inflections of the Russian Noun.

On points of grammar it is always possible to get the facts; on historical episodes this is often less easy, and it was to history rather than to grammar that Chambers' imagination usually drew him. He tells us in this same section—*The Third Rome*—which contained the Russian lesson, a blood-curdling story about Russian spies. He heard this story from a man whom he knew as "Herbert" or "Otto" or "Karl" and who was "in fact the tank commander of the Leningrad military district"; he does not explain why this man was spinning yarns in New York instead of commanding tanks around Leningrad; perhaps he was on a reconnaissance. On one of the two "conversations of length" he had with this person—one for each pseudonym and a half—he learned how Russian spies in Paris killed an old White Russian General, took the body to the Russian Embassy, dismembered it there, and dispatched "his head and hands" per diplomatic bag to the Kremlin, as proof that the old party had indeed passed away. I happened to have a thermometer in my mouth when I was reading this affecting narrative, and I noted that the point where my blood ran coldest was where I realized the dread implications, in the context, of the words "and hands." The object of the unusually composed despatch was to convince the Kremlin that the general (whose name appropriately enough was Kutepov) was well and truly dead. In most Western diplomatic bags, in such circumstances, it is usually considered enough (as far as my own experience goes) to include the head; the effete unprofessional minds that rule our chancelleries are then apt to jump to the conclusion that the man concerned is dead. But the cold and crafty minds which are planning our destruction in the Kremlin are not satisfied with literally *prima facie* evidence. "This is his head all right," they are to be thought of as saying, "but how do we know he is not still typing counter-revolutionary manifestos? The hands too, please. *Both* of them." (Professor William Empson, with whom I have discussed this question, thinks the inclusion of the hands a sensible routine precaution, but points out that ambiguities would arise should the face not correspond to the fingerprints or should the hands not be a true pair.)

One may think that those who believe Chambers' gory tale

The Perjured Saint

show themselves considerably less exigent, in the matter of evidence, than the Kremlin is supposed to have been on this picturesque occasion.

We have to remind ourselves at this point that Chambers has to be taken seriously—very seriously indeed. Largely on his testimony a respected public figure, who denied and still denies his charges, was sentenced to several years in prison—for, of all things, perjury. Well-known writers have taken Chambers at his own valuation; that is to say as a saint, who heard voices like Joan of Arc and was crucified like Christ. (I shall concede the validity of the latter comparison if I am present for his resurrection; in matters of evidence I incline to a Kremlin-like caution.) Miss Rebecca West sees in him "a Christian mystic of the pantheist school, a spiritual descendant of Eckhard and Boehme and Angelus Silesius. Mr. Arthur Koestler (according to the jacket of *Cold Friday*) thinks his act of "moral suicide" in the Hiss case was an atonement for the guilt of our generation. His former employers in *Time* see him as the publican in the parable, with Hiss cast of course for the pharisee; an analogy which would be a mite stronger if the publican had been smart enough to get the pharisee put in clink, and to write a best-seller about how he did it. In any case all concerned, beginning with Chambers, have spread a thick fog of religiosity over his person and actions.

Everything hinges on our judgment of the nature of Chambers' "witness." What was the act of "moral suicide" remarked by Koestler? Surely not Chambers' admission of his own past career as a traitor and spy. The admission (as distinct from the career) is generally regarded as creditable; and a public confession, if true, cannot possibly be thought of as "moral suicide." Nor can his denunciation of his "friend"—if true, and patriotically motivated, as he claimed—be moral suicide. If he made his disclosures to save his country and the world from the clutches of "absolute evil"—which is what he says he thought communism was—then his act of denunciation, painful though it is supposed to have been, would have been clearly justified, brave and virtuous; no question of suicide.

Matters, of course, were not as clear as that, and this is why God has to be called in, always a bad sign. The fact has to be accounted for, that this splendid and useful fellow Chambers indubitably and inescapably committed perjury. His most meritorious action in the eyes of his admirers was the production of the Baltimore Documents, with the charge that Hiss had given them to him: a charge of espionage. But Chambers had, up till then consistently denied, and denied under oath, that he and Hiss had been engaged in espionage. So, if he was not lying when he produced the documents, he must have been lying earlier. "But," to adapt a phrase of the late Stalin's: "we do not want him to have been lying when he produced the documents. No, comrades, we do not want that." So he was lying earlier, perjuring himself earlier. No way out of it; the most sympathetic and anti-communist people, those who could at worst suspend judgment about other parts of his testimony, which looked on the bare evidence remarkably like perjury, had to insist that he did in fact commit perjury on the occasions when he swore Hiss had *not* been involved in espionage.

Pity. How could this just man swear falsely? The answer suggested is: pity. The biggest set-piece in *Witness* asks us to believe that Chambers' affection for Hiss was so compounded that, while he could bear to accuse his friend of traitorous conspiracy and subversion—"messing up policy," to help Joe Stalin and scupper Uncle Sam—he just could not bring himself to accuse him of espionage, although that is what Hiss had really been at. Chambers felt so badly about this that when he was about to make the charge—with maximum publicity, and the pumpkin in the wings —he tried, he says, to commit suicide (like Scobie, the classic "pity-and-guilt" man), with the aid of a strange and inefficient contraption which he describes in his book. He survived to ram his new charge home and put Hiss in jail.

There are those who find this story convincing and moving; these are good souls and will inherit the kingdom of Heaven; on earth they are a little lacking, intellectually speaking, and in point of information. Well-informed anti-communist intellectuals, people like Miss West, who are not mugs and do not want to be taken for mugs, cannot be seen to fall for this kind of thing, or for much of Chambers' testimony. Miss West, in her *Atlantic Monthly* review (June 1952), refers, with cautious regret, to "the encouragement he gave his non-Communist opponents to believe that he was a liar." He gave this encouragement in the most effective possible way: to wit, by telling lies. Apart from the lie which his admirers have to admit and even insist on—"no espionage"—there are many contradictions in his testimony, for which by far the simplest and most probable explanation is that he was lying. Perhaps the most flagrant example is that of his original charge against Hiss's brother, Donald Hiss, whom he said he knew as a Communist and from whom he said he collected Communist dues. Donald Hiss flatly denied that he had ever met Chambers, and no attempt at all was made to prove that he had; the thing was simply dropped. In his book Chambers, while not withdrawing the charge, coolly remarks that Donald Hiss's answers to the charge were "forthright" and reflected badly on—Alger Hiss, who by comparison had seemed to hedge. Yet, if Donald Hiss was telling the truth—as seems to be recognized in the adjective "forthright" as well as in the dropping of the charge—it was Chambers who had been guilty of a most odious lie: a lie, also, by no means explicable by the excessively merciful disposition, brought in to account for the *admitted* act of perjury. About the Donald Hiss charges Lord Jowitt has written, in measured words:

This, at any rate, seems clear, and must leave a most damaging impression of the truth of Chambers' evidence as a whole: that the allegations were demonstrated, so far as human testimony can demonstrate, to be entirely without foundation. There was, as it seems to me, no scope for explaining away the discrepancies as mere differences of recollection.

Similarly when Chambers made the charge—subsequently demonstrated to be altogether false—that Alger Hiss had swindled his stepson Timothy for the benefit of the Communist party, it can hardly be contended that this lie—again it cannot be just a legitimate mistake—is accounted for by his overflowing affection for his dear old friend.

Chambers testified that Thayer Hobson (the boy's father) was paying for his education, but the Hisses had told him, Chambers, that "they were diverting a large part of the money to the Communist party . . . and they took him out of a more expensive school and put him in a less expensive school for that purpose." This was actually the reverse of the truth. Thayer Hobson has recalled that "When Timothy was transferred to a far more expensive school, he protested . . . and the Hisses paid the additional money out of their own pockets." (Fred Cook, *The Unfinished Story of Alger Hiss*) "The accuser," says Mr. Cook, "was the same man who was later to justify his own radical shifts of testimony by picturing himself as nobly protecting a former friend."

If we are to love and admire this particular anti-communist hero, divine aid is urgently necessary, and down it comes. "This is an act," says Miss West, speaking of the admitted perjury, "which is explicable only by reference to the egotism of the mystic. In the light of that clue it is quite comprehensible. Without that clue, it is troubling and enigmatic." Mysticism also covers, presumably, other "troubling and enigmatic" business, like the false charge against Donald Hiss and the false charge about Hiss's stepson. It is a serviceable attribute, even in this world's affairs. In the Hiss case the non-mystic was indicted for perjury, found guilty and sent to jail. The mystic, admittedly guilty of the same offence, was never even indicted. He was secure in the Cloud of Unknowing, safe in the bosom of the God of Dostoevsky and Graham Greene—a God who bears a marked resemblance to the Father of Lies.

Much in the Hiss case remains puzzling, and anyone who says a word against Chambers is likely to be hit on the head with that Woodstock. The fact remains that it was Chambers' testimony, *plus* the documents accepted as typed on the Woodstock, that convicted Hiss—the documents alone, whatever we may think of them, would not have sufficed. Yet it is clear to any rational person—exception made of temporary mystics like Miss West—that Chambers was an inveterate liar. He was, however, a successful one and in a patriotic cause, and this is why he is admired. "Your unlucky forgery," wrote Charles Maurras about Colonel Henry—exposed as the framer of Dreyfus—"will be acclaimed as one of your finest deeds of war." "Your lucky perjuries," an American Maurras might aptly say of Chambers, "were your most effective prose." All those who, while considering communism "absolute evil," also believe in fighting it with its own weapons, are forced to concur. Chambers himself was one of these.

The Perjured Saint

When Richard Pigott—the key witness in the "Parnellism and Crime" case of the eighties—was first exposed as having committed perjury and forgery, the judge asked him incredulously whether he thought certain of his admitted acts compatible with the behaviour of an honourable man? He replied:

"No, my lord; I have never claimed to be an honourable man."

The response has a certain bleak dignity, compared with the current style. In our day, a successor to Pigott replies: "I am something more than a mere 'honourable man,' my lord. I am a saint and mystic, engaged in a suicidal struggle against Absolute Evil. If you seem to trip me up in an odd lie here and there it is either because of some extreme, and pertinent, virtue of mine (like mercy) or because, at the time I was on the stand, I was in communion with God and didn't pay attention to what I was saying." And that, in the view of some respected commentators, would be the "clue" to the "troubling and enigmatic" business of perjury.

I prefer Pigott.

VII

THE UNITED NATIONS AND THE DEVELOPING COUNTRIES

CONFLICTING CONCEPTS OF THE UNITED NATIONS

The United Nations organization has now survived seventeen years, covering several periods of intense international strain, and great specific strains on the structure of the organization itself. It has survived; it has helped to avert threats to peace and above all, during the worst periods of the cold war and during actual periods of "hot war," it has provided a permanent meeting-place for great powers which often seemed on the verge of hostilities, and which sometimes were actually engaged in indirect hostilities. Through all this time it has provided, both in the Security Council and, above all, in the General Assembly, a forum where bitterly conflicting opinions could be expressed—a verbal, taking the place of a material, warfare—while in the corridors, through the meetings of permanent representatives and others, and sometimes through the mediation of the Secretary-General, compromise solutions were worked out, aimed at preventing the battles from becoming material. It is true that the successes were often equivocal, and that the compromises had often a bitter taste. I shall come, in a moment, to look at these aspects of the matter. At this stage it is enough to say that the United Nations has achieved a life and an apparent volition of its own—or partly of its own—in a sense that the old League of Nations never knew; that it is universal—or almost universal—in a way that the old League never was, and that it is sensitive to the opinion of smaller countries in a way which, while somewhat more apparent than real, is yet real in a sense that would never even have occurred to the League. This last factor—the sensitivity of the United Nations to the opinions of the smaller, formerly subject, nations—reflects, and is reflected in, the attachment of these countries to the United Nations. It was Hammarskjöld who asserted, in September 1960, speaking of the smaller powers, that "the organization is, first of all, their organization." This statement contained an element of exaggeration, but it did strike a most responsive note among the small nations, with hardly a single exception.

This mutual attachment has become probably the most important single source of strength for the organization as such. The reason for this is that the great power systems strive, especially in Africa and Asia, for influence over the smaller powers—or to exclude the influence of their rivals, which usually amounts to the same thing—and since these smaller powers like to work through the United Nations, it becomes important for the great powers to be as active and exercise as much authority inside the United Nations as they can. Thus the basic factor in the political life of the United Nations is the triangle of pressures exerted by America and its allies, the Soviet Union and its allies, and the Afro-Asian countries. None of these can afford, as it were, to "let go" of the United Nations—as Germany and Italy did with the League—and none has power to expel any of the others, as the Western controllers of the League did with Russia. Thus the United Nations has become, as the League never did, a centre of intense, competitive, oblique diplomacy, combined with equally intense open propaganda.

Whatever else may be said about it, the United Nations is an extremely lively organization and, as life is the condition of growth, all who count the growth of international institutions as a necessity for human survival must rejoice at the abundant signs of life on the shores of Turtle Bay. Not only is the United Nations lively now, but its continued life may be predicted with reasonable safety. An organization which has survived the bitterness and confusion of Palestine, Korea, Suez, Hungary and the Congo has demonstrated, among other things, its vital tenacity.

I shall take it, then, as axiomatic that the United Nations—at the very least in its functions as an international forum and centre of mediation—is a necessary human institution and likely to survive as long as organized human society, however long that may be. If we take that for granted, we are enabled to set aside the argument of those who would stifle criticisms of the organization's imperfections and its sometimes inflated pretensions, by alleging that such criticisms endanger the last, best hope of man. The United Nations, at seventeen, is by no means so fragile as those critics would suggest. On the contrary, it is quite a tough organization, served by some reasonably tough people and used, in varying ways, by tough, though mostly mildly spoken, representatives of various powers and especially of one power. No light we can shed on the organization's actual ways of working is likely to bring it to an untimely end, or to prevent the fulfilment of the purposes which it was set up to serve. On the contrary, as, like most if not all human institutions, its practice has a pronounced tendency to deviate from its professions, it is in the common interest that such light should be shed. It is by the shedding of light that practice is most often encouraged to move up a little closer to profession. In any event, we shall be helping to diminish the area of optimistic illusion which at present has such an unhealthy grip over public opinion in international affairs.

From this introduction I may have given you the impression that I am about to produce some sensational revelations about the inner workings of the United Nations. This is not so. In what follows I shall be doing no more, for the most part, than presenting and reasoning from some of the assumptions about the facts of international life at the United Nations which are habitually made by those who work there, whether in the delegations or in the Secretariat. I refer to the assumptions which they make while they are actually working, as distinct from those which spring almost unbidden to their lips when they are addressing outside audiences in their American environment, or in their puzzled homelands.

The first working assumption, which every professional makes, and few professionals publicly refer to, is that if the United States does not want a given course of action to be taken, then the United Nations—that is to say the Security Council, the General Assembly and the Secretariat—will refrain from taking that course of action. The same assumption is not made about any of the other permanent members except in function of their degree of influence, at a given moment, with the United States. The second assumption, the converse of the first, is that any action taken by the United Nations must fit in with the United States' estimate of its own diplomatic interests. The third assumption is the corollary, that extensions of the power and influence of the

United Nations are likely to be more at the expense of the Soviet Union and its allies than of the other sovereign members. The fourth is that the United Nations is unlikely to encroach on the interests of America's allies, unless it should be expedient, on a wider view of American interests, for the United States to permit the United Nations to do so. The fifth assumption is that if, in the judgment of the State Department, it is expedient to sacrifice the real or supposed immediate interests of any of America's allies, for the strengthening of America's over-all diplomatic position, then the United Nations is likely to act in a manner disrespectful to these particular allies and their interests.

Up to 1958, the sixth assumption—nay, the first assumption—would have been that any proposition which the United States desired would become United Nations policy. By 1958, however, at the time of the Lebanon crisis, it became apparent that because of the intake of new members, the United States could no longer carry through any proposition which ran flagrantly counter to Afro-Asian opinion, as a whole. The new sixth assumption then emerged: that any proposition on which the United States and a considerable number of Afro-Asian states can agree will become United Nations policy. This sixth assumption has now become a cardinal one, for practical prognosis, as distinct from academic speculation, about United Nations activity. Major propositions which are intended to be carried are now invariably worked out between the United States and at least some African and Asian delegates before coming to the floor. Naturally other consultations also take place, but the critical ones, as far as voting is concerned, are between the United States and the Afro-Asians. Both the Soviet Union and the Western European powers are, for different reasons, very reluctant to oppose openly a solid American–Afro-Asian consensus, although they will usually strive hard, at different ends, to prevent such a consensus coming into being. This new sixth assumption does differ significantly from the old one, whereby American control over the United Nations was virtually complete. The shift is healthy as far as it goes, in that it encourages the development of real negotiations, instead of pure propaganda demonstrations at the United Nations.*

---

* Mr. Andrew Boyd (*United Nations: Piety, Myth and Truth*, p. 16) holds the following two assumptions to be "oversimplified": "that throughout the UN's

Conflicting Concepts of the United Nations [*199*]

The gap, however, between the two assumptions is not quite so great as one might at first suppose, and this for two reasons. The first is that the United States, through its widespread network of diplomatic and technical aid missions, and the pervasive influence of its great financial, commercial and industrial corporations, has a considerable and probably an increasing say in the foreign policies of a number of Asian and African governments. The second is that the Asian and African countries by no means form a solid bloc and it is therefore possible for the United States to acquire the necessary accession of Afro-Asian votes for one phase of its policy from one end of the spectrum, and for another phase from the other end. Thus, to take a recent example, the United States, in supporting and deciding military action in Katanga, could have relied, if necessary, on the left and centre of the Afro-Asian group at the Assembly to give, together with the safe Latin American and other votes, the necessary two-thirds majority in any voting. In the second phase, when it was United States and United Nations policy, just after the end of the secession, to maintain Tshombe and his government at the head of provincial affairs in South Katanga, the United States could still, if necessary, have found a majority for this policy—but a different and somewhat more vulnerable one, the right and centre, instead of the left and centre, of the Afro-Asian group, combined with the

---

first ten years there was an automatic Assembly majority at the disposal of America, and that there is now one controlled by the Afro-Asian members." The second assumption is indeed oversimplified, if only because it ignores the fact that the Afro-Asian members seldom act as a united group. I cannot see, however, that the first assumption is oversimplified in any serious way. Mr. Geoffrey L. Goodwin, writing of these same ten years, observed that "the attitude of the U.S. is usually decisive" (*Britain and the United Nations*, p. 218). Mr. Boyd gives only one example to show the limitations on American influence in the period he names. The example given—the case of Palestine (November 1947)—is hardly convincing, since the American administration got its way in that matter, though not without, as Mr. Boyd says, "exceptional pressure." *United Nations: Piety, Myth and Truth* is the best introduction to the United Nations which exists, and one of the very few works which give any clear idea of how that institution functions in practice. The only serious weakness of this valuable book is an apparent tendency to underestimate, as here, the importance of American influence in the United Nations, both in the past and now. One of the most realistic comments I have seen on United States influence and attitudes at the United Nations comes from a Canadian observer, K. A. MacKirdy: "The nation which pays a third of the budget, like the boy who owns the football, wants the game played his way or he will go home" (*Queen's Quarterly*, winter 1961).

safe votes. Thus, today, by the exercise of a sophisticated kind of parliamentary diplomacy, the United States can get almost as good results as by the cruder methods prevalent up to 1958.

I have deliberately stressed the preponderant American role at the United Nations. I have done so for the sole reason that this is a major fact of international life, well known to all professionally concerned with these matters, but often glossed over, minimized or simply ignored, in public discussion and even, or perhaps especially, in discussions of a serious academic kind. In preparing this lecture I read through a certain number of textbooks and similar writings by learned men, sometimes jurists and sometimes political scientists, often attached to, or writing for, some foundation. I was astonished by the regularity with which most of them discussed the deliberations and decisions of, for example, the General Assembly, as if that body were responsive simply to world opinion generally, without the marked specific weighting which it in fact has in favour of the State Department point of view.*

In drawing attention to this large and obvious, but relatively neglected, phenomenon it is not at all my wish to denounce the United States. Any great power which was in a position to exercise such authority in an international organization would have made use of its opportunities, and on the whole I think the other powers would have made a worse use of it than the United States has done. The United States, despite certain aberrations on Formosa and Cuba, has never—so far at least—shown the reckless disregard for the possible consequences of its actions which Britain and France showed at Suez and the Soviet Union showed in Hungary. On the whole, the United States administration handled the combined Suez-Hungary crisis through the United Nations with a caution in relation to its potential foes and a firmness in relation to its imprudent allies which were what, at the time, the interests of world peace as well as the particular

---

* Professor Benjamin V. Cohen, an eminent legal authority, tells us that the effectiveness of a request addressed to the General Assembly under the "Uniting for Peace" procedure "depends primarily upon the extent to which the request expresses the reasoned will and elicits the support of an alert and aroused worldwide conscience" (Cohen, *The United Nations, Constitutional Development, Growth and Possibilities*, p. 19). "Primarily" this may in some sense be true; "secondarily," however, such a proposition needs to have State Department support, without which it is certain to fail in the Assembly.

interests of the United States probably demanded. Since it is more or less inevitable, in a world of unequal sovereign states, that one great power should have far greater influence in the international organization than others, humanity has probably reason to be glad that the key decisions should have been in the hands of Eisenhower and Kennedy, rather than of Eden, Guy Mollet, Macmillan, Chiang Kai-shek, de Gaulle, Stalin or Khrushchev. I might add that, of all those named, Khrushchev might well be the safest second choice.

It will, of course, be pointed out that the United States control over the United Nations is not, and never has been absolute, because of the famous Soviet veto in the Security Council: that is to say, the rule that decisions of the Security Council require the approval, or at least the acquiescence, of the five permanent members. As, in principle, *decisions* are taken only in the Security Council, while the General Assembly only has power to *recommend,* this should mean—and Stalin probably believed that it did mean—that the United Nations could never act in a way to which the Soviet Union objected. In practice, however, once the deep divergence between the blocs emerged after the war, and once it became apparent—as was the fact at that time—that the United States had a safe majority in the Assembly, it was natural and possible for the United States and its friends to build up the authority of the Assembly as against the Security Council. This trend was foreshadowed by Warren Austin as early as October 1946, when he said: "the General Assembly wields power primarily as the voice of the conscience of the world ... we foresee a great and expanding area for the General Assembly."* Warren Austin's prediction of expanding responsibility for the General Assembly came true in 1950. At that time the Truman administration had judged it expedient to resist the attempt made by the Communist government in North Korea to reunify Korea by force, and had very naturally taken advantage of an ill-advised Soviet absence from the Security Council to get its decision covered and converted into a United Nations action by the votes of its allies and supporters on the Security Council. When the

---

* The Soviet Union, being in a minority, was less impressed by the moral authority of the General Assembly. "And it might in fairness be admitted that if the roles were reversed a not dissimilar attitude would probably be taken by a minority West" (Geoffrey L. Goodwin, *Britain and the United Nations,* p. 214).

hurried return of the Soviet representative to the Security Council threatened to obstruct the operation, the United States took the momentous decision of throwing the matter into the General Assembly with the "uniting for peace" resolution. The safe American majority in the General Assembly enabled the entirely American-directed action in Korea to be continued under the United Nations flag.*

In 1956, on the other hand, when Soviet troops moved into Hungary, in what seemed to many a clearer case of aggression than the Korean one, it might have been expected that the "uniting for peace" procedure would have been invoked once more to launch a new United Nations action in resistance to aggression. This was not done, nor was it ever formally proposed in the Assembly. The reason for this, of course, was that the United States, which was ready to undertake war against the North Koreans, and risk war against the Chinese, on the Korean peninsula, was not ready to risk war against the Soviet Union in Central Europe. This perfectly rational calculation found expression at the United Nations by rather devious means, and greatly increased the confusion about what the United Nations is, and what it could be. I remember myself, at the time of my own first arrival at the United Nations as junior delegate in a minor delegation, the corridor activities on the Hungarian question, which now seem rather strange in retrospect. This was before the actual armed Soviet intervention and at a time when the Nagy Government was holding out under great pressure for its new non-aligned position. At this time, before the Soviet intervention which crushed the Nagy Government, it is possible that some

* Senator Taft, for once in agreement with a Soviet view, questioned the legality of the United Nations position on Korea, "because Article 27 of the Charter clearly provides that decisions by the Security Council on all matters shall be made by an affirmative vote of seven members including the permanent members. There was no concurring vote by Russia, but we overrode this objection without considering how it might be used against us in the future" (*Congressional Record,* January 5, 1951). In the same speech Taft, with great prescience, declared that it would be "most unwise" to build up the power for actions of Assembly, adding that "we should only have one vote among 60 which sometime in the future, even in the very near future, may be inconvenient for us" (*ibid.*). Similar, but more lively and even better founded, apprehensions were entertained by the British Government, which foresaw the growing anticolonial tendencies of the Assembly (Goodwin, *Britain and the United Nations,* p. 229).

kind of United Nations presence in Budapest—the sending of the Secretary-General or even a group of his aides—might have induced the Soviet Union to refrain from risking a new and worse Korea; on the other hand, it might not have had that effect at all, but might have left the United Nations, and through it, the United States, in a position of moral commitment to defend Hungary even against the armed intervention of the Soviet Union. The United States Government, after no doubt a very careful assessment of the situation, decided to run no risk. The United States delegation at the United Nations, therefore—a delegation then headed by Henry Cabot Lodge—was active in the corridors in the phase before the Russian intervention, but active not in support of the Nagy Government, but against it. American aides would insistently tell one that Nagy was just as bad a Communist as Khrushchev, that the whole dispute was a falling out of thieves, that the Nagy representatives at the United Nations had an appalling Communist record and so on. It was only after the Hungarian rising had been definitely crushed, and no possibility or danger of effective United Nations and United States intervention remained, that Nagy and his colleagues came to be hailed as heroes and martyrs by the same people who had assiduously smeared them when they may have been within reach of help.

In all this, the policy of the then United States Government, that of Mr. Eisenhower and Mr. Dulles, was rationally defensible. It was rationally defensible not to run a risk of world war over Hungary, as it also was to curb, with the help of the United Nations, the simultaneous sally of rash friends at Suez. All this was quite defensible, but not on any terms which the Republican Administration could consistently and effectively use to its supporters. Mr. Dulles and his friends, after all, had promised to roll back the Iron Curtain, and when it came to the pinch they decided not to roll back, but to climb down. This was a very difficult operation, because millions of Americans, including large immigrant groups, were passionately concerned about Hungary, while those Americans who cared at all about Suez were mainly on the side of Israel, Britain and France—in that order—and detested Nasser. In these circumstances, the Republican Administration used the United Nations, and used it very ably, as a lightning conductor. It was the United Nations which, in the public legend, halted Britain and France in Suez; it was the United Nations which, in the same legend, failed to cope with Soviet aggression in Hungary. Hence the myth of the United Nations' double standard: severe on the nations of the West and soft on communism. In actual fact, of course, what the General Assembly did in both cases was much the same—that is, it passed resolutions calling for a withdrawal of the British and French forces from Egypt, and of the Soviet forces from Hungary. If there was any double standard, it was at the expense of the Soviet Union, whose actions, unlike those of Britain and France, were stigmatized as aggressive and condemned. The British and French obeyed, not so much, one can reasonably assume, because of the voting majority in the Assembly, but because both the United States and the Soviet Union were against them and there was a risk of having to fight the Soviet Union without American support. The Soviet Union did not obey, because it well knew from the posture of the United States in the early and more critical days, and from the failure of the United States to invoke sanctions under the "uniting for peace" procedure, that the United States would not intervene in support of Hungary.

These attitudes of the powers were determined by rational, though perhaps mistaken, calculations of their own interests—which did however include, and this is important, the common interest in peace—and those of them who could so do, made use of the United Nations to mask their positions. Thus American Republican spokesmen regretted, after the event, that the United Nations had failed in the case of Hungary, and Americans forgot, if they ever realized, that if there was any failure, it was a failure of the United States Government which failed to propose sanctions and dissuaded others from doing so. Similarly, the British Government, withdrawing under Russian and American pressure from its ill-judged Suez venture, made some parade of its law-abiding deference to a decision of the United Nations and emphasized how very different its level of international morality was from that of the Russians, and how defective an instrument the United Nations was for dealing with Russia. In this way, the government of Mr. Eisenhower used the United Nations with great success, as a scapegoat, while the government of Sir Anthony Eden, with less success but still with some, used the United Nations as a means of saving what remained of its face. The peace was saved, adventures were liquidated, the public was misled.

In the United States the United Nations came to be thought of as a powerful but suspect almost supra-national body with a mysterious authority over United States policy. This illusion continues to be useful for any American government which finds it necessary to pursue a domestically unpopular line in foreign policy. The government can refer the issue to the United Nations, obtain the decision it wants, and let the United Nations shoulder the unpopularity. In Britain and France, many after Suez thought of the United Nations as a hypocritical and irresponsible mass of small nations applying a double standard and ignorantly intervening in grave matters of policy which should be reserved for experienced statesmen. This, of course, was the reaction of what is called the "wider public."* Some British and French politicians, who well knew that United States policy was the main factor involved, found it more convenient to denounce the blind hysteria of the United Nations than to complain too much about the stinging and calculated rebuff administered by the senior partner in the NATO Alliance. Similarly today, Lord Home, who resents the policy which the United States has been pursuing in relation to the Congo, does not attack the United States directly, but denounces the United Nations and the supposedly irresponsible smaller powers. The United States Government, of course, perfectly understands what Lord Home is saying; the public at large does not.

Senator Robert Taft, who had in his own country a reputation for being an honest, as well as an able, man, said twelve years ago that the United States should use the United Nations as "a

---

* Not only of the wider public, and not only in Britain and France. Professor Benjamin V. Cohen believes that the "irresponsible exercise of voting power by the small and relatively weak states may threaten the future of the United Nations" (*The United Nations, Constitutional Development, Growth and Possibilities*, p. 94). This fear prevailed in the League of Nations also. "The great powers," according to Lord Robert Cecil, "were obsessed with the wholly unreal danger that the small powers might band together and vote them down" (quoted in Andrew Boyd, *United Nations: Piety, Myth and Truth*, p. 27).

diplomatic weapon."* No spokesman of the United States Government has, I believe, used this language, but successive United States Governments have acted, and with much success, in accordance with the Taft doctrine. The major decisions of the United Nations on Iran, on Palestine, on Korea, on keeping China out of the United Nations and keeping Formosa in China's Security Council seat, on Suez, on Hungary and on the Congo have one thing in common: they were all in line with United States government policy: in the case of the Congo, United Nations policy changed after a change of United States administration. The only partial exception I can think of is that of Lebanon, in 1958, where the Arab countries, working with the Secretariat, reached agreement, ratified by the United Nations, which fell short of what the United States delegation had hoped for at the outset of the special session in question. In reality, what Lebanon marked was the transition from a state of affairs in which the United States was the sole determinant of General Assembly decisions, to one in which it exercised predominance on condition of working together with the Afro-Asian group—the sixth assumption to which I referred earlier.† That is what the case of Lebanon represented in reality, I believe, but it repre-

* "But for the present we can only make use of the United Nations as best we may, as a diplomatic weapon, and through it we may hope that perhaps more friendly relations can be established with Russia. But as far as military policy is concerned I see no choice except to disregard the United Nations . . ." (*Congressional Record,* January 5, 1951). It is clear from the general context of this strongly anti-communist speech that Senator Taft, while he genuinely believed in the United Nations as "a forum for discussion," and a safety-valve, did not envisage a "diplomatic weapon" primarily as a means for bringing about the problematical "more friendly relations . . . with Russia" (see above, page 202, footnote). A British observer was more explicit about the real functions of the diplomatic weapon: "And however clear the need to defend Western outposts might seem to ministers and officials, on an issue that might easily appear both obscure and remote to the electorate the moral backing of the U.N. might well be instrumental in rallying the necessary public support [by an] U.N. endorsement of military action by the NATO powers" (Goodwin, *Britain and the United Nations,* p. 248). The same observer realized, however, that a diplomatic weapon was something one could cut oneself with. It was not, he wrote, "impossible to envisage cases in which a two-thirds majority [in the Assembly] against Britain might be mobilized" (*ibid.*).

† "By 1958, it was noted in Moscow, the Afro-Asian states held a third of the Assembly's seats. This gave them a collective veto, since important Assembly resolutions require a majority of two to one and can be defeated by a 'blocking third.' Soviet commentators gleefully argued that 'the American voting machine was no longer working' " (Boyd, *United Nations: Piety, Myth and Truth,* p. 38).

Conflicting Concepts of the United Nations [207]

sented something else in the mind of Mr. Hammarskjöld. It represented for him an important stage in the growth of the Secretariat, and especially in the office of the Secretary-General, towards independent authority in world affairs. This was the theory of the "dynamic instrument" of which Mr. Hammarskjöld often spoke.* It is not easy to express this theory briefly, because it developed over the years in Mr. Hammarskjöld's mind, while remaining wrapped in the translucent envelope of his prose style, but roughly speaking, the theory was this: the Secretary-General represented the general will of the international community as a whole, independent of the will of any individual member or group of members; where the other organs of the Charter, the Security Council and the General Assembly, had failed to reach agreement or, as more often happened, had reached only ambiguous agreement, the Secretary-General, and under him the Secretariat, could be, and ought to be, trusted to act in the general interest of all. In this way, and through such situations, the authority of the Secretary-General and the Secretariat were to be gradually built up in the direction, it was hoped, ultimately of a genuinely supra-national authority—a world government.

* *Servant of Peace; a Selection of the Speeches and Statements of Dag Hammarskjöld, Secretary General of the United Nations, 1953–1961*, edited and introduced by Wilder Foote. See especially pp. 37, 46–7, 136, 150, 198, 227, 259, 353. The evolution of Hammarskjöld's thought on this matter is too complex to be analysed here. It can, however, be said that in his thinking the "instrument" tended to become more important and the "agents" (Council and Assembly) rather less. Compare:

"The Secretary-General does not suffer from the fact that he has nobody to refer back to provided that the main organs of the United Nations—the Security Council or the General Assembly—have taken clear decisions on general terms of reference, short of which, of course, the Secretary-General is forced to undertake a kind of policy-making which from the point of view of member governments I feel may be considered unsound" (Press Conference of April 4, 1957; in *Speeches*, p. 136).

"If negotiations are necessary, or if arrangements with a certain intended political impact are to be made, but Member nations are not in a position to lay down exact terms of reference, a natural response of the Organization is to use the services of the Secretary-General for what they may be worth" (Statement of May 1, 1960; *Speeches*, p. 259).

The shift in emphasis is remarkable. Failure by the main organs to provide clear terms of reference is regarded in the 1957 press conference as a regrettable situation from which the Secretary-General "suffers" and in which he may be "forced" into activities which "may be considered unsound." By 1960, the note of misgiving has entirely disappeared and it becomes simply "natural" that the Secretary-General should act without "exact terms of reference." But the 1960 line is foreshadowed in some of the earlier statements (*Speeches*, p. 150).

Now for all of us who are frightened by the anarchy of sovereign states, the cold war, the armaments race and so on, this is an exceedingly attractive concept, and it has enlisted the loyalty of many able and admirable men and women throughout the world. As I now propose to subject this concept to some criticism, I should perhaps say first that I believe it tends in the right direction, that is to say that the strengthening of a genuine focus of international authority is obviously in the common interest. I do not believe, however, that we are helping the tendency in that direction by pretending that we have already reached a stage which we have not in fact reached: a stage where the Secretary-General and the Secretariat can be implicitly relied on as an impartial instrument in the service of the international community as a whole, influenced by no national policies. I believe that the role of the Secretariat, from the foundation of the organization up to now, has to be seen in relation, not directly to the international community in the rather mystical manner imagined by Hammarskjöld, but in relation to its own immediate and real environment: those buildings on the East River, in which the Security Council, the General Assembly and the other organs work. In that environment, the influence of the United States was, as I have suggested, once supreme, and is now conditionally predominant. In the Secretariat also—that is to say in the executive service of these American-led organs—American influence was once supreme, and is still predominant. The powerful personality of Hammarskjöld partly disguised and to a lesser extent deflected the reality of American pressure on the Secretariat. For a clear view of the basic situation it is therefore well to go back to the days of Trygve Lie.

Trygve Lie possessed neither Hammarskjöld's ability nor his obliquity, and his book *In the Cause of Peace,* so much more candid than anything Hammarskjöld is known to have left us, is still in many ways a better guide to United Nations realities than are Hammarskjöld's speeches or most textbooks. As regards the Secretariat, Lie tells us that he was "especially concerned about American recruitment." "The trouble was," he says, "that so great a proportion of the staff were of United States nationality, and the United States Government"—he is here referring to pre-McCarthy days—"gave so little help towards choosing among the applicants." Towards the end of Mr. Lie's tenure in 1952–53, the then American Government turned its attention to this problem, and began to comb out, with Mr. Lie's help, any Americans in the Secretariat who could be suspected of being soft on communism. Lie, having pointed out that nothing in the Charter or the staff regulations bars a Communist from being a member of the Secretariat, and that every Secretariat member has full freedom for his personal, political and religious convictions, nonetheless goes on to say that "if there was even one American Communist in the Secretariat, I wished to get rid of him. I would do it quietly and in accordance with the Staff Regulations."* He refers, a few pages later, without apparently being conscious of any inconsistency and even with some pride, to the fact that he declined to discharge, as the Russians demanded, White Russians employed in the Secretariat, and refused to consider sacking Czechs and Slovaks disapproved of by Prague.† On the other front, the McCarthyite outcry in the United States continued, and Mr. Lie tells us: "On the one hand, the sweeping attacks upon the standing and integrity of the Secretariat were vicious and distorted and out of all proportion to the facts. On the other hand, there was no question in my mind that the cases involving the Fifth Amendment ought to go, as a matter of sound policy entirely divorced from the public hue and cry."‡ This meant in practice that Mr. Lie, who was able to stand up against the pressure of the Russians and their friends—and indeed could not have afforded to give in to it—yielded to the much more powerful pressure of the United States. The F.B.I. installed a kind of inquisition in the Secretariat building; the Fifth Amendment cases, and others, did go, and Mr. Lie's trusted friend and legal counsel, an American citizen, Abraham Feller, jumped out of a twelfth-story window.

The Secretariat inherited by Hammarskjöld was therefore one which contained not only a large number of American citizens, but a particular body of such citizens, a body which had been purged of all who, in the McCarthy time, could be shown to have deviated in some degree from the then very stringent norms of

* *In the Cause of Peace*, p. 388.
† *Ibid.*, p. 394.
‡ *Ibid.*, p. 397.

loyalty to the United States. The American survivors of this system would, it could reasonably be assumed, have a distinct tendency to identify loyalty to the international community with conformity to United States policy, since the penalty for radical noncomformity with United States policy had been shown to be dismissal from the service of the international community. These survivors included the most important people in the Secretariat next to Hammarskjöld—and it was a closer "next" than the public generally were in a position to see. Hammarskjöld himself, with greater diplomatic resources and cooler judgment than Lie, managed to conduct relations with the State Department with a greater degree of international decorum than Lie had achieved, but the reality of a sort of right of oversight by the State Department over the American Secretariat members—and probably indirectly over other Western members—continued. So, and rigidly, of course, did Soviet control over Soviet citizens in the Secretariat. The difference was that the Americans, under the more supple, but perhaps no less strong, rein of the State Department, remained at the centre, where political decisions were taken, while the Russians, although occupying high-ranking posts, were kept out in the political cold in ignorance of what was really going on. This practice may have originated with the Korean War—that it did prevail then Mr. Lie has recorded—I saw it myself in operation in relation to the Congo, and I believe it is still in force. In Hammarskjöld's time, his closest associates and advisers were all Americans—Cordier, Bunche and (for Congo matters at least) Wieschhoff—and they were all Americans who had the approval—although, in one case, against a background of Congressional criticism—of the State Department. This state of affairs was quite a faithful reflection of the situation in the other organs—the Security Council with its safe (though constitutionally limited) American majority, and the General Assembly with its less safe, but still conditionally reliable, American majority. All this, in turn, reflected the realities of a world in which the United States was the most powerful and the wealthiest country, the greatest in trade and finance, and in diplomatic influence, and of course the greatest contributor to the United Nations. It was entirely natural and quite unavoidable that this influence should permeate also the United Nations Secretariat, which is a service

Conflicting Concepts of the United Nations [211]

belonging not to some Rousseau-like disembodied general will of the international community, but to the real world, with its real balance of forces.

Hammarskjöld's subtle mind, although quite at home in this real world, conceived the idea that, working through contradictions and ambiguities, in the instructions coming to him from Council and Assembly, he might still make the Secretariat somehow, despite its composition, and its conditions of working, into an instrument genuinely serving the international community in some higher sense. It was a heroic endeavour, and a sincere one, but I am not sure that it was successful. Save for the lonely and transitional issue of the Lebanon, and perhaps the case of Laos—though that is much less certain—it would be hard to think of an issue on which the Secretariat differed to any significant extent from United States policy and succeeded in carrying its point. On what might be called the McCarthy issue, Hammarskjöld bowed, more gracefully and inconspicuously than Trygve Lie, but bowed none the less, to prevailing American opinion. On Suez, naturally enough, and perhaps with more questionable propriety on Hungary, Hammarskjöld worked with the United States, and the services of the Secretariat may not have been without importance in enabling the explosive Hungarian issue to be buried. It may be urged, and with truth, that the interests of world peace were involved here, but if the United States had decided to protect Hungary, I think it likely that the United Nations, including the Secretariat, would have asserted that in Hungary, as in Korea, peace could only be defended by resisting aggression.

On the Congo issue, the United Nations was from the beginning and still is generally responsive to American policy. There were some partial or apparent exceptions, which are themselves significant. Thus, when the Republican Administration wanted to seat a Kasavubu delegation as representative of the Congo, at a time when there was no recognized legal government, the Secretariat used its influence against this move. Similarly, when the United States, in concert with Great Britain, wanted to get rid of M. Dayal, the United Nations representative in the Congo, the Secretary-General for a time demurred. Two things, both important, have to be noticed about these exceptions. The first is that it was the United States Government, not the Secretariat, which, in both cases, carried its point; the Kasavubu delegation was seated and Dayal was dropped. The second point is that these happened to be cases on which the Republican Administration acted with relatively little deference to Afro-Asian opinion. It could, I think, be said with truth that when the United States unconditionally controlled the General Assembly, the Secretariat served the United States, and that now that the United States, working in concert with a sizeable section of Afro-Asian opinion, controls the Assembly, so also the Secretariat works for an American–Afro-Asian consensus—with the emphasis still, as it is in the General Assembly, in favour of the United States. The relation of countries like Britain on the one hand and the Soviet Union on the other to this situation is important but intermittent and peripheral. In certain conditions, in particular if United States policy is hesitant and United States public opinion divided, British and French policy may inflect the United States attitude and also and simultaneously that of the Secretariat. Similarly the Soviet Union strives, with less success, to influence the policies of the Afro-Asian nationalists.* The vacillations of United Nations policy in the Congo were mainly due to American hesitations under conflicting Anglo-French and Afro-Asian pressures. When the United States finally makes up its mind to go ahead, however, the United Nations goes ahead also. Thus Andrew Cordier, a senior American on the Secretariat, helped the United States Ambassador to break Lumumba in September 1960. A change in United States policy produced another kind of firm action in Katanga, especially following the despatch of the American Military Mission to Elisabethville and the use of American aircraft to transport United Nations military equipment. The settlement in the Congo—to the degree that we can regard the Congo as being

* ". . . one of the UN's most striking characteristics is the extent to which it has frustrated the Communist powers' hopes of directing the Afro-Asian anti-colonial movement" (Boyd, *United Nations: Piety, Myth and Truth*, p. 182). There is truth in this, but it must be remembered that the Afro-Asian group at the United Nations is far from being fully representative of the Afro-Asian anti-colonial movement. Many of the African delegates in particular, notably most of those who speak French so well, represent governments which were set up precisely as barriers against the anti-colonial movement, and their philosophy of "African independence" is very similar to that of Moise Tshombe. It is true, however, that the genuinely "anti-colonial" governments do also—for different reasons—reject any Communist attempts to give them a lead, and that this is reflected in the United Nations.

settled—was one determined on in Washington—"Thant Plan" and all—and implemented by the Secretariat through the forces supplied by neutral member nations. The achievement of the United Nations, which may, or may not, have prevented the Congo from becoming the focus of general war, was a rather equivocal success for international action, a partial success for Afro-Asian opinion in relation to the Katanga fraud, a partial defeat for Great Britain, at the very least a major tactical defeat for the Soviet Union, and a triumph—at this moment apparently unqualified—for United States diplomacy. We see therefore that the difference between Senator Taft's concept of the United Nations as a diplomatic weapon for the United States and Hammarskjöld's concept of a dynamic instrument in the hands of the international community is less wide in practice than in theory.

The most hopeful element in all this—the point of growth—is the element of the conditional. United States policy—working through the United Nations—cannot simply dictate, but must bargain for support. This need—combined with the diplomatic competition between the great power blocs in Asia and in Africa—gives to the smaller and weaker countries an influence which they would otherwise not possess. This influence is felt not only in the Assembly but in the Security Council, for any potential veto-wielder fears, as Mr. Andrew Boyd has rightly pointed out, "the sword of Damocles" of the "Uniting for Peace" procedure, and thus the Council has, in Mr. Boyd's words, "been revived by the Assembly."* The form of this revival has operated to the benefit of the smaller and weaker countries. The influence of these countries—mainly Afro-Asian—tends both towards the mitigation of the cold war, and towards other unexpected ends—for example, towards a rapid growth in racial equality and therefore in human freedom on a very large scale throughout the world. The part which the United Nations plays in obliging the great powers to carry out their professions regarding racial equality is one of the organization's greatest contributions. The world, on the whole, is both a safer and a better place than it would be without the United Nations. That, however, is no reason for pretending that the world is already safer and better than it has,

---

* Boyd, *United Nations: Piety, Myth and Truth*, pp. 32–33.

in fact, become, or that the United Nations has attained, or is likely soon to attain, a sphere of detached and impartial virtue, remote from the real political environment in which, by many curious and often questionable expedients, we are contriving to live together on this planet.

THE UNITED NATIONS,
THE CONGO AND
THE TSHOMBE GOVERNMENT*

This morning at the Carnegie Endowment Institute in Diplomacy seminar I was asked a significant question: whether the government which has just been formed in the Congo is not conclusive proof of the failure of the United Nations in the Congo? The answer is clearly "yes" if we look at the matter from the viewpoint of the government—Lumumba's government—which invited in the United Nations force. Lumumba asked the United Nations forces in so as to get rid of the Belgian forces which had then invaded the Congo, and so as to enable his government to re-establish its authority over the whole country, ending the secession of Katanga, organized by Tshombe and Munongo in the interests of the Union Minière and other powerful foreign companies. Today Lumumba is dead, and his followers deprived of influence in the capital. The secession of Katanga is indeed ended, and by the United Nations, but the rulers of Katanga, Tshombe and Munongo, with their Western financial backing and Western state backing are installed in power over the whole Congo. When Lumumba called in the United Nations against Tshombe and Munongo and their Belgian backers, he certainly did not imagine—and neither did anyone else—that when the United Nations forces left the Congo, it would be a Congo ruled by Tshombe and Munongo, generally, and I believe rightly, regarded as Lumumba's murderers.

The part played by the United Nations in this chain of events was important, though it has not yet fully emerged. It is certain, however, that the United Nations representatives in Leopoldville

* This address was delivered at Makerere University College, Kampala, Uganda, on July 11, 1964. At that time, it seemed possible that Tshombe might attend the Cairo Conference of the Organization of African Unity.

played an important part in Lumumba's downfall, and in bringing about the situation in which Western influence became predominant in Leopoldville. The United Nations after long hesitation and after Lumumba's death also played an important, indeed decisive, part in ending the secesssion of Katanga. The net outcome of Lumumba's downfall and death, followed by the ending of the secession of Katanga, has been the unexpected and paradoxical one of the installation of the former secessionists, Lumumba's murderers, at the head of the state from which they seceded, Tshombe taking the place of his victim.

Nothing quite like this has ever happened before. If we were to take a parallel in American history, it would be as if, at the end of the Civil War, Jefferson Davis had been elected President in place of Lincoln, with, for Vice-President, John Wilkes Booth. The parallel is not exact—for there was no United Nations in those days—but it does give an idea of the dimensions of the paradox and of the feelings about the present government of those Congolese—and they are not few—who felt about the murder of Lumumba as the North felt about the murder of Lincoln.

This is how the situation seems if we look at it from what we may imagine to be Lumumba's viewpoint. The United Nations intervention, from that viewpoint, seems not so much a failure—the word is too weak—as a ghastly betrayal and catastrophe. As a precedent it is, still from this point of view, a sinister one. Any future prime minister of a newly independent country, facing a situation in which he has to consider calling in the United Nations, will be slow indeed, thinking of the fate of Lumumba, to come to a positive decision. And African countries generally will be more cautious than they would have been in 1960 about looking to the United Nations for intervention in places like Angola and Mozambique.

When I move, as I now propose to do, to consider these events from the point of view, not of what Lumumba was asking the United Nations to do, but of what the United Nations itself came in to do, I shall have to present a somewhat different picture, or rather, the same picture but in a different perspective. This does not mean, however, that I think that what might be called the Lumumba's-eye view of the transaction—what I have just tried to present—is either irrelevant or insignificant. On the contrary, as one who played a part in the United Nations effort in Katanga, a part which I believed to be in the interests not only of world peace but of the Congolese people and of Africa, I cannot help feeling horror and indignation at an outcome in which, as it seems to me, foreign interests have clearly prevailed, not without some collusion on the part of some members of the United Nations Secretariat, over those of the Congolese people. If the net result of all that effort was to put Tshombe and what he represents in the place of Lumumba and what he represented, then many of us were indeed naïve about what we thought we were doing in the Congo.

Let us, however, without losing sight of what actually happened in the Congo, now try to look at matters from the point of view of the United Nations. The primary purpose of the United Nations is not to help member countries to preserve their unity and independence: the primary, and overriding, purpose of the United Nations is to prevent international war from breaking out: to avert threats to the peace.

The situation in July 1960 constituted not merely a potential threat to the peace but an actual breach of the peace: mutiny followed by invasion. It was invasion—for the Belgian troops intervened without any request from the Government of the Congo, as required by the Treaty of Friendship. This limited breach of peace constituted a potential threat to peace on a large scale. Antoine Gizenga's appeal on behalf of the Government of the Congo to the United States (July 12, 1960) for military intervention in order to expel the Belgians put the United States in a dilemma because of its relation to its NATO allies. The United States did not accept, but a simple refusal might lead to a Russian "takeover." Therefore the United States favoured a United Nations solution. The Soviets could have blocked this but did not because they were reluctant to fly in the face of African opinion and also to run the risk of war. They therefore agreed to the sending of a United Nations force.

The result was that the threat to world peace was for the moment averted, and a situation was created in which Belgium's allies could quietly press her to extricate herself from her untenable position. The withdrawal of Belgian troops—the troops of the Belgian state—was completed in the latter part of 1961. This ended the actual breach of the peace—the war situation between two sovereign states.

Thus, the United Nations could claim that, in the Congo, it succeeded in averting a threat to the peace of Africa and the world, that it liquidated the military adventure of a colonialist power against an ex-colony, and that that in itself rendered such adventures less likely for the future. Since it was not in the interest of Africa as a whole, any more than of the Congo in particular, that the Congo should become a Korea, or that the former metropolitan powers should deem themselves at liberty to ignore the governments of the new states and interfere at their good pleasure, the United Nations can therefore claim to have rendered, in the Congo, important services to Africa as well as to the world.

Now there is a considerable measure of truth in these claims. The outbreak of a world struggle in the heart of Africa would indeed have been a hideous disaster and not least for the continent of Africa. We cannot, of course, be sure that without the United Nations there would have been an international clash over the Congo in 1960; but certainly without the mechanism of adjustment, the face-saving equipment, which the United Nations provides, the risk of such a clash would have been much greater. It is true that, if any of the great powers had been bent on war, in this or any other situation, there would be very little the United Nations could do about it. But the United Nations does provide, and did provide in this case, the means whereby the powers can avoid the kind of confrontation in which it becomes very difficult for them to avoid war without grave loss of face. An organization like the United Nations if it had existed in 1914 might, with luck, have prevented a war which none of the really great powers desired. It could have done this by helping to gain time, by arousing world opinion to the general danger to humanity, by providing an open forum in which the powers could let off steam and give satisfaction to public opinion at home, and by providing also, at the same time and in the same building, private meeting-grounds where the public antagonists could seek a formula based on their common interests in preventing general war.

These are the ways in which the United Nations works and they represent a form of functional adjustment on the success of which the lives of all of us depend. We cannot therefore afford—even when we criticize most strongly a given United Nations action or operation—to talk as if the United Nations were not indispensable. When we say, as we may on this or that occasion, that the United Nations has "failed" we must remember that as long as the United Nations continues to function as a mechanism of adjustment, and as long as world war remains averted, the United Nations has not yet failed in its primary purpose. None of us, whether we live in the West or in the communist countries, or in the non-aligned world, can afford to ignore or neglect, or underestimate the United Nations.

Let us accept the hypothesis that, by sending troops to the Congo in 1960, the United Nations averted, or helped the major powers to avert, an occasion of international war.

Two things remain to be said: first, the peace was not preserved without bargains and sacrifices, and the sacrifices were of a specific kind; second, as a result of these bargains and sacrifices the threat to the peace, which existed on the arrival of the United Nations forces, has arisen again on their departure in a new and perhaps more intractable form—a form, moreover, which may have the gravest implications for Africa as a whole.

As regards the first aspect—the bargains and sacrifices—it is necessary to make one or two preliminary points. The first is that we are apt to assume too easily that the only people who play power politics are the war-mongers. This is not correct: the peace-mongers like, for example, the late Dag Hammarskjöld, have to play their version of power politics too, because international politics *is* power politics. Peace is preserved by compromises, and compromises between great powers are usually at the expense of someone else. I shall take an example remote from Africa—the case of Hungary in 1956. This was a case in which one great power, the United States, found itself on the brink of war, by reason of a limited aggressive action by the other great power, the Soviet Union. The position of the United Nations in relation to the "Warsaw Pact" situation in Hungary was comparable in many ways to the Soviet position in face of the "NATO-backed" intervention in the Congo. In each case the power which might have considered itself provoked and have come to the rescue of the injured party decided instead—and it is well for world peace that it did—to "play it cool" and to use the United Nations as the instrument for playing it this way.

In the Congo, somewhat similar considerations applied. Mr. Hammarskjöld had to negotiate the departure of the Belgian troops, who were—from the international point of view—the most obvious danger to peace. In this he had Congolese opinion behind him and African opinion also; he also had United States support, but only conditionally. The implied conditions of United States support were that the United Nations forces should not come into conflict with Belgian forces and that the conditions of departure of these forces should not be such as to benefit the Communists. Britain, France and Belgium insisted that this meant "hands off Tshombe," and the United States under the Eisenhower government accepted this view. Mr. Hammarskjöld, perhaps perforce, accepted it also. But the policy of "hands off Tshombe" brought Lumumba's government into collision with the United Nations and the United States and—once he had appealed for Soviet aid—sealed his doom. The United Nations, in the person of Mr. Andrew Cordier, took the critical decision—the closing of the radio and airports—which made a Lumumba comeback impossible.

In effect, Lumumba was sacrificed because he had become an obstacle in the way of the only kind of peace Hammarskjöld felt he could make workable in the United Nations—a peaceful withdrawal of the Belgians negotiated with the West European NATO countries, through reliance on unconditional African, and conditional American, support.

That the sacrifice was rational does not make it any less bitter or its consequences less grave. Not only Lumumba but Hammarskjöld also paid the price of these consequences with their own lives. The destruction of Lumumba, his principal colleagues and his party meant the destruction of the only—albeit rudimentary—national movement in the Congo. It left no Congolese parties except parties based on a single tribe or on outside support and these categories overlap widely. That is to say that, when after long delays and vacillations, the secession of Katanga was liquidated—as a result of African pressure and the change of policies of the United States in the revulsion after Lumumba's murder—by the time this happened, Congolese Constitutional politics had become about as real as those of, say, eighteenth-century Poland. Political circles in Leopoldville, purged, corrupted and intimidated, became more representative of opinions in board rooms in Brussels, London, Paris and New York than of any real currents of opinion in the Congo. So Tshombe, the tried, tested friend of such board rooms, became Prime Minister of the Congo.

The new threat to the peace comes sharply to the fore. For the new government in the Congo will have against it not only dissatisfied tribal groups—as any Congo government is likely to have—but also all that widespread and tenacious, if badly organized, national feeling which the name of Lumumba has come to represent. And these forces have on their side, if as yet rather impalpably, a far more implacable and adventurous enemy of Western influences than the Soviet Union ever was: the People's Republic of China. And the mere shadow of a possibility of Chinese influence is likely to lead the United States, in line with its present policies elsewhere, to commit itself ever more deeply behind puppet regimes. In short the Congo, formerly threatened with the fate of Korea, is now threatened with that of Vietnam.

The United Nations efforts to avert war in the Congo cannot be said, as yet, to have achieved more than the gaining of four years of time, at a high price.

What can other African countries—within or without the United Nations—do to prevent war in the Congo, and to help the emergence of a genuinely independent Congolese state?

It would be quite wrong to pretend that the Congo, after all that has happened there, can be easily or quickly stabilized or that a general election—for example—is likely to give serious results. It is not likely by now that the troubles of the Congo can be solved without going through further agonies of civil war. All that the African states can perhaps do is to attempt to hold the ring to check the involvement of outside powers, whether the United States or Belgium or China, in the Congolese struggle. An all-African observer force, approved by the United Nations and limiting itself to observing and reporting the degree of foreign military intervention, would serve a purpose. The African countries will also, I believe, be helping the Congolese and protecting their own interests if they make it absolutely plain that they understand and wholeheartedly reject the latest exercise in puppetry which the new government in Leopoldville represents. The African governments rightly understood the threat which Tshombe in Katanga represented; the danger which he represents in Leopoldville is not less but greater.

The African states cannot and should not look to the United Nations for their salvation. The United Nations' function is not primarily to help Africa, but to protect the peace from dangers arising in Africa and elsewhere. If African public opinion recognizes that, it will not expect more from the United Nations than it really has to offer and it will not be disappointed. Within the United Nations Africa already wields considerable acknowledged influence. With greater cohesion in policy, greater alertness to common interests and a realistic willingness to use its "nuisance value" constructively, it can wield a great deal more. Until it does so it remains probable, given the nature of the world and of the United Nations, that when sacrifices have to be made to save the peace the interests sacrificed will be those of Africa rather than of the stronger powers.

Only the younger generation in Africa—the generation which includes the students at your famous University and at the University of Ghana which I can be proud, for the present, to call my own—only this rising generation, the hope of this great continent, can see to it that when peace is being preserved—as it must be for all our sakes—the interests sacrificed will no longer be those of the peoples of Africa.

MERCY AND MERCENARIES*

What the Voice of America called "the Congo-Belgian-American Mercy Mission to rescue and evacuate hostages held by the rebels in the Stanleyville area" is over. A number of whites have been rescued, the deaths of a number of others were precipitated by the landings themselves; we are not told how many African lives were lost as a result of the humanitarian intervention of the Belgian paratroops.

In Europe there was jubilation. African ears, listening to European radios—including the B.B.C.—heard that note of jubilation; they also heard the detailed reports about Europeans rescued or dead. They heard—so far as I have learned—nothing, not even a global estimate, of how many Africans died when the paratroops came down, or how many more died when Tshombe's mercenaries entered to mop up in the city which the humanitarian intervention had left open to them.

"Meanwhile," said Radio South Africa on the day the intervention ended, "tales of atrocity, brutality and horror continue to flood out of the Congo. It's a hideous war out there, so hideous that some of the South African mercenaries have opted out of the armed forces. Here is one of them . . . who speaks of the war and the part children are playing in the campaign. One of the most horrible things is that so many children have been trained by the rebels. They act as scouts and some are under eighteen years of age. . . . [inaudible passage]. The question now being asked is: what next in the Congo?" It is doubtful whether the mere fact that children gave information to the rebels so horrified certain South African mercenaries as to make them desert; the horror must have come, I believe, from what was done by the mercenary-led army to children suspected of carrying information

---

* The gist of this article appeared under the same title in the *Observer*, London, for December 6, 1964. The *Observer*, however, primarily for reasons of space, found it necessary to make some cuts in my text. These cuts have been restored in the version printed here.

to the enemy—that is to say, to their own people. That much is conjecture. That atrocities were committed by the mercenaries who entered Stanleyville in the wake of mercy is fact, attested with photographs by Western correspondents. Belgian spokesmen have been at pains to establish the distinction that the Belgians who committed the atrocities were mercenaries, and had no connection with the mercy-intent Belgian para-commandos, although it seems they wore a virtually identical uniform (United Press International despatches). Unfortunately, as Mr. Colin Legum points out, "There are few African minds sufficiently detached to see such a distinction."

In practical terms, though not in legal theory, the Belgo-American Mercy Mission, called in by the Tshombe Government, struck a heavy blow in support of the mercenary-led army created by the Tshombe Government, and the Tshombe Government itself, with its mercenaries and mercy missions, is regarded throughout Africa as the creation of Belgian interests with American backing.

It is not surprising, therefore, that many Africans regard the "Congo-Belgian-American mercy mission" as the use of a humanitarian pretext for the extension of the rule of Belgians and their associates, through the complaisant government of Leopoldville, over the whole of the resources and the strategic space of the former Belgian Congo. The condemnations of this intervention by African governments and by the OAU Commission in no way exaggerate the bitterness of African opinion on this; if anything, they understate.

Two objections will be urged: first, that there were genuine humanitarian reasons for the intervention; and second, that the Congo government which invited the Belgian forces in is not a puppet but a properly constituted legal and representative government. I shall try to deal with these two points.

There is no doubt that the plight of the hostages, their sufferings and their dangers were real, and no doubt either that European and American opinion—almost totally indifferent to the sufferings of Congolese—was moved to compassion for the hostages and anger against their captors. It cannot be pretended that this was just an abstract sentiment of pity and indignation on behalf of *any* prisoners ill-treated by *any* guards. The surge of racial solidarity was unmistakable: the paratroops came to rescue the whites from the blacks. The blacks, of course, feel the same way: Africans would like to be able to send paratroops to Dixie and to South Africa to rescue Negroes from their brutal white guards, but they are not yet in a position to do this. The white countries obviously still have the power to do it. The question is whether it is wise for them to use this power. Are white people in Africa to be regarded as covered by a sort of Caucasian-providence insurance policy, with a guarantee that if the natives get rough, the metropolitan forces will once again come to the rescue? And if so, will this doctrine, in the long run, increase or decrease the security of white people in Africa and elsewhere? Similar policies in China contributed eventually to the total exclusion of all white influence, missionary and other, from that country. A similar outcome in the Congo and in the rest of Africa has been made more likely by the intervention at Stanleyville. The only real security for white people in Africa lies in convincing the Africans among whom they live that their presence is genuinely useful to Africa, and that they are not out to trick, rob or murder Africans. Belgians and other whites in the Congo have not succeeded in making this favourable impression, and that is why they have to be bailed out by paratroops from time to time. One does not need to go all the way back to Leopold's Congo Free State to account for the hostility to whites which is widespread among Congolese. Many of the realities of the Congo Free State continued throughout the period of the Belgian Congo, and the attitude of many Belgians towards the Africans continued to be symbolized, up to the very verge of independence, by the practice, widespread among them, of using *macaque* (monkey) as a term of address for Africans. It is also appropriate to recall at this particular juncture that Leopold's Congo undertaking—now generally admitted to have been an exercise in unmitigated rapacity—was originally presented to the public as a humanitarian enterprise. The British public, in particular, generally accepted it in that light until much later its sanguinary character was exposed by Roger Casement and E. D. Morell. It is little wonder that the news of a new humanitarian undertaking in the Congo evoked so little enthusiasm in Africa. It is true that some of the hostages were missionaries, and therefore presumably there not to exploit the Congolese, but to help them. Unfortunately, in the Congo these distinctions are not clear-cut. Such missionaries as I met in Katanga were almost all warm and active political supporters of the Tshombe regime against, at that time, the United Nations; several of them worked as scouts, and some were used for psychological warfare directed, in particular, against the Irish contingent. It would be natural, and prudent, for Mr. Gbenye's forces to regard any Belgian missionaries in their territory as at least a potential fifth column. Nor is it easy to see the logic of rescuing these men of peace by the use of violence, killing the Congolese whom they supposedly came to help.

Much is made of the legal point that there is no comparison with, say, Suez or the Bay of Pigs, since the paratroops came in at the request of the Government of the Congo. It seems to be forgotten that this is not the first, but the second, time that Mr. Tshombe has invited in Belgian paratroops to "save lives." The first time was on July 10, 1960, and he was acting in his capacity as provincial Premier of Katanga. On the arrival of the Belgian troops he declared the independence of Katanga, and was able, with powerful European support, to maintain this secession for two and a half years. On that occasion, Tshombe's invitation, and the Belgian intervention, were totally illegal, but that fact did nothing to inhibit the intervention from taking place. The "legality" argument is convenient, if available, for justifying afterwards the decision to intervene. In the actual making of the decision, the legality concept has proved irrelevant, as far as Belgium is concerned. It is true that for Great Britain and the United States, with their wider interests and greater need for international punctilio, the legal consideration must have had weight.

Most African opinion will, however, be interested not so much in the exact legal status of the Tshombe Government as in its representative, or non-representative, character. African opinion, though disturbed, seems to have accepted the calling in of British forces to quell the East African mutinies because there the inviters were African leaders with undoubted mass support in their own countries. A Tshombe invitation is quite a different matter. Hardly any African can believe that the forces which, through President Kasavubu, installed Tshombe as Prime Minister of the Congo, had anything to do with any movement of Congolese opinion. Mr. Tshombe's native support, such as it is, comes (mainly in the form of loyal addresses) from the chiefs and elders of the Lunda people in Western Katanga and some other Belgian-appointed chiefs in other parts of Katanga. Outside this rather somnolent section, and such tribesmen as they can influence, or are enrolled in his gendarmerie, or are otherwise on his payroll, Tshombe has no African support, even in Katanga, and in the rest of the Congo his name is only known as that of a rebel and a traitor. African opinion, therefore, understandably cannot credit the thesis whereby he is now supposed to speak and act for the Congolese people as a whole. Most Africans believe him to represent not the people of the Congo but the people who control the resources of the Congo: a very different matter. Mr. Colin Legum and others have argued that he is not a puppet, but an astute politician with a will of his own. One need not perhaps quibble about whether the term "puppet" is an entirely appropriate one, but Tshombe's whole record shows that his astuteness as a politician lies in working closely with those who control the resources of the Congo, and with those states in which the controllers of those resources have allies, influence and support. He and the political party which obtained power in Katanga were launched in politics in 1959—just in advance of the Congo's independence—by the agents of the Union Minière du Haut Katanga; it was the Union Minière which supplied his government with the sinews of war throughout the secession, and financial interests throughout the world, allied with that great company, gave him aid and comfort wherever their influence extended. He sent an economic mission, headed by his brother, to South Africa which reported favourably on conditions there. He himself, whenever in difficulties, sought refuge in Welensky's Rhodesia. His gendarmes found asylum for a time in Salazar's Angola, and were repatriated from there by arrangement with the Portuguese authorities when he had acquired control, through Kasavubu—another tried "friend of the West"—of the government in Leopoldville. Throughout this time his rule, first in Katanga, then in the Congo generally, has been maintained by intervention of Belgian regular troops, and by white mercenaries drawn from South Africa, "Free Cuba," "French Algeria," Southern Rhodesia, and so on. With this record Tshombe cannot conceivably provide, to African opinion, a moral warrant for another armed intervention in a nominally independent African country.

It is important, I believe, that the British Government should draw back from any further involvement in the Belgian and American policy for the Congo, which is to restore the realities of the old Belgian Congo behind the rather threadbare screen of Africanization provided by Tshombe. It is now more than three years since Baron Rothschild cabled from Elisabethville on the news of the fall of Lumumba: "Success of Katanga experiment will probably bring about the political reconstruction of the Congo on an Elisabethville line" (*à partir d'Élisabethville*). That is exactly what is happening today. It is a policy which makes sense from the point of view of the Société Générale and of Wall Street. It surely cannot be a policy which a British Socialist Government could support. The use of Ascension Island as a springboard for the Belgo-American Mercy Mission was no doubt intended solely as a contribution to a humanitarian effort. Unfortunately it also helped the Belgians, and their American backers, to continue their application of the Rothschild Doctrine.

In most parts of Africa—everywhere except where there were numerous white settlers—British rule, unlike Belgian rule, has not left a legacy of hatred; on the contrary, there is a real fund of good will towards Britain in English-speaking Africa—a fund which was increased by Mr. Wilson's declaration on Southern Rhodesia, and by other matters such as the appointment of Sir Hugh Foot to the United Nations. Those in Africa who were most pleased by those developments, and looked forward, under a Labour government, to closer and happier relations with Britain, were the most dashed by the news of Ascension Island. They hope that the help given by Britain to the Mercy Mission was an isolated episode, occurring under exceptional humanitarian pressures; they fear it may be a symptom of a tendency to bring Britain's policy in Africa into line with the policies of her NATO allies, even where these policies are resented throughout Africa and denounced by the genuinely independent African states. If that fear is not justified it is urgent that it be dispelled.

The real tragedy of the twentieth century may prove to be a

deepening of racial antagonisms—on that ominous line of fissure which is also an economic and social gap—to the point where global racial warfare becomes a prospect for the beginning of the next century. With such possibilities in mind, and considering the past history, and much of the present practice, of white peoples in relation to the other branches of mankind, it might be well for Europeans and Americans, having rescued some hundreds of whites from blacks, now to set about rescuing several millions of blacks from whites.

CORRUPTION IN DEVELOPING COUNTRIES

The subtitle of this book* reflects a kind of good feeling common enough among British liberals, which never quite conveys to its supposed beneficiaries the desired impression. The writers clearly and properly wish to dissociate themselves from the suggestion: "The people in the poor countries are corrupt because they are inferior to us." In order to effect this severance they are saying in effect: "We too were once miserable sinners like you. You too can, if you take our advice, become decent people like us today." This implication, although basically less offensive, is today found more irritating than the first. One African who saw the book on my desk asked what the subtitle meant: "Which did they do in 1880—did they stop being corrupt, or did they stop developing, or both?"

It is a great pity that this supposedly conciliatory theory—"we too were once like you"—ever suggested itself to the authors, because it has distorted their book and deprived it of much of its possible usefulness. The book is divided into three sections, of which the central section, which takes up more than half of the whole text, is devoted to eighteenth- and nineteenth-century Britain and to the presentation of a series of interesting but generally not unfamiliar theses about the prevalence of graft in the eighteenth and early nineteenth centuries and the increase in probity in public and private life with the emergence of the Victorian middle class. In particular, and this is a pivotal area in the book, stress is laid on the character and ethos of Britain's civil servants overseas. These are assumed—and the assumption is almost universal in English writing on the subject—to have been uniformly or almost uniformly incorruptible; the tableau of independence

---

* Ronald Wraith and Edgar Simpkins, *Corruption in Developing Countries, Including Britain up to 1880.*

thus becomes a tragically ironic one, of the alien but upright administrator handing over to the native but crooked successor. So the populations concerned are, it is implied, actually the losers by the freedom on which they have insisted.

Few people outside Britain, I think, find this picture entirely acceptable. To begin with, personal bribe-taking, although obviously a serious vice in an official, can be less grave than a form of corruption much more general at various periods among servants of the Empire: that vicarious form of corruption which consists in being an unquestioning agent of collective rapacity. Thus Sir George Trevelyan was, according to the conventional view, an upright civil servant. It would have been far better for the Irish people who were unfortunate enough, during the famine of the 1840s, to have their fate decided and sealed by Sir George, if he had been a drunkard and a bribe-taker with some compassion in his heart and less complacency about "iron laws" which enriched those whom he served.

There is an area also—which the writers of this book ignore—where the satisfactions of being an instrument of collective rapacity cease to be entirely vicarious. Thus certain British administrators in Southern Africa in Cecil Rhodes's time—and that was later than 1880 and they were true sons of the Victorian middle class—ignored, condoned or were collusive in illegalities committed by Rhodes, retired from the service and accepted seats as directors of Rhodes's company. Almost certainly there was no explicit corrupt bargain involved in these cases. Rhodes, it was generally assumed, picked these men for his board because he was struck by their experience, prudence and ability. These qualities had, however, manifested themselves to him by the benevolent non-intervention (at the very least) of the officials concerned in relation to his activities during the time when they were still public servants. Other public servants could easily realize, without a word spoken on either side, how best to impress Rhodes with their ability, prudence and experience.

Many people in the developing countries and elsewhere outside Britain are inclined to believe that by way of this kind of structure of tacit assumptions, corruption has been not so much eliminated from British public life as distilled into a more refined essence the nature of which tends to elude even those who are saturated in it. Thus we may be sure that Sir Sydney Shippard, at the very moment when he retired as Her Majesty's Commissioner for Bechuanaland and took his seat on the board of the British South Africa Company, would have heartily despised and condemned any employee of his who took a bribe of £5. Such an action would have been "corrupt." Yet Shippard, by his collusion with Rhodes, inflicted far more lasting damage on his African "wards" than any petty thief could have done.

Developing countries—that is, poor countries—have not reached such a pitch of sophistication. Corruption, when it occurs in such countries, takes crude and often fairly open forms, forms often falling more precisely under the head of extortion than of bribery: a minister puts pressure on a bank to lend him money on inadequate security; a petty official exacts a "dash" for forwarding an application, and so on. No one can deny that these are serious social evils, that they are widespread in all the poor countries—although less widespread than is sometimes supposed in Europe—and that they help to keep them poor. I would agree with much that the authors have to say in their conclusion about cures for corruption: passage of time, spread of education, evolution of public opinion, growth in commerce and industry and in the professional class, and so forth, but the most disappointing feature of the book is that it makes no attempt to compare progress made in this direction in different kinds of developing countries. Their own experience is mainly with Nigeria—and what they have to say about Nigeria is interesting and instructive—but they seem inclined to assume that what holds good for Nigeria holds good for Africa and, indeed, the "emerging" world as a whole. This is an assumption which should be tested. For the regimes in the African countries differ very widely in character—and especially in their relation to the former metropolis and in the degree of evolution of political parties—and it seems rash to assume that these differences in regime have no bearing on the degree and character of corruption practised and tolerated. Are states like Guinea and Mali, where political power is really in native hands, less or more corrupt than states like Ivory Coast and Cameroon, which are managed by the former colonial power through a system of indirect rule? Such little evidence as I have suggests to me that in the genuinely independent states there is significantly greater effort to end corruption than there is in the nominally independent countries. If a serious study of corruption is to be made, this question surely deserves to be examined, and examined in conjunction with others—contrasting, for example, not merely nominally independent with genuinely independent, but also relatively poor with relatively rich: Mali with Ghana, Upper Volta with Ivory Coast. Admittedly the whole subject of corruption by its very nature tends to elude analysis, but a methodical effort at comparisons between situations in the various African states, classified in some such ways as I have suggested, would seem to be a more helpful starting point than a comparison between twentieth-century Africa and eighteenth- and nineteenth-century Britain. A comparison between African states would, however, have to take into account the extremely important factor of the degree and kind of influence of the former colonial powers. This is a subject which most British, French and American writers on African subjects seem to avoid as if by instinct. Yet unless this factor is adequately and explicitly considered, it is impossible to write anything really illuminating about the political, social or economic life of Africa today.

THE SCHWEITZER LEGEND

It is more than fifty years since Albert Schweitzer went to Lambaréné, in what is now Gabon, to practise medicine and found a hospital. In that time he has become a symbol, to a large white public, of altruism, self-sacrifice and dedication to the Negro. To educated Africans and Afro-Americans on the other hand—with a few exceptions—he represents the most irritating, if not the most noxious, aspects of the white man in Africa: paternalism, condescension, resistance to change. A by no means revolutionary African thinker, Dr. Davidson Nicol, Principal of Fourah Bay College, Sierra Leone, was applauded by a large student audience in Ghana some months ago when he subjected Schweitzer's writings about Africa to severe criticism, pointing out in particular that in his famous "respect for life" Schweitzer tends to equate African Negroes with insects as two inferior forms of life which must none the less be "respected," since *all* life is sacred. It is not likely that Schweitzer would have been moved by this criticism. He would readily concur with the view of a British nineteenth-century administrator: "the educated African, the curse of the West Coast." The Africans in whom he is interested are the "simple" ones—the more primitive the better—and for their sakes he keeps his hospital also "simple," that is to say primitive. The photographs, which are the best part of *Verdict on Schweitzer*,* show this clearly. They show Dr. Schweitzer and his helpers wearing solar topees—long since abandoned by everybody else, except some of that class of Africans known as "migrant madmen"—and fondling pelicans in the middle of a chaotic and artificially preserved medical slum. There are several—though far from enough—modern hospitals in Africa, and it seems clear that Schweitzer's fame has brought him enough financial support to turn Lambaréné into such a hospital. He keeps it as it is because

---

* Gerald McKnight, *Verdict on Schweitzer: The Man Behind the Legend of Lambaréné*.

he believes that "simple people" would not come to a modern hospital: an opinion disproved by the experience of the modern hospitals of Africa. When he first came to Lambaréné in 1913, Schweitzer and his wife were running real risks, enduring real hardships and making a real contribution to the health and welfare of those among whom they chose to live. Today, by refusing to admit that anything has changed, this proud and obstinate old man has become a tragic anachronism.

This is the story that any doctor who has visited Lambaréné tells his friends; it is therefore widely known throughout Africa and in the medical world generally. Mr. McKnight now tells it to the general public. So far, so good. But having shattered the Legend of Lambaréné—no difficult task, since the camera does most of it—he pursues the Man with a dull, pertinacious hostility, an obsessive anxiety to find discreditable interpretations of the most innocuous biographical data, which can only make one reflect how much greatness must still smoulder, even in the wreck of Schweitzer, to arouse so much envious malice. Mr. McKnight's writing has the worst features of the kind of British mass-circulation journalism which formed it; cockiness, ignorance, carelessness, prurience, innuendo, and lip-service to the highest moral standards. Schweitzer, Mr. McKnight is shocked to find, falls below these standards. When Schweitzer receives him, the old man permits himself the unsanctified luxury of sitting in a "chair padded with several layers of foam rubber," while leaving the young journalist to sit on "a hard wooden stool." His diet also is pretty lax: he has two hen's eggs "specially reserved" for him each day: "Thus the jungle doctor whom the world sees as a saint ensures that his strength is kept up whatever happens to anyone else."

The old man's depravity is in part explained by the tendencies of his early youth. He liked Wagner, a fact which when interpreted by Mr. McKnight gives us this sinister picture: "The music that later inspired the Kaiser's and Adolf Hitler's goose-stepping soldiers made a thunderous impact on the young man sitting alone in the stalls." Schweitzer's responsibility for the war was, however, even closer than this. The year 1905, in which Schweitzer gave up his academic post to study medicine was, as Mr. McKnight tellingly establishes, "nine years before Europe was brought to war by his Kaiser." Having noted this chronological link with Hohenzollern aggression, we are not surprised to find that Schweitzer prefers "savages and cannibals" to his own family. Did he not refer, in an autobiographical work, to the "pain of parting" from Africa, although he had not used these words about leaving his wife and daughter in Europe?

> *If the man who turnips cries,*
> *Cry not when his father dies,*
> *'Tis a proof that he had rather*
> *Have a turnip than his father.*

Proof enough for McKnight on Schweitzer, certainly. Schweitzer's early life was a sad business altogether. Snobbery and sex reared their ugly heads. He is entertained by Countess Melanie de Pourtales: "How cosy and titillating these aristocratic associations sound . . . and how hard it is to imagine them culminating in a life of abnegation in the jungle!" He goes for walks with a Miss Herrenschmidt. Mr. McKnight licks his lips: "Together we can imagine them roaming the student quarter and enjoying the piquant life of the city. Though he makes no excuse [*sic*] or explanation for alluding to her in an exclusive paragraph of his memoirs except to say that they 'saw a good deal of each other,' doubtless Schweitzer's usual reticence about everything private in his life is reflected here."

One could forgive the debauchery, the writer seems to feel, if the fellow wasn't so furtive about it. Even after he went to Africa his goings-on have something to do with sex, although Mr. McKnight cannot, greatly to his disappointment, find out just what, except that the nurses are women and tend to admire Schweitzer. Some of them are a little odd, and all have come a long way. One lady's journey, by bicycle from Abidjan to Gabon, gives Mr. McKnight an opportunity to display his Africamanship:

When the ship reached her port of destination, Mrs. Clent trundled her bicycle down the gangplank, mounted it, and rode towards the jungle. Her path to Schweitzer lay across nearly 1,000 miles of jungle, bush, scrub, wild-land, bad-land, swamp, river, tundra, forest, lake and plain. The tribes she would pass among contained many with savage reputations. Cannibalism is not extinct, by any means. (While I was in Lambaréné, there were seven convictions for it in Sierra Leone, farther up the coast.) A few miles east of Abidjan Mrs. Clent crossed the border into Ghana. Farther in the same direction she entered Togo; then Dahomey, Nigeria and the Cameroons. Here she turned south, though by now she had parted with her map and went only on the directions given her by friendly natives. Having cycled her way across the high Cameroon and skirted tiny Spanish Guinea, she entered Gabon. The end of her journey was unbelievably in sight.

On this journey the lady was hardly in more danger of being eaten by cannibals than of freezing to death in all that "tundra." Apart from mosquitoes and saddle sores, the greatest risk she ran was that of being knocked down by a truck on the busy stretch of highway between Sekondi and Accra. Catty about Schweitzer though he is, Mr. McKnight has uncritically acquired the Schweitzer vision of Africa: the Africa of 1913. All references to "the natives" in *Verdict on Schweitzer* reflect Schweitzer's basic assumptions, to the effect that these primitive creatures are at their best when they are most "unspoiled." "They are no good any more," as a Belgian hired assassin once told the present writer, "when they are polluted by the Town."

Verdict on Schweitzer has its comic aspects, but the total effect of the constant drip of feeble spite is most depressing. Take, for example, the chapter boldly entitled "The Tragedy of Madame Schweitzer." Here the writer wrestles flabbily with meagre data to get such holds on reality as these: "Schweitzer [in his autobiographical writings] deliberately avoided mentioning Hélène whenever possible. This could have been, and is believed by his admirers to have been, praiseworthy reticence ... Nevertheless the rigorous skirting of Mme. Schweitzer's role in events he was describing gives an altogether different impression from chivalry. And where she is mentioned the reader can be pardoned for wondering what special reason lay in the Doctor's mind for choosing to reveal her." If one starts from the assumption that Schweitzer is a thoroughly bad hat then it is clear that, whether he leaves her out or puts her in, he must have some discreditable motive, which, if one had sufficient imagination, one might even find. What the tragedy was I have been unable to discover from Mr. McKnight's account, except that Mme. Schweitzer like other mortals was sometimes ill, may sometimes have been lonely, probably found the tropics hot, and eventually died. The culminating passage is a quotation, from Norman Cousins's *Dr. Schweitzer of Lambaréné:*

> January 1957. The first time I saw Mme. Schweitzer I could see she was not well. The blue veins stood out in her forehead and seemed stark against the pure whiteness of her skin . . . When she spoke it was with considerable effort. Her breathing was labored . . . Once I saw Mme. Schweitzer start out across the compound, her weight bent forward on her stick and her whole being struggling for breath. I rushed to her side and took her arm. She looked up at me, somewhat puzzled, as though I did not know the rules of the game at Lambaréné.

What a brute Schweitzer must have been—the whole context of this chapter in McKnight's book implies—to reduce his wife to such a condition! The message loses some of its impact when one realizes, by comparing dates, that this description is of Mme. Schweitzer a few months before her death, which took place in Zurich at the age of seventy-five.

It is discouraging that the Schweitzer legend still lingers on; it is no less discouraging that it can now be debunked in this particular way—a way that displays the maximum meanness towards the man, while leaving intact that dangerous illusion: the pasteboard Africa which he and his admirers think he is living in.

TWO ADDRESSES

In mid-September 1961 when United Nations headquarters in Elisabethville was under fire, mainly from mercenaries and local Belgians, the President of Ghana, Osagyefo Dr. Kwame Nkrumah, addressed to United Nations headquarters a message of concern for my personal safety.

When this message was transmitted to me by Dr. Bunche I was particularly grateful to Dr. Nkrumah because I knew that messages of a very different character about me were reaching United Nations headquarters from other governments at that time.

I had met Dr. Nkrumah briefly before this on two occasions. The first time was in May 1960 when he made an important address in Dublin in which he stated that if South Africa, having become a republic, was allowed to remain in the Commonwealth, Ghana would leave: a statement which was generally and rightly regarded as a prelude to South Africa's extrusion from the Commonwealth. The second time I met him was in New York in September 1960 when he addressed the Secretary-General's Advisory Committee on the Congo—a committee on which I was representing Ireland at that time. I was impressed by his analysis of the Congo situation—an analysis which led me to reconsider my own approach to this question, hitherto largely conditioned by the atmosphere on the East River—and also by the patience and good humour with which he replied to some very aggressive questioning.

After my resignation from the United Nations Secretariat and from my own country's service in December 1961 in the circumstances related in my book *To Katanga and Back,* I received a telegram from Dr. Nkrumah inviting me to become Vice-Chancellor of the University of Ghana. Despite the high regard which I had for Dr. Nkrumah as an African leader, I had considerable hesitation about accepting this offer. I knew that relations between state and University had been strained and I had no wish either to appear as one imposed by a state on an unwilling university or to be caught in a similar though less tangible cross-fire to that which I had encountered in Katanga. Dr. Nkrumah invited me and my wife, however, to come to Ghana without commitment so as to see for ourselves how matters stood. We went there accordingly in February 1962. We were attracted to Ghana as all who know that country have been, and I found that not only the President but also the leading members of the teaching body at the University whom I met were in favour of my accepting the appointment—on the principle, I apprehended, that if I did not accept it somebody worse might be found. I agreed to accept it and in my first address to the Academic Board on October 12, 1962, I told the representatives of the teaching body some of the principles which would govern my tenure as Vice-Chancellor. The text of this address follows.

Since I am addressing you for the first time as your Vice-Chancellor, I think it would not be appropriate for me on this occasion to limit my remarks to a progress report or to routine notifications.

I shall try, therefore, to speak to you of some of the more basic questions which affect our University life, and our own lives within the University.

I am not speaking about these things in order to try to impose some doctrine on you, or to instruct you in any way. All of you have much more experience in the world of education than I have; almost all of you have much more experience of academic life in Ghana, and of Ghana itself. If I talk to you now about certain important questions, within the area of your concern and experience, it is not because I can claim to offer any ideas which will, in themselves, be new to you. It is because I believe you have a right to know what are the ideas—whether you judge them to be good or bad—of your new Vice-Chancellor on two questions which are vital to you. In general terms, these questions concern the role of the university in a newly independent country, and the nature and conditions of academic freedom. In specific terms they concern the role of this university in this independent country, and the nature and conditions of our academic freedom, here and now. These questions are, of course, closely linked.

The role of the university in a newly independent country ... There is a thesis, which has powerful and respectable defenders, that the role of a university is everywhere and always exactly the same, and that whether that role is exercised in a newly independent country, or in a rich and advanced one, makes absolutely no difference. Philosophically, if one of you should come to uphold that thesis, I am sure I should find it hard to refute. Historically, however, I believe the evidence is against the theory. Universities have adapted themselves differently, throughout the world, to changing historical circumstances. The change from the status of a colony to that of an independent country is a very great change, even a revolutionary one. All historical precedent suggests that an institution like a university must adapt itself, in a number of important ways, to vital changes in its environment. The coming of independence to this country constituted such a vital change. I think you will agree with me that the University College of Ghana—great as had been its services to the country—was rather slow to adapt itself to that change in its environment. That slowness gave rise, as the years passed, to frictions and mutual distrust. Finally it produced the form of the transition, as brusque as it had been long delayed, from University College to University. The circumstances of the transition were such that it constituted, I believe, something of a traumatic experience for the academic body. There is little point in entering into the details of those events. Our common interest now is that the University, without either brusque transitions or a stubborn rejection of change, should develop a relationship with its environment—that is, with independent Ghana—which will favour a steady, healthy and undisturbed expansion of the University's work: an expansion in which the University itself will be setting the pace.

We cannot here avoid the question of our attitudes to independent Ghana and what it represents. The words "what it represents" are important, for Ghana is not just a country which is content with the name of independence or with the passive enjoyment of its own independence. It is recognized throughout the world, by enemies and friends alike, as the symbol of a certain concept of African independence: a concept which challenges all aspects of external dominance on the African continent. I shall not, myself, affect on this matter an aloofness or a detachment which I do not feel. I support this concept of independence, believing it to be a part of the movement of the idea of freedom in the world. I believe in independent Ghana, and in the Ghanaian idea of independence, and if I did not believe in them I should not be here.

I am not, however, pressing these views on you or asking you to share them. Many, perhaps most, of you will feel that political affairs are quite peripheral to your concerns; some will be sceptical about politics in general; many will feel that the important thing for University people is to get on with their own teaching and their own research, leaving political affairs to sort themselves out as best they can.

I have no quarrel with any of these attitudes, and no wish to politicize the University: on the contrary indeed. The only attitude which I think should *not* have a place here is that of radical rejection of our environment—the spirit which detests, not perhaps the abstract idea of independence, but the actual exercise of that independence by a former colony, now a sovereign state; the concept that the only legitimate liberty of an ex-colony is the liberty to imitate the institutions of its former rulers.

Such attitudes, and the resentments which they inevitably evoked, have done some harm here at Legon in the past. I believe there is little danger of their doing so in future, because hardly anyone—I hope, indeed, no one—can now conceive of the University as an enclave of the old order, with a duty to hold out against the new. On the contrary, all the discussions I have so far had with you lead me to believe that there is, in this University, among Ghanaians and expatriates alike, a great determination to serve Ghana—and through Ghana, Africa—in all the many ways in which a university can contribute to developing countries.

The second question on which I think it is right to state my views is that of the nature and conditions of academic freedom, in our context here and now. This is obviously something of great practical importance to us all. A lecturer cannot get on with teaching his subject, a scholar cannot get on with his research, if he feels that in these activities he is subject to some kind of extra-academic surveillance and interference. Speaking purely pragmatically, a university, in any large sense of the word, could not flourish in those conditions and the defence of academic freedom in that sense is a necessity of university life. If academic freedom in that sense were ever to be assailed here, it should be my duty as Vice-Chancellor to defend it by all means in my power, and I should do so. But I have no reason whatever to believe that this basic freedom is under attack or likely to become so.

There are, however, some extensions of the theory of academic freedom which I should not consider it my duty to defend. There is for example the view that a university, even if financially dependent on the state—as this University is—has the right, or even the duty, to ignore the views of the state as regards, for example, the number of students which should be accepted for higher education, or the categories of graduates which the country most needs. I must make it clear, in this complex, important and delicate set of questions, that I do not assert that the University should have no will of its own and should merely acquiesce passively in external decisions. On the contrary, the University must argue and defend its own viewpoint; I believe that it will find a hearing and that it is quite possible to produce a harmony between the needs of the country and the character of the University. My contention is, however, that the best method of achieving this end, in this field, is not by brandishing the flag of academic freedom on little or no pretext. Academic freedom, in the central pragmatic sense, is a flag well worth fighting for; that is all the more reason for not unfurling it without good and sufficient cause.

Another concept of academic freedom which seems to me unacceptable is that which was known in mediaeval times as benefit of clergy; the concept that academic people, we as *clerks,* enjoy, or should enjoy, a privileged position in relation to the general laws of the land in which we live. The assertion or even the implicit maintenance of such a claim, far from favouring real academic freedom, seems to be calculated to jeopardize the core of such freedom, which concerns the University as a centre of teaching and learning.

I hope you will forgive me both for having spoken at some length—and yet too briefly in relation to such large themes—and also for having asserted, rather than established, views on some highly controversial matters. I have done so, not in order necessarily to convince you of the merits of these views in themselves, but so that you may not feel in the dark as to what my ideas are on these matters.

Since these remarks have been about, essentially, academic borderlines and sensitive areas, they may have sounded to some of you unduly negative. So indeed in some ways they are. These doubtful regions of academic and national interest are not at all likely to become centres of active controversy, provided the University is living on terms of reasonable discussion, based on an acknowledged harmony of interest, with the authorities of the nation of which the University is a living organ. Far from being unattainable, such terms are within easy reach. This country, according to UNESCO figures, spends a larger proportion of its national income on higher education than does any other country for which statistics are available. That figure is a certain index of the state's sincerity in this question: it also expresses expectations—expectations which for us in the University should be not an intrusive irritant, but a most welcome challenge, and an opportunity of fruitful activity for all of us in our different domains.

I am quite certain that, whatever range of social and political opinions there may be in this room, there is a consensus of opinion here in favour of accepting that challenge and seizing that opportunity. It is in that spirit that I look forward to working with you all. I am sure that I may count on your co-operation, as you may count on mine.

I thank you for hearing me out so patiently.

In retrospect this statement seems a rather sanguine one, but for the first year the hopes expressed seemed to be fulfilled. Tensions began in my second year and, at the beginning of 1964, mainly because of grave events outside the University, the University had to go through a phase of acute difficulty.

Two Addresses

The Address to the Congregation of the University of Ghana, which follows, is hardly fully intelligible without some information on the exceptional circumstances of its delivery. The background was as follows:

On January 2, 1964, a policeman had made an attempt on the life of the President of Ghana, Dr. Nkrumah, and killed one of his security officers. Following this, a state of emergency was declared. The state of emergency coincided with preparations for a referendum making certain controversial changes in the constitution of Ghana. This state of emergency, combined with the mobilization of opinion required for the referendum, led to considerable excitement in the country and to the adoption in the press of increasingly militant and, at times, vituperative language. The press attacked various persons and institutions whom it suspected of disloyalty, and the latter category unfortunately and wrongly included the University of Ghana, of which I had been Vice-Chancellor since September 1962, and which during my first year of tenure had enjoyed a relatively untroubled existence and harmonious relations with the state and press.

On January 17 the Government ordered a seventeen-day recess for all the university institutions of Ghana. On the same day a sizeable contingent of police came to the University and searched the apartments of two University teachers, Dr. de Graft Johnson, Director of the Institute of Public Education, and Dr. D. G. Osborne, a senior lecturer in physics. Then they took these two gentlemen into custody. A crowd of some hundred students then began to demonstrate against the recess and the arrests, but dispersed on my requesting them to do so. I was informed that a number of students intended to remain in their halls and refuse to disperse for the recess unless expelled by force. I warned student leaders that, if they took this course at such an excited time, there was a serious danger that force would be used and that the repercussions of this would result in irreparable damage to the University. I addressed the entire student body on the following day, urging them to disperse forthwith for the recess without manifestation of any kind. They took this advice and dispersed quietly. At the same time I made representations to the President for the release of the two members of the University who had been taken into custody. One of these, Mr. Osborne, was a British subject, and the Acting High Commissioner had been refused access to him.

Immediately after an interview I had with the President on January 24, I was notified that Dr. Osborne would be conditionally released provided I would give certain undertakings on his behalf—undertakings that he would not leave the country without the consent of the security authorities, that he would avoid all contact with Ghanaians, and that I would produce him on the request of the security force. I said that I was prepared to give such undertakings if Dr. Osborne wished me to do so. I was then allowed to see Dr. Osborne, obtained his agreement to my making the undertakings, wrote and signed the undertakings at police headquarters, and took Dr. Osborne out of the police station in which he had been confined since June 17. The police officers on duty at the station, who had obviously conceived affection and respect for Dr. Osborne, carried his bags to his car and stood on the verandah waving him goodbye. Dr. Osborne was subsequently permitted to return to the United Kingdom. Dr. de Graft Johnson, who had been politically active for many years, formerly in the opposition United party and latterly in Dr. Nkrumah's ruling Convention People's party, is still in detention at the time of writing. Two students who were arrested a little later (in early February) remained in detention until the following August, when they were released on the order of the President.

During the recess, the press campaign continued to increase in violence. On January 30 I received a visit from two high-ranking members of the security forces. They informed me that they had reliable evidence that four senior members of the University, whom they named, were engaged in subversive activities prejudicial to the security of the state. The persons named included the Professor of Law, Professor W. B. Harvey; the Senior Lecturer in Law, Mr. R. B. Seidman (both American citizens); and a person referred to as "Mr. Chester" (who later turned out to be Professor L. H. Schuster, a newly appointed member of the School of Administration). The fourth name, which I shall not record here, was that of a person of French nationality. I informed the security officers that I could appreciate the fact that people employed by the University did not thereby enjoy any licence to engage in treasonable activities, and if reliable and adequate evidence was forthcoming that any of them had been engaged in such activities, then I would agree that the people concerned must face the consequences of their acts. The security officers stated that they had such evidence but that they could not reveal it to me. I said that I could take no action on the basis of evidence which I was told was available to others but which was not made available to me. I could therefore take no steps for the dismissal of the persons concerned or for any other sanction against them.

I also urged that no action should be taken by the security forces until I had had an opportunity of seeing the President about the matter, as I believed there was grave danger of a miscarriage of justice. I suspected that at least two of those affected, Professor Harvey and Mr. Seidman, might be the objects of malicious denunciation; at this point one of the security officers made a gesture which I interpreted as meaning I was on the right track. I said I knew that neither of them could conceivably have been engaged in treasonable activities, as they were wholly dedicated to their profession of teaching law. "Mr. Chester" I could not identify at this stage, though later, when it became clear to me who was intended, I made similar representations on behalf of Professor Schuster. I could not vouch for the fourth person, not named here, as his Head of Department had recently reported to me that he was not attending to his University duties and had received an official warning that disciplinary action would be taken against him if this state of affairs continued. In the light of this I did not feel warranted in including him in the representations which I made on behalf of members of the University in good standing.

I then made an urgent request to see the President about this matter. I had not yet received any reply to this request when on the following day (January 31), while walking across the campus, I was stopped by a security officer who wished to serve on me a deportation order in the name of "Professor Chester." As Professor Schuster is an American Negro, it became clear that both his physical appearance and his correct name were unknown to those who were seeking him. Deportation orders expiring within twenty-four hours were served on that day on Professor Harvey, Mr. Seidman and the French national referred to above. Similar orders were served on the following day on Professor Schuster, on the Reverend Mr. Stewart, a British subject, Chaplain of Legon Hall, and on an American lecturer in African studies, Mr. Jean-Pierre, who were included in our subsequent representations. The Academic Board of the University carried on February 3 a resolution supporting *nem. con.* the representations which I was making on behalf of members affected by deportation orders or in detention.

Still unable to see the President, I succeeded in seeing the Minister of the Interior, who granted a stay of execution up to February 8 (with a further extension in the case of Professor Harvey, who was at this time seriously ill). It was not until February 7 that with Mr. (later Sir) John Fulton, Vice-Chancellor of the University of Sussex and a member of our University Council, I succeeded in seeing the President, who heard my representations but told me that the Government decisions on deportations were final.

The press began to devote more space to attacking the University as a "centre of subversion," and one journal asserted the doctrine that it would be better to have a university with no professors at all than one that harboured subversives. The students returned to the campus at the end of the recess on February 3 and 4, and it soon became clear that there was considerable unrest among them as a result of the recess itself, the detentions, the deportation orders and the press attacks. Reports reached the President that a big student demonstration against the Government would be held on February 8, the day on which the deportations were due to take effect. It was clear that there was some danger of matters getting out of hand, with the University becoming a political storm centre and a wide variety of possible results, the most likely of which would, in my opinion, have been the closing down of the University for a prolonged period, the alteration of its constitution in such a way as to deprive it of the degree of autonomy that it enjoys, and its reopening on a new footing. With the support of the academic body I therefore decided, while continuing my representations on behalf of the members affected by deportation orders, also to do everything possible to prevent any kind of student demonstration, or even retaliation to provocation.

I addressed the students to this effect at 8:00 A.M. on the morning of February 8, the day when the deportations took effect. I warned the students that in my opinion some of the attacks by extremists in the press and elsewhere were intended to goad students into some gesture which would be the pretext for remoulding the University and entirely changing its character. I therefore urged that all students who wished to uphold the existing character of the University, and academic freedom at the University, should in this excited time exert rigid self-control even in the teeth of severe provocation. I had no sooner finished this address than word reached me that a mass demonstration was on its way to the University. The vanguard arrived between 9:30 and 10:00 A.M. There were between two and three thousand demonstrators of all ages and both sexes, including a number of school children. They were led by Nathaniel Welbeck, organizing secretary of the Convention People's party, who had with him other prominent members of the party. Most of the demonstrators were orderly and good-humoured, but a fringe of activists did some damage to property, broke doors and windows of the halls and committed two minor assaults. Subsequently, the damage having been assessed, I sent a bill to the party for £130, 14s. 6d., which was not paid. The object of the demonstration, as was later confirmed to me on good authority, was to overawe the students and prevent, or blunt the effect of, the student demonstration which was anticipated for that day but which never took place as the students, without exception, obeyed the injunctions of the University authorities. If the student demonstration—which had been seriously discussed—had taken place together with the party's demonstration or if the students had responded to provocation, there would have been an obvious risk of serious violence.

I sought out Mr. Welbeck and pointed out to him that no student demonstration was in progress or intended and that therefore his manifestation was unnecessary, and that I hoped he would disperse his followers. Mr. Welbeck, however, directed a part of his followers to "occupy" Commonwealth Hall with orders not to withdraw until I had summoned the whole student body to hear addresses from himself and his colleagues. I then left the campus and went to the Government officers at Flagstaff House, where I saw the Secretary to the Cabinet and told him how matters stood at the University. He was most distressed by these developments and left to inform the President, then residing at Christiansborg Castle, and to ask him to have the demonstration called off. I then returned to the University where I found Mr. Welbeck and his associates seated round the table in the University Council Chamber engaged in discussions with the Pro-Vice-Chancellor and the Registrar, who were attempting to explain the University's position. Mr. Welbeck repeated his demand that the students should be convened to be addressed by him and his colleagues. I pointed out that we should be happy to offer him facilities to speak at the University, in the ordinary way and on an ordinary day, to any students who wished to hear him, but that I could not convene the student body to hear him under such circumstances, and in the presence of a quite unnecessary and undesirable mass demonstration. After much further discussion and after the arrival of the Chairman of the University Council, Nana Kobina Nketsia IV, who added his authority to the request of the other University officials that the demonstration should disperse, the demonstrators and their leaders departed from the campus.

On this day some of the deportees left Ghana, and the remainder followed within a few days.

In the weeks that followed, press criticism and other forms of pressure continued and it was evident that an influential section of opinion wished to continue what it considered to be the good work accomplished in January and early February, to force politically trusted people into key posts, and to put an end to the University's autonomy. It was also evident, however, that other influential sections of opinion in and close to the Government regarded these developments with apprehension and displeasure. This was the background to the delivery of the Address to the Congregation which follows and which was delivered on the occasion when the University of Ghana conferred for the first time its own degrees. Those parts of the Address which dealt with the basic principles of academic freedom were received by the student body and graduates with unmistakable marks of approbation which were heard by a large audience, including many people prominent in public life. The solidarity and discipline shown by the student body and by the academic body at this difficult time enabled the University to survive this particular crisis, battered indeed, but in essentials intact. The public attacks on the University soon slackened in volume and finally ceased altogether; they have not, at the time of writing, been renewed.

When I read over the Address I realize that parts of it may seem to some readers, in more tranquil settings, rather platitudinous. I can only say that, at the time and place of its delivery—Legon, March 14, 1964—it did not sound platitudinous to its hearers.

It is the custom, on these occasions, to give a review of the work of the various departments of the University. Such a review would be interesting, for there has been no lack of constructive achievement at the University during the past year. I propose, however, on this occasion to cause a review of the work of departments to be reproduced and circulated, so that I may devote my present remarks to some general considerations which seem to me of importance in this phase of the University's history.

I have said some perhaps ungenerous words, from time to time, about the architects who designed and built our University, and it therefore gives me a special pleasure to pay them a deserved tribute today. We know that the buildings which make up our University are earthquake-proofed, and the architects have been widely criticized for having taken this expensive precaution, since it was believed that Legon Hill was not in the earthquake belt. When I felt the floor of my office heaving the other morning, I must say I felt a surge of unaccustomed gratitude to the prudence of our builders.

The vibration which shook our campus was a reminder—of a kind which it is said academics need from time to time—that we stand on the same soil as the rest of the community. Just as physical changes in our environment affect us, so must all other changes, including political change. All Africa is going through a process of revolutionary change, and this country in particular has been living through a time of national emergency which has produced, among other effects, a drastic intensification of security measures. It would have been idle to expect that these changes would not have affected the University and they have, in fact, affected it. In a university, changes should be a stimulus to thought, to re-examination, to self-criticism, and this University has responded to this stimulus. Our Convocation has been in special session, members have proposed certain reforms in our customs and practices, and a special *ad hoc* committee has been set up which will, I understand, shortly present me with a program of recommended changes. I not merely welcome this development; I have helped to promote it. It is right that the academic body should cast a critical eye from time to time on our customs and practices, and that habits which are outmoded, or misleading, or simply inessential, should be dropped. It is, for example, not essential to the life of a university that students should wear gowns, or be waited on at table, or that dons should sit at high tables. These things are not essential; they may even in some small way be harmful because of their implications. I personally would welcome a simplification of our life here. I believe that such a simplification would be quite as much in concord with the true purpose of an academy as with the manners and ideals of a socialist society. It would be a mistake, however, to exaggerate the importance of these externals. What is important at a university is not the colour of the piece of cloth that a student wears on his back; what is important is what is going on in the student's mind. This—the process of learning—is for the university the domain of the essential. Changes that would affect this domain would require careful and anxious scrutiny by the academic body. A time of rapid change in our environment, in the social and political context in which we live, must certainly challenge us to re-examine our own ways; but it also demands of us that we be true to our responsibilities, faithful to the values of teachers and of scholars. Such fidelity is put to the test, in the most advanced societies, in some very subtle ways. We who live in a rapidly developing society are in a sense fortunate, in that the tests are more readily recognizable.

The slight seismic shock which interrupted our trains of thought on Wednesday morning was not the first shock our peaceful community has experienced during this term. The question which must occupy us is this: can we emulate the success of our builders? As they, in their caution, reinforced our fabric even against what seemed a very remote danger, will we also find, in time of trial, that the moral and intellectual fabric of our University is such that it too will stand proof against shock, so that those values which are more important to us even than the University's organization, or its physical fabric, will be handed down to future generations in all essentials intact?

Much depends on the answer to this question: much, not only for Ghana, but for Africa. There are now a considerable number of universities in Africa, but there are few—perhaps not more than four others—comparable to this one. We are able to draw upon a more developed secondary-school system than is available in most other parts of Africa, and we can therefore maintain exacting standards in relation both to entrance qualifications and to degrees. The Government's enlightened policy in relation to scholarships means that no student who can meet our minimum entry requirements need, at that stage, be debarred by lack of money from continuing his studies. This is a feature not matched in some other African universities which are, in many other ways, comparable to ours. We have been fortunate enough, up to now, to be able to attract a diverse and highly qualified staff, and we have enjoyed all the advantages which are requisite to the growth of a university. None of this could have been accomplished without the financial support of the Government of Ghana and the Ghanaian taxpayer. In this again, our position is unlike that of some of our sister universities in Africa, some of which depend entirely, and many to a considerable degree, on subventions from outside Africa. In our case, outside contributions, welcome as they are, have been statistically negligible in comparison with the massive contribution which Ghana itself has made.

When we adhere, as we try to do, to what we regard as essential in the life of the University we do so not, as some have suggested, with indifference to the sacrifices of the Ghanaian workers and farmers who have made all this possible: we do so in order that their sacrifices shall not be in vain: in order that this place shall be not merely an assemblage of bricks and mortar and educational functionaries, but a real university in mind and spirit. That, surely, and nothing less than that, is what the people of Ghana want for their children, and it is therefore our duty not to be content with anything less than that.

Nor is it only a matter affecting the next generation; it has a bearing on Ghana's plans and problems here and now. The Seven-Year Plan, which rightly calls for such great efforts from the whole nation, expects the universities to make their special contribution. This University is eager to play its part in helping on the success of this great Plan. It can help in many ways—the University's Volta Basin Research Project may have, for example, a significant bearing on the success of the Plan—but of course what is chiefly expected of us is to provide the graduates, on whose availability the planners' assumptions often turn. Now it is important not only that these graduates be available in sufficient quantity, but that they should meet a required standard of quality. Only a university where well-qualified teachers can work freely in congenial conditions can produce such graduates, and the existence of such a university is therefore an assumption of the Plan. This assumption is a welcome one; all of us must do our best to see that it is realized.

Some of our detractors assert, or imply, that when we use such language—when we speak, for example, of "a real university"—what we intend is the perpetuation of colonialist and neo-colonialist values, subtly alienating our students from the rest of the people and imbuing them with loyalties to countries and systems of government not their own. Now it is certainly true that servants of a withdrawing colonial power may desire to leave behind them such an institution as that, and that some have even been successful in this. It is, however, simply not true to suggest that this University today is a colonialist or neo-colonialist institution, or that, behind a screen of concern for academic freedom, it seeks to promote colonialist or neo-colonialist purposes. Those who suggest that this is so have not produced any evidence in support of their allegations. Nor can they produce such evidence, for it does not exist. It is sad, and it is wrong, that the people of Ghana should be told that this University, for which they have sacrificed so much, is working against them. I should like, if my voice could reach them, to tell them that it is working to give them that for which they have made their sacrifices: a better future for their children.

The values to which we adhere have nothing in common with colonialism or with any other system of oppression, nor have they anything in common with neo-colonialism or any other system of deceit. They are forces of their nature hostile to such systems as colonialism and neo-colonialism, and they have served to bring about the downfall of the first system and the exposure of the second. Respect for truth; intellectual courage in the pursuit of truth; moral courage in the telling of truth: these are the qualities essential to the life of learning and teaching; these are the qualities of a real, of a living university. Since the days of Socrates in Greece and Mencius in China these values have been asserted, and have been attacked. None of us, alas, is Socrates or Mencius—and philosophy seems to have fallen on evil days—but no member of an academy can forget, without being unfaithful to his calling, how Socrates lived and how he died. A teacher may, in the eyes of the world, be a rather battered and insignificant sort of person, but he knows, if he is a good teacher—as he so often, almost inexplicably, is—that he carries responsibilities, and must try to live up to examples, which are on the highest plane of human achievement. This is not, as is sometimes suggested, curiously enough, by both colonialists and some of their adversaries, a question of "introducing European values into Africa." These are not European values; they are universal values. Mencius taught in China very much in the same spirit as Socrates taught in Greece. They were almost contemporaries. The geographical and cultural gap between them was the widest possible, yet it is clear that they would have understood one another.

In Europe, and in America, these values have had at least as many enemies as defenders, as the names of Dr. Goebbels and Senator McCarthy remind us. This ancient continent of Africa, which gave the world one of its first and richest civilizations, has the right to share in and contribute to the universal intellectual heritage which we associate with the names of Socrates and Mencius. The University has the duty, not only to transmit intact that heritage, but to provide intellectual conditions in which a modern African genius can make his own fresh and unpredictable contribution to the development of the human mind. We are here to provide, in Yeats's phrase:

> ... *not what they would,*
> *But the right twigs for an eagle's nest.*

Is this idea of the teacher's role too lofty, too high-flown, to be relevant? There are certainly those who think the teacher's role is not, essentially, different from that of the plumber: a specialist technician whom you call in to do a particular job, and whom you expect to get on with his job and keep a civil tongue in his head. A speaker said the other day that if a teacher takes money for his teaching "then he cannot in honesty say that he will not teach what we want him to teach." This is certainly true in the sense that if you engage a teacher to teach elementary mathematics, and he insists on teaching Sanskrit instead, you will have the right to get rid of him. But there is another sense—a sense which I hope was not intended by the speaker—in which the words are not true. It is not true if it means that he who pays the teacher has the right to determine how he should teach his subject. Few would maintain that he who pays the mathematics teacher can oblige him to disseminate the doctrine that two and two are five—or that the historian's paymaster can exact acquiescence in the theory that the battle of Waterloo took place in 1923. Yet in many countries, at various times, the doctrine of "paying the piper and telling him how to play his tune" has led to distortions scarcely less gross. Thus, in South Africa, the government which pays the teachers requires teachers in return to acquiesce in, or at least not to challenge, its disreputable and unscientific racialist theories. Yet the South African Government would have a right to do this if we were to accept the theory that the teacher's paymasters have a right to whatever kind of teaching they want to pay for.

In this country, we are fortunate in this degree, that our Chancellor, Osagyefo Dr. Nkrumah, has gone on record with a statement which categorically and in strong terms denies any doctrine that would encroach on the proper sphere of the teacher's freedom. I should like to quote this important passage from a speech made by our Chancellor a little more than a year ago, on February 24, 1963:

> We know that the objectives of a university cannot be achieved without scrupulous respect for academic freedom, for without academic freedom there can be no university. Teachers must be free to teach their subjects without any other concern than to convey to their students the truth as faithfully as they know it. Scholars must be free to pursue the truth and to publish the results of their researches

without fear, for true scholarship fears nothing. It can even challenge the dead learning which has come to us from the cloistral and monastic schools of the Middle Ages. We know that without respect for academic freedom, in this sense, there can be no higher education worthy of the name, and, therefore, no intellectual progress, no flowering of the nation's mind. The genius of the people is stultified. We therefore cherish and shall continue to cherish academic freedom at our universities.

The Chancellor in his speech laid stress not only on academic freedom, but on the need to serve the community, and we wholeheartedly accept the ideas which he propounded on both subjects. We remain faithful to the aims placed before us in the Statute of this University's foundation: "That students should be taught methods of critical and independent thought, while being made aware that they have a responsibility to use their education for the general benefit." These aims are logically interdependent, for if the University graduate has not been encouraged to think critically and independently, then he will have no education worthy of the name which he can use for the general benefit.

The existence of the University as a centre of critical and independent thought is therefore no luxury, but a necessity.

In times of rapid social and political change, such as those in which we are living, centres of critical and independent thought seldom enjoy unalloyed and universal favour. In the long run, the survival of such centres is secure, for it is in the nature of the human mind to question, and to check and test the answers to the questions. In the short run, however, at any given point in space and time, the future of a particular centre of critical and independent thought may be in doubt. What of the future of this particular centre now? If the spirit of those noble words of our Chancellor's which I have just quoted will prevail in all the practical relations between the University and the authorities, as surely it ought to do, then this University's future will be as secure as any institution has a right to expect. The Constitution of the University, the Act and our University Statutes which, although of recent enactment by our Council, enshrine principles of academic freedom which are very old, will be respected, and our academy will flourish. We must hope that this will be so. We cannot, in the light of some recent events, and the comments of certain publicists, simply take it for granted that our intellectual freedoms are unchallenged.

In many lands, and in widely different political contexts, in America, in Germany, in the Soviet Union, and elsewhere at various times, people have sought to call down on scholars, on teachers, on writers, the hand of authority. The pretexts for this have varied widely: in America, teachers have been dismissed or disciplined for being sympathetic to communism, in the Soviet Union they have been dismissed or disciplined for revisionism. Whatever the language used, however, the nature of the operation remained the same, and its motive the same: the need to overawe and, if possible, inhibit the working and expression of a free intelligence. People driven by this impulse of coercion are heard from in disturbed times, and it would be surprising if we did not hear from them; we have heard from them, and we have recognized what they represent. What we do not know is to what extent their voices may prevail. For the University it is vital that they should not prevail but that the enlightened policy proclaimed by our Chancellor in the passage from which I have quoted, should stand firm.

We hope, naturally, that this will happen and that we shall enjoy a resumption of the pleasant and fruitful conditions of work which characterized the last academic year. But even if we face, as well we may, a time of difficulties and of painful silences, we should not allow ourselves to become despondent. Respect for learning, for truth, for justice and for intelligence are enduring human qualities which are present in ample measure in the people of Ghana. These qualities may be obscured for a time, but in the long run they are tougher and more resourceful than their impatient adversaries. It is a reasonable faith, therefore, that the flame of free learning which has been lit on this hill will not be suffered to die out. In that faith, and in the hope that we ourselves may see that flame burn with renewed brightness, we can face the future, and whatever it may now bring us, with serenity. The values which a university represents, the values which we ourselves individually strive to represent, are infinitely more important than we are. They do not die when we die, or depart when we depart. We should be speaking loosely if we spoke of ourselves as their defenders, for it is we, rather than they, who need defence. We should be altogether wrong if we thought, or acted as if we thought, that these values could be in some way protected or upheld by evasion or compromise on principle. These values do not depend on what we do, or fail to do, nor do they need our feeble protection. Rather it is we who shall be judged—we who in our own minds and consciences must judge ourselves—by the measure of our fidelity to these values. Insofar as we have held to them in our lives and in our teaching, and insofar as we have transmitted, to even a few others, a sense of their abiding and transcendent importance, then we have done all that we can do; we have in fact fulfilled our task, whatever the immediate material outcome may be. The various forms of instruction that go on at a university are important in themselves, both practically and as disciplines, but the soul and life of a university is the spirit of learning, which is the love of truth. If a university has instilled this spirit even into some of its students, then no matter what happens to the organization, or even to the physical shell, of the place in which the teaching was done, the university lives on, and will, in the fullness of time, flourish anew.

Among you, the new graduates of this University, there will certainly be some, and I hope there will be many, who will carry this spirit into your future life and work. Much—more than you know perhaps—depends on you for the future of this great and stormy continent. From what I know of you I think you will not fail. I hope that your generation, and you among its leaders, will see the consolidation of African freedom: the growth of intellectual freedom within the political freedom of the continent. I wish you, therefore, something more than success in your careers—I wish you success in that phase of African history on which your generation is now entering, and which is likely to be of momentous significance, not only for Africa itself, but for the whole world.

Our thanks to the following, for permission to reprint:

NEW YORK REVIEW OF BOOKS—For "The Schweitzer Legend," by Conor Cruise O'Brien (August 1964), Copyright © New York Review, Inc. 1964, and for "The Perjured Saint," by Conor Cruise O'Brien (November 1964), Copyright © New York Review, Inc. 1964.

NONPLUS—For "Michelet Today," by Conor Cruise O'Brien (October 1959), © 1959 by Irish Channels Limited.

WILLIS KINGSLEY WING—For "Love Without Hope," by Robert Graves, from *Collected Poems 1955* by Robert Graves. Copyright © 1955 by International Authors N. V.

We wish to thank the following, in which the selections indicated first appeared:

BRITISH BROADCASTING CORPORATION—"Monsieur Camus Changes His Climate" (radio broadcast, January 1957).

LEEDS UNIVERSITY PRESS—"Conflicting Concepts of the United Nations," Montague Burton Lecture on International Relations (pamphlet, 1964).

NEW STATESMAN—"Sartre as a Critic" (August 1955), "Irishness" (January 1959), "Orwell Looks at the World" (May 1961), "Our Wits About Us" (February 1963), "Chorus or Cassandra" (April 1963), "A *New Yorker* Critic" (June 1963), "Varieties of Anti-Communism" (September 1963), "Journal de Combat" (December 1963), "White Gods and Black Americans" (May 1964), "Critic into Prophet" (May 1964), and "A Vocation" (October 1964).

MANCHESTER GUARDIAN—"Corruption in Developing Countries" (December 1963).

THE OBSERVER—"Communists and *Communisants*" (June 1964), and "Mercy and Mercenaries" (December 1964).

RADIO ÉIREANN—"Somerville and Ross" (radio broadcast).

THE SPECTATOR—"Poetry, Inspiration and Criticism" (July 1955), "The People's Victor" (April 1956), "Some Letters of James Joyce" (June 1958), "Queer World" (November 1958), "The Great Conger" (May 1959), "Mother's Tongue" (August 1959), *"The New Yorker"* (July 1959), "Re-Enter the Hero" (September 1959), "Free Spenders" (March 1960), "Generation of Saints" (January 1960), "Bears" (April 1960), "Serpents" (May 1960), and "The Fall of Parnell" (1960).

REPORTER (University of Ghana)—"Congregation Address" (March 1964).

TRANSITION (Kampala, Uganda)—"The United Nations, the Congo, and the Tshombe Government" (Speech delivered at Makerere College, July 11, 1964).